Management
by
Baseball

The Official Rules for Winning Management in Any Field

Management

by

Jeff Angus

Collins

An Imprint of HarperCollins*Publishers*

HarperCollins books may be purchased for educational, business, or sales promotional use. For information, please write to: Special Markets Department, HarperCollins Publishers, 10 East 53rd Street, New York, New York 10022.

Designed by Joy O'Meara

Library of Congress Cataloging-In-Publication has been applied for.

ISBN-13: 978-0-06-111907-1
ISBN-10: 0-06-111907-5

08 09 10 / 10 9 8 7 6 5 4 3 2

Contents

Acknowledgments

Above all others and to more than all others combined, STEVE MANES, whose vast, constant support, wisdom, and navigation of the publishing world saved me slings and errors of outfielding fortune. Steve Rees for unending moral and logistical support, connections with knowledge, bulk printing, and for keeping that rhythm on percussion. For this book's editor, Herb Schaffner, who graciously put up with me and the turbulence of too much material and too little time, and who came out to the mound at the exact right times to remind me how to throw strikes.

But without the generous insight, research, and teaching of these others, there would not be a book worth reading: Earl Weaver, Dick Williams, Al Hrabosky, Martín Dihigo, Ray Miller, Seans Gallagher, and Forman and Lahman, Tom Ruane, Alan J. Kaufman, Don Malcolm, Mikes Emeigh and Scioscia, Bill McCarthy, Darren Viola, Dick Cramer, Steve Steinberg, Erik Hansen, Tom Peters, Biz Stone, Frank Patrick, Joe Ely, Mike of MLB Center, Rico Carty, Michael Dineen, Rick Peterson, Dave Perkins, Jen Grogono, Bob Buckman, Dr. Mike Kositch, Dr. Grant Sterling, Dr. Logan Davis, Dr. David Weinberger, Susan Madrak, Rep. H. John Heinz III, Terry Gilliam and Salman Rushdie, Anita Fore, Stuart Johnston, Lisa Gray, Rich Levin, Clint Wilder, Raymond D. Watts, Buckminster Fuller, Ray Calamaro, Connie Marrero, Barry Mitzman, Bill Veeck, The Twelve, Steve Gillmor, Martin Marshall, Doug Dineley, the Dixie Peach, Mario Machado, and Bob "Death to Flying Things" Ferguson. To the editors who sharpened the content: Diane Bruch, Pam Beason, Bill Anscheutz, Maria A. S. Ward, D. S. Aronson, and Adam Goldberger. And to my Management Hall of Famers (Underappreciated Wing): Rachel K. E. Black, Gary Brose, Greg Smith, Scott Boutwell, Alexis Laris, Mark "Mad-dog" Eppley, Chris Logan, and my evil antipodal twin, Paul Heath.

Management
by
Baseball

Introducing Management by Baseball

Managing is getting paid for home runs someone else hits.
—Casey Stengel

Management consultant by day, major–league-baseball writer by night, I didn't see the connection between my two jobs. Then came the day I witnessed a remarkably self-destructive client insist on a foolish decision—and in the evening watched the worst manager of post–World War II baseball destroy his team's slender chances for the season with a boneheaded move hauntingly identical to my client's.

I'd spent a too-long day trying to convince my consulting client that he had lots of wasted talent working for him. An experienced manager recently hired to run a chronically low-performance work group, he had re-organized the group to match his own ideal structure, then unilaterally rebuilt job descriptions to correspond to his new structure. He delegated too rarely. When he *did* delegate, he assigned tasks strictly on the basis of employees' job descriptions, not their individual skills. He completely ignored the people as individuals, imagining they'd just step up to the plate and deliver what the new structure required. He knew *he* could do it, so they could, too. I tried to explain to him the fallacy limiting his group's success. My words just wouldn't reach him.

That evening, I was working at my baseball-writing job, watching the struggling Seattle Mariners, not paying as much attention to the game as I should have. I kept sifting through my brain for some hook that would make clear to my client why he needed to modify the way he operated . . . and then *it* happened.

Jeff Burroughs, a massively muscled, barely motile Mariner slugger, was on first base. He took off, trying to steal. What happened next unfolded like an auto accident you're involved in—in slow motion so you get to savor every ugly detail. Burroughs started lugging. Then, at the speed of a tectonic plate, the lug went into the least graceful slide I'd seen since Little League. Finally, to add injury to insult, he crashed into the infielder tagging him out. He had to be scraped off the field like some ignominious roadkill—existential humor at its most unsightly. Burroughs missed a chunk of the season, thereby weakening an already anemic offense.

Was the slug-like Burroughs afflicted with a sudden dementia? Nope. After the game, Mariner manager Maury Wills explained that the signal to steal had come from the skipper himself. Wills had once been the premier base stealer in the majors, a compact, efficient speed merchant with an unerring ability to read pitchers and their moves, an exceptional talent that made him famous. Like most people, he came to believe that the talent most important to *his* career was the talent most important for winning. It's a classic management blunder.

Moreover, any intelligent baseball observer would have understood that this particular steal was a low-yield idea. First, the 30-year-old Burroughs had no history of success stealing bases. For every base you get thrown out stealing, you need roughly two successes just to break even. Burroughs's history with stealing was net deficit; for every base he stole, he had been thrown out once, costing his team scoring chances.

Second, Burroughs was a key player with a good batting average, and unlike almost everybody else on the Mariners squad, he was also able to deliver the single most valuable offensive event, the home run. Third, the Mariners were playing their games in the Kingdome, a park that boosted offense at the cost of bludgeoning pitchers. The games the M's played there were far more likely to be decided by a big offensive inning than by squeezing out a run from a steal.

So by sending the steal sign, Wills had risked the health of one of his least replaceable resources—a power hitter. He had done it in a park that was the worst possible environment for a steal. And he had done it with a player whose record shouted, "Stay on your base, Sparky!"

As all this was spinning through my head, I realized two critical things.

I realized Wills's decision flew in the face of something Dick Williams, one of the two most successful modern baseball managers, had said to me. Williams stressed that managers needed to make moves based on the contents of their roster, always considering the abilities of each player in specific situations. I also realized my client was making the exact mistake Maury Wills was making. He was trying to make his "roster" succeed at a game he himself had mastered, but one that they hadn't.

That night in the press box, the epiphany hit me as hard as a Randy Johnson inside fastball. I could apply my interest in the management, strategy, tactics, business, and sociology of baseball to the practice of management in general. Once I opened myself to the thought, baseball lessons started appearing in my consulting practice all the time.

Baseball management, I realized, reflects more general management principles, more clearly and more broadly, than any of the academic teachings we normally use in organizations. I started experimenting with baseball models to coach managers in business, government, and non-profits, especially those with no formal training in the profession—the majority. Using lessons from the National Pastime turned out to be a dynamic, effective method for accelerating my clients' learning process.

The client I was working with the day Maury Wills imploded was a casual baseball fan. He'd never heard of Steve Dalkowski, but two days after Burroughs went on the disabled list, I saw the client again and told him about the legendary pitcher, almost an apocryphal figure in minor-league history. I thought the Dalkowski story would show him what he needed to know about teaching, personal limitations, and maximizing his employees' contributions better than I could in three hours of business-speak.

Steve Dalkowski was a fireballing lefty. Some minor leaguers, including Ron Shelton (who went on to write films such as *Bull Durham* and *Tin Cup*), believed he was the hardest thrower in the history of the game. Shelton said he blew pitches past Ted Williams in spring training, and quoted Teddy Ballgame, who called Dalko the "fastest ever" and added, "I never want to face him again." Earl Weaver, the other top modern baseball manager, managed the pitcher at two minor-league levels. He stated that Dalko had thrown wild pitches through two different steel-mesh backstops, breaking one of them 60 feet behind the catcher. In his first pro season, the southpaw struck out 10 of the first 12 batters he faced without anyone touching the ball with a bat. He probably threw close to 100 mph.

But Dalkowski had limitations. He had only two pitches, a fastball and a slider. In the Orioles system, they liked guys who threw at least a third pitch at a slower speed (usually a curve) to keep the hitter worried about the fourth dimension, and Dalkowski couldn't learn the off-speed pitch. Plus, he usually had zero ability to control his pitches.

Shelton cites a no-hitter where Dalko struck out 21 and walked 18, and the 1960 season at Stockton, where in 170 innings he struck out 262 . . . and walked the same number. Weaver wrote about a game where Dalko threw 280 pitches (starters usually go about 110 now) and lost no velocity on his fastball while striking out 16, walking 17, and winning 4–3. All three runs scored on bases-loaded wild pitches.

The O's knew what a rare asset they had, but baseball teams, like most large organizations, have rules that are accepted as commandments. For the O's, the commandment read "All pitchers shalt have an off-speed pitch." Paul Richards, the mastermind behind three decades of Oriole pitching dominance, kept trying to teach Dalko the pitch, and the moundsman kept not learning it.

One season, still-minor-league manager Weaver got permission to give a Stanford-Binet (IQ) test to all the entry-level players in the system. It turned out, Weaver wrote, that "the test indicated that Richards was wasting his time. Dalkowski finished in the 1st percentile in his ability to understand facts. Steve, it was sad to say, had the ability to do everything but learn. . . . The more you talked to Dalkowski, the more it confused him."

Halfway through the 1962 season, Weaver taught him one simple idea: that if he didn't throw strikes, all the batters would walk, and he'd lose. In the second half, Dalkowski threw 57 innings, gave up one earned run (ERA = 0.16), and racked up 100 Ks with only 11 walks. Weaver figured if the man could do that with only two pitches, let him ride it until he failed. But higher-ups insisted on the curveball and kept making him work to master it until Dalko blew out his arm trying.

End of career.

Weaver knew what Dick Williams did about how to manage the talent. He did the right thing: go with his employee's strength. But the organization pulled a Wills by trying to make Dalkowski do what he couldn't. It destroyed a rare asset.

My client was touched by the story and readily saw the connection. It helped him make important behavioral changes that led to both his personal improvement as a manager and higher productivity in his group.

Weaver and Wills, Dalkowski and Burroughs are just two petits fours from a monster banquet table of illuminating and true stories from the National Pastime. I use field-tested, easy-to-understand stories to teach management skills to people interested in improving their abilities as managers. Each story delivers new ways to examine a problem and shows one or more guidelines for action. Many will add to your store of knowledge about baseball's fine points and the game's lush history.

Management by Baseball delivers lessons structured around a model: the baseball diamond. Like that diamond, the model has four "bases": four distinct skill sets managers have to master to be effective at their jobs. Like a baseball player scoring a run, a successful manager has to touch all the bases and do it in sequential order.

First Base—Managing the Mechanics

Every day of the baseball season, skippers skillfully juggle complex decisions from choosing a lineup to calling for a steal. In the dugout, they handle abstract concepts such as time management and training techniques. In the office, they pore over research reports and apply them to the problems at hand. You'll learn from the masters the methods of successful operational management—and lessons in what to avoid from baseball's biggest bunglers.

Second Base—Managing Talent

Great baseball managers know how to get the most out of a team over a long season by understanding how to evaluate and motivate players, and when and how to hire and fire them. You'll learn models to squeeze better performance out of your own team.

Third Base—Managing Yourself

The most successful managers in and out of baseball learn enough about their own habits, biases, and strengths to overcome preconceived notions. You can boost your own skills through examples of how baseball's best and worst came to grips with intellectual and emotional blind spots that undermined their effectiveness.

Home Plate—Managing Change . . . and Driving It

The best baseball managers know how to adapt to significant changes in the game. So should anyone who works outside a ballpark. Lessons from baseball will improve your ability to thrive in times of change and actively drive changes to your organization's advantage—and your own.

If you look closely enough, baseball can teach you almost everything you need to know about management, whether it's project management, getting the most out of staff, strategic planning, facing difficult organizational challenges, or engaging big changes in a specific industry or the entire economy.

At a time when managerial ability is both scant and absolutely necessary for hard-pressed organizations' survival, *Management by Baseball* gives you some new notions of management and slings you some practical examples and proven, practical tools. It gives you a dash of new perspective from the national pastime to trigger and polish your own approaches to the challenges that chew up your peers and competitors.

Drawing from my frontline management and consulting experience, exclusive interviews from my own baseball reporting, and fascinating research from baseball's best contemporary observers, I will arm you with practical and entertaining lessons from over a century of the National Pastime, whether you're a baseball fan or a manager planning to hone your management skills in business, professional practice, nonprofits, government, the military, or in academia.

Management by Baseball Web Site: Resources, Glossary, Tools

This book is just the beginning of our ongoing conversation. At www.ManagementByBaseball.com I host a community of managers who, like me, want to work on their skills and exchange knowledge and advice. If you come, you'll find a range of resources. Those who have a copy of the book can register for free, and registered users get access to management tools with instructions on how to use them, an invitation to participate in a discussion group, and a glossary of concepts and words in this book. Join us.

1

The View from the Blimp

If I have seen further it is by standing
on the shoulders of The Giants.
—Sir Isaac Newton

Winning at managing in organizations is much like winning baseball games. In baseball, the team that wins is the one that scores the most runs, so the act of scoring a run is the key objective. To score a run, you have to touch each of the bases safely, and you have to do it in order.

You can't reverse the order, like the Philadelphia Athletics' Harry Davis tried in 1902. In a game with the Tigers, Davis attempted a double steal with a teammate on third. The idea of this play is to force the catcher to throw to second under pressure; an off-target throw, or a bobble on the play by the infielder, will allow the runner on third to break for home with a strong likelihood of scoring. In this game, Davis's attempt didn't draw a throw, and he successfully stole second, but it wasn't the run-scoring play he had in mind. So on the next pitch, Davis took off from second base for *first* base, stealing in reverse in an attempt to coax a throw out of the unyielding catcher. A few pitches later, he stole second again, this time drawing a throw, and his teammate scored from third. A couple of other players tried this maneuver, and two succeeded, but umpires stopped allowing it after 1907. In baseball, you can't change the order you run the bases.

Neither can you cut corners running from first to third by hustling straight through the pitcher's mound while skipping second base—you'd be called out. Besides, Roger Clemens would throw a broken bat at you, and with his velocity and from that distance, he'd skewer you like a kebab.

In the practice of management beyond baseball, there are four sequential stops as well. Your best chance for success at managing requires you to master or at least be adequate in four main skill sets: operational management, people management, self-awareness, and meeting change. As in baseball, you can't skip any. If you don't touch a base on the way to the next one, learning each skill set in sequence, you're likely to fail in your goal of being a good manager.

Safe at First—Starting a Rally With the Basics

A fellow bossing a big league ballclub is busier than
a one-armed paperhanger with hives.
—Ty Cobb

The first skill a manager must master to be a success is operational management, working with inanimate objects. These objects include resources such as time, money, and tools of the trade. Other objects are conceptual designs, such as work processes, rules, and guidelines (and the skill of knowing when to ignore them). Operational management also involves setting goals and objectives, negotiating, recognizing patterns, and knowing how and when to delegate.

In the early 20th century, professional management was all about using this process/procedure/tools skills set, and it pretty much ignored everything else. In large part, that's because management as we know it was something that had been developed, as Peter Drucker has explained so tidily, by government to improve results on governmental projects (translation: very big, very complex projects that brook no creativity once set in motion).

Large corporations, looking for greater success in the mass production of hard goods (which factory owners saw as analogous to the mass production of soldiers), asked, "Why can't business be more like government?" Corporations adopted government's model of professional management, and with that, inherited government's values and limitations. That's why it's inevitable that most giant companies have the same kind of strengths (and weaknesses) that government agencies of the same size do. That's why the management practices taught in the generic MBA programs (funded by and for giant companies and government agencies) fail so universally in smaller, more entrepreneurial businesses and other types of organizations. And why they fail to blunt the mass dementia of certain management beliefs, such as the "More with Less" cult that has undermined so many outfits.

Rant follows. I won't do this often.

The Most Dangerous Management Cult

The fact that a believer is happier than a skeptic is no more to the point than the fact that a drunken man is happier than a sober one
—**George Bernard Shaw**

American management has been in the thrall of an incredibly dangerous and brain-damaged cult since the late 1980s. If management just examined baseball, they'd know the cult's teachings were hot air, the gauze would be drawn from their eyes; their bodies would be turned to face the front of the cave; the fantasy spell would be broken.

The cult is the "More with Less" fad, the faith that an organization can achieve net gains in work output while downsizing staff talent or investment in R & D. The "More with Less" cult has run its intellectual course. A decade ago, you heard this dementia all the time; now, organizations behave the same way, but outside of a small handful of delusional amateurs, the chanters know they're mouthing an empty platitude.

Operationally, real managers are always looking to either (a) do more with the same, or (b) do the same for less. They take one step at a time, examine the results, then try the next step, iteratively and incrementally. A real manager would never try to do more with less; if you hear somebody saying that, he either has tertiary syphilis, or knows nothing about managing either time or process or technology. If you are working for an organization with executive management that says this and actually believes it, get out before the whole bubble implodes. Only in Communist Chinese prison labor camps and in for-profits that are monopolies is "More with Less" a net-gain strategy.

Real managers know this intuitively. Megan Santosus, a columnist for *CIO* magazine, delivered some hard numbers in a 2003 analysis, "Why More Is Less: Recent Evidence Shows That Multitasking Is an Enormous Waste of Your Time and Your Company's Money."[1] She summarized studies proving that the multitasking that ensues from the serial killing of staff slots is a lethal drag on effectiveness and even productivity. One example: administrators with four projects lose 45 percent of effective work compared to those with just one project.

The multitasking that results from the cult's power flies in the face of what has been known to be state-of-the-art people management, too. Since the mid-1980s, when the book *Peopleware* by Timothy Lister and Tom DeMarco popularized effective management of development teams, practitioners have known that if you interrupt someone who's working in a "zone," it takes an average of 20 minutes for her to return to a productive pace. Load multiple rôles on a person, make him cover them in the same day, and it's a test lab for creating waste. It strip-mines the victims while undermining the quantity and quality of work the organization gets.

So how does baseball fit in? Baseball is the perfect simple lab to test management theories. If you can't do more with less in baseball, you'd better have a perfecto explanation about why it works elsewhere.

What team believes it can replace an all-star with a scrub and garner more wins? None. "Moneyball" has made the Oakland A's stingy ways widely known, but their general manager (GM), Billy Beane, isn't trying to do more with less. He's trying the proven manager strategy I mentioned earlier: to do the same with less.

Could the Los Angeles Angels of the OC dump Vladimir Guerrero in exchange for ex-Yankee utility man Tony Womack and expect to win more games with less talent? I don't think anyone who manages a baseball roster believes that for a second. They might try to cobble together other talent using the salary savings they gained in the trade, but that'd be trying to do the same with the same. They might try to work on fundamentals and invest in advance scouting to get additional value from the diminished portfolio they had, but that'd be the Beane (the same with less) approach. Marketing departments of major-league teams or their minions, the broadcasters, might try to tell you a stripped-down home team was on the verge of turning it around, but no serious baseball manager believes this.

Beyond baseball, you can't do more with less talent. The rare purge that's done intelligently can dump lower-talent people while retaining the talented, but there's no *more* talent or output than there was before. They are not going to get "more with less."

"More with Less" is a laughable but dangerous cult. Using baseball as a yardstick makes the obviousness of that inescapable.

Successful management, however, is about the distance of a Barry Bonds home run away from just mastering operational management, as we'll see as we motor around first base later in the book to build on additional, vital skills. I'm not underestimating how critical operational management is—without getting to first successfully, you're never going to score, and as Casey Stengel was quoted as saying, "You can't steal first base." If you master operational management, you'll be better than 65 percent of your peers, because that's how many managers *never* get safely to first base.

Part 1 covers a lot of what you need to know about operational management and provides some of the rules for mastering it. This form of management is like the major leagues' spring training, where a good record doesn't guarantee a winning regular season, but if a team expects to have a successful campaign, it has to be diligent and serious during February and March.

Getting to Second Base— People Are the Keystone (Corner)

A manager wins games in December. He tries not to lose them in July. You win pennants in the off-season when you build your teams with trades and free agents.
—**Earl Weaver**

On our Field of Schemes, it's only when you've gotten safely to first that you try for second base: managing people.

As numbers- and operations-driven a dude as Earl Weaver is, he considered the individual batter-versus-pitcher performance tracking he did only a small edge, not a foundation of his success. Again and again, he reminded his own management and the press that the *players* won the games, not him. If you think it was just hyperbole, look at the most successful contemporary managers. They have what's called high "emotional intelligence," a set of attributes defined by researchers John Mayer, Peter Salovey, and others, and then popularized by Daniel Goleman in the book *Emotional Intelligence.* The aptitude includes an individual's ability to recognize the meanings of emotions, and to reason and problem-solve on the basis of emotions, as well as the capacity to perceive, understand, and manage them.

Emotional intelligence, combined with the knack for evaluating talent, makes for successful management in a range of environments as diverse as the star-saturated New York Yankees and the smoke-and-mirrors magic act the San Francisco Giants put on so frequently. The Giants' general manager, Brian Sabean, and their ex-manager, Dusty Baker, used their people-management skills to optimize performance and cobble together combinations that succeeded on the field out of a roster that looked—on paper—to be lucky to play .500 ball. Yankee manager Joe Torre uses people-management skills in an entirely different way. Torre

Binary Thinking Is Dangerous

Sadly, modern executives—the people who hire and fire managers—tend to make decisions in a binary yes-no, black-white, always-never way. As a result, when good operational managers with rough edges or low people skills start to wear out their welcome, executive management looks to replace them with people who have a good record of managing people, but without evaluating their operational abilities. Executives, about 85 percent of them lacking one or both skills themselves, tend to see this as an either/or decision, which it isn't at all. Almost no one is simply "good" or "bad" at operational or people management; it's a shaded spectrum of overall abilities shaped by component skills at each of them. So instead of looking for someone who's adequate at both, executives tend to look for the antithesis of the washed-out predecessor. More often than not, the department ends up with someone whose strength is the predecessor's weakness and whose weakness is the predecessor's strength, merely trading one imbalance for another.

You see it in baseball all the time. The easygoing, everybody's-favorite-uncle manager who gets a pink slip when the team disappoints usually gets replaced with a stern disciplinarian. And that usually harvests an immediate, ephemeral boost of some kind (this is because of the Law of Problem Evolution, which I write about in chapter 4). And when the disciplinarian's team wears out on him, ownership will usually replace him with an easygoing, everybody's-favorite-uncle manager, or sometimes a quiet tactician, with the same kind of immediate short-lived uptick the previous switch generated.

soothes egos of stars who frequently have to share playing time (something no one as competitive as a pro athlete ever likes to do). He keeps bench players alert and fresh enough that when they do get into a game, they more frequently contribute, and the manager still squeezes out some playing time for prospects.

In baseball, managing people involves building a roster of complementary talents: setting daily lineups and pitching rotations; providing coaching; setting goals; observing individual strengths and weaknesses relative to situations the team might be facing. It involves delivering pats on the back and kicks in the rear, and keeping morale high in the low times and not too high in the flush times.

Beyond baseball, managing people involves staffing (hiring, succession planning, firing, promoting, setting goals); coaching (giving training and guidance); evaluating (assessing each individual's strengths and weaknesses, judging which aptitudes can be improved with additional coaching and which can't); motivating (assessing what makes each individual tick and which positive and negative reinforcements work for each); and exercising leadership.

Only a minority of managers in large organizations—about 35 percent, I've found in my years of experience—are good at people management. Some of the ones who *are* good haven't succeeded at mastering the operational techniques that get you to first, and that's a problem. There are very few management positions where you can succeed by being good at people management while failing to cut the mustard in operational skills.

The managers who successfully get through first and arrive safely at second base usually generate a big productivity advantage for their departments. Part 2 describes details of people management and delivers suggestions in the art that will add to the abilities of most managers.

Sliding into Third: If God Is Not Your Co-pilot, Can Jiminy Cricket Be Your Third-Base Coach?

We don't know who discovered water,
but we're certain it wasn't a fish.
—John Culkin

Getting to third base from second should be easy because the cluster of talents that forms third base in our model is actually a specific flavor of the aptitude of understanding people: self-awareness.

In my years of work in the field, I've accumulated a ton of evidence that shows achieving self-awareness *isn't* easy. Most managers who have people-management skills haven't applied those observation and analytical aptitudes to themselves. Self-awareness is complicated. Why? Without waxing philosophical, let's just say some nearly autonomic behaviors we have are actions we tend not to think of as behaviors at all. Frequently, they're invisible to us.

If you've ever seen the 1948 movie *The Babe Ruth Story,* you know what I'm talking about. The Bambino started out as a (very successful) pitcher. The movie shows his character hitting a rough spot—after a lot of success, batters are starting to, well, batter him, and mercilessly. Finally a fan tells The Babe he's been tipping off hitters when he's going to throw a breaking ball by sticking his tongue out of his mouth during his windup. Because the hitters know what the pitch is going to be, they have a better chance to hit it successfully. This may or may not have happened to the Babe when he was pitching; it may just have been written into the script. Even so, this happens in real baseball all the time. When we learn to do complex sets of behaviors in sequence (like wind up and throw a curve), most of us have small cues we give ourselves to make it all work in the right order and proportions. A hurler, without realizing it, unconsciously tips the specific pitch to an observer by using a cue he doesn't even realize is part of his sequence.

This subliminal response to the outside world can be physical, as in the Babe Ruth movie example, or it can be purely emotional or intellectual. One of the most difficult human challenges is to see ourselves the way others see us, to understand our own ingrained motivations, automatic responses, and tacit assumptions.

Some new age manager-clients I've consulted with have the exact opposite set of skills—while they've been through enough therapy or group consciousness-raising of one form or another to understand themselves well, that self-knowledge maxes out their quota for people awareness. Men and women who match this pattern feel sometimes that what they've accomplished in this area is quite enough, and that others just need to meet their own needs.

But so what? Why is self-awareness important in managing? One important reason is that a lot of people's strengths and weaknesses are invisible to them. All of us have this blindness to some degree. People tend to feel that whatever they do is normal, and what they can't do is either hard, merely trivial, or not normal. Take Maury Wills. In his mind, it seems, not only was stealing a valuable tactic (we all like to think the things we do are valuable), but that with practice, awfully easy, too. Hitting home runs wasn't easy for Wills (his acme for homers was six, in 1962, the same year he stole 102 bases). So even though the only team he got to manage in the majors played in the Kingdome, a home-run-stimulating environment, and even though his roster was thin on fast guys and larded with slow guys, when he viewed his team through the filter of his own extraordinary skill set, one that he viewed as the norm, he didn't see what could make his *team* successful. He could see only what made *him* successful.

Eighty-five percent of all managers never get safely to third base, that is, achieve adequacy at first, second, *and* third. But it's worth trying to master self-awareness, not just because it makes you more successful, but because it protects you emotionally when your work situation is stressful.

Part 3 includes self-awareness lessons from the National Pastime, lessons that may illuminate your own non-baseball management approaches.

Getting Home: 1918 Is Much Closer to 1968 Than to 1920

Everything in the universe is in constant flux.
The only constant is change, and change changes in
ever-changing directions at an ever-changing rate.
—from Heraclitus

It's not too difficult to score a runner who's standing on third base, especially with no outs (88 percent of them score) or just one out (69 percent).[2] A safe hit will always do the trick, but there are other events that will get the base runner home, such as a fly out that's long enough for the runner to tag up and score before the throw comes back from the outfield. There are wild pitches, passed balls, and balks, too.

In the diamond of management skills, getting home is more of a challenge, because even with the foundation of skills that gets you to third base, there's nothing rarer than reaching home plate successfully: managing, or better, driving change.

The skills that get you to every base up through third are fueled by the ability to recognize lessons from both past and present experience. Change is not. Change is about the future, a set of circumstances that haven't happened yet, where the lessons one's learned from experience have as much chance of hindering as they do of helping. I'm not suggesting the first-, second-, and third-base skills don't require induction or intuition based on pattern recognition and hunches. On balance those skills are about the past. Adapting to the future requires analyzing the past and then escaping from it.

Major-league baseball in 1919–1920 was at a critical juncture, the first major turning point it had come to since the turn of the century. Rapid changes in the game on the field were triggered by the post–World War I economy and vastly altered social values. The pace of change was accelerated by ownership's need to counter skepticism about the sport that bubbled up in the wake of rumors about the 1919 World Series being thrown by the AL champion Chicago White Sox in exchange for bribes from gamblers (the "Black Sox Scandal"). But those were just the environmental factors that made change desirable and possible. For a change to actually happen, you need a mechanism to provide the spark.

That spark was the surprise hitting performance of a pitcher named Babe Ruth, and it was applied by the most important management innovator most management experts have never heard of: Ed Barrow. If the Baseball Hall of Fame had a Sistine Chapel and Michelangelo had painted it, the picture of God touching Adam's hand and transmitting the sacred spark would have featured an Adam modeled after The Bambino, and a deity modeled after Barrow.

Ed Barrow managed the Boston Red Sox in 1918. He inherited a team that in '17 led the league in most pitching categories and in defense but had below average offense. That team had finished in second place, trailing the first-place Chicago White Sox by nine full games.

But Barrow's Red Sox had lost two well-regarded outfielders, Duffy Lewis and Tilly Walker—excellent players very similar to Andruw Jones and Bernie Williams at their peak. The best replacements available were Amos Strunk and George Whiteman—more on the less appetizing order of today's ultra-mature Craig Biggio and Todd Zeile. The 1918 team featured a glut of very good pitching (Carl Mays, Bullet Joe Bush, Dutch Leonard, Sad Sam Jones, Ruth), but hitting and defense that had finished the previous season with less potency than Chicago's and was further weakened in the off-season. The one out-of-the-ordinary asset Barrow inherited was pitcher Ruth's hitting.

In Ruth's three full seasons as a Sox hurler (1915–17), he'd managed in his hundred or so plate appearances each year to exceed American League average batting production. Even though Ruth wasn't getting a ton of plate appearances, he was exceeding the league in every measure: batting average, getting on base, hitting for power.

With lush pitching choices and thin outfield choices, Barrow experimented with getting Ruth more appearances at the plate in 1918. Barrow cut Ruth's starting pitching in half, used him in the outfield for 59 games, and subbed the left-handed Ruth for the right-handed starting first baseman Stuffy McInnis in another 13 games. Barrow's move was very bold, but it wasn't radical. He still had Ruth starting 19 games as a pitcher and relieving in one. The Babe went 13–7 as a pitcher that year. But look at the sidebar's chart (page 21). Ruth came to the plate 380 times, led the American League in slugging percentage, tied for the home run lead with Philadelphia's Tilly Walker (with 11), and outproduced league averages by 94 percent.

Most managers, in and out of baseball, imitate others' success. The Red Sox won the pennant and beat the Cubs in the World Series, and it was the beginning of a sea change in the way first the American and then the National League played baseball.

In 1918, the entire American League hit 96 homers. In 1919, Ruth hit *29* all by himself. While home run records didn't have the cachet they've acquired since, this feat broke through the previous record of 27, set in 1884 by infielder Ned Williamson. So little were home runs considered a marquee statistic, it wasn't widely noted at the time that Ruth had broken the record.

But opposing managers, coaches, and players noticed the home run changed the relative value of various strategies, boosting the utility of some while diminishing others. Teams concentrated on producing more power hits. The 1919 AL totaled 240 homers. League batting average climbed 14 points, players collected 33 percent more doubles, and stolen bases started tailing off, by about 5 percent that year.

In 1920, Ruth hit *54* homers, the league 369. Stealing declined another 18 percent. Every team but one scored more runs than it had in the previous year, and all but one had more homers (the exception: Boston, which had sold Ruth to the Yankees). All but two had fewer steals.

The league was playing the game differently. The benefit of stealing second base had gone down in an environment where a home run could

Boom, Boom, *on* Goes the Light: Babe Ruth's Early Hitting

Year	PA	BA	lgBA	OBP	lgOBP	SLG	lgSLG	OPS	lgOPS	OPS+
1915	103	.315	.252|	.376	.330|	.576	.330|	.952	.660|	**188**
1916	150	.272	.257|	.322	.331|	.419	.335|	.741	.666|	**122**
1917	142	.325	.254|	.385	.324|	.472	.328|	.857	.653|	**162**
1918	380	.300	.258|	.411	.329|	.555	.329|	.966	.658|	**194**
1919	542	.322	.269|	.456	.334|	.657	.361|	1.114	.695|	**219**
1920	616	.376	.296|	.532	.361|	.847	.407|	1.379	.768|	**255**

This table, courtesy of www.baseball-reference.com, lists for each year the following: PA = plate appearances, BA = batting average, OBP = on-base percentage, SLG = slugging average, OPS = on-base plus slugging, OPS+ = the percentage of the league's OPS the hitter achieved. The four columns that start with "lg," like lgBA, are the league composite average for that stat that year.

There are definitions for all the stats in the *Management by Baseball* Web site glossary, but the final column, OPS+, is one that really matters. The goal of many baseball researchers is to find a single number that, alone, describes a batter's offensive value. OPS+ is a good single number developed by contemporary baseball researchers that compares a batter's offensive production relative to the league. For example, Ruth's 1915 OPS+ is 188, meaning he performed at 188 percent of the league norm, 88 percent better than average, an extraordinary feat. Note that that feat, though, was achieved over a mere 103 plate appearances. As a pitcher, he hadn't been in the lineup every day.

bring a runner in from first base as effectively as from second base and the offense hadn't invested in the risk of being thrown out trying to steal second. Recruitment changed because if a fellow could hit for power and greatly increase your run potential, you might suffer along with his sloppy fielding or slow baserunning.

Managing a team in 1920 with the tactics assumed by 1918 managers would have guaranteed poor results. In fact, a 1918 manager ripped through the space-time continuum and deposited unscrambled into a 1968 dugout would have had an easier time winning with his assumptions than he would have had in 1920. In '68, experiments with strike-zone boundaries produced an offense-starved year that delivered batting averages and earned run averages more like the deadball era game of 1903–1909. Carl Yastrzemski led the American League in batting average with .301, the lowest for a champ since Elmer Flick's 1905 mark of .308 and the lowest batting average leader's mark ever. League composite on-base percentages were similar, though 1968's slugging average was higher than 1918's because 1968 batters were still able to hit home runs when they made good contact with the ball.

The change from the teens to the twenties was sudden, and it rewarded those who could adapt quickly. Those who tried to continue optimizing what was successful in the past were disadvantaged. Change was the enemy of past success.

Baseball has had many changes. Some were premeditated, as when the major leagues intentionally deadened or juiced up the ball to lower or raise run scoring. Some changes were externally imposed but foreseeable, such as World War II's effects on player retention and fan interest. And some unforeseen events completely remade the economics of the game. The Major League Baseball Players Association won a 1975 decision that a player can be bound to the team that owned him for only a single year after the contract expired, and not forever. This undid the previous assumption of the reserve clause, which had confined players in a professional skilled-slave category for three-quarters of a century.

Outside baseball, change is the enemy of whatever skills you master: operational management, people management, and (to a lesser degree) self-knowledge. Change alters what is useful, what is optimal, what is possible. Change alters your tools, and how you should solve problems. Most important, change alters the way you *avoid* problems.

Being effective with change, managing it, driving it, is the rarest skill of all. Only 5 percent of managers cross home plate safely. Part 4 delivers techniques and tips for being effective with change, and some inspiration to drive it. If you can be in the 5 percent of managers who are good at all four skill sets, you can probably write your own ticket.

To the luxury box.

Part One

Getting to First Base—
Mastering Management Mechanics

Hold 'em, boys. I'll think of something.
—**Charlie Dressen, Brooklyn Dodger manager, to his team**

In management in baseball and beyond, getting safely to first base requires putting together the lineup, keeping progress both happening and apparent, devising strategy, choosing tactics, and making decisions in an environment unfriendly to dawdling or dithering. No matter how good you are at the other aspects of the job, you'll never be adequate unless you master this initial step I call "operational management."

In baseball, operational management includes roster management; designing, scheduling, and executing practices; pregame research and analysis and other planning based on opponents' and one's own team's past performances; and in-game strategy and tactics. In most other organizations, operational management is stewarding money, time, people resources, tools, designing processes, rules (and guidelines for knowing when to ignore them), delegation, setting goals and objectives, and negotiation.

Some people have a natural knack for this, others don't. Some get serious training, but everyone learns by doing, starting with his very first management job. How do you start as a manager? By using common sense and history. By knowing something about how to organize, but also about the specifics of the work performed by the people you'll manage.

That's exactly the way the baseball managers started their craft in the 1840s. Ever wonder why other sports have "coaches" but baseball has "managers," and why the corporate entities that operate major-league teams are called "clubs"? The two oddities spring from the same origin.

Why Only Baseball Has Managers, While Other North American Sports All Have Coaches

Baseball clubs originated from urban areas' social cricket clubs,[3] membership organizations that existed to collect dues from well-off men and to coordinate all the equipment, the playing field and supporting transportation, the catering, and other logistics required to play the English sport. Given the resources of such clubs, there was not a lot of specialization with separate managers for on- and off-field management; they generally did both.

By the 1840s, a U.S. nationalist movement created a groundswell to finally establish an "American" culture differentiated from the British roots. Americans quite intentionally invented new behaviors that would make their fellow citizens feel uniquely American. Sometimes these were simplifications. While Noah Webster's new rules created permanent differences with British English, they rationalized spelling to make it a bit more phonetic. Other changes just created a difference for difference's sake that actually wasted energy, such as the complex choreography of knife and fork that expends more ergs than the European two-fisted model.

Replacing cricket with simpler native substitutes as the game of choice became part of the nationalist urge, and cricket clubs started playing "base ball" and like games. Cricket clubs became baseball clubs, and the manager function remained the same.

That set of job requirements—managing schedules, facilities, equipment, personnel, and finances, amid frequent changes in the game on and off the field; getting the most out of contributors for the benefit of the organization; and all in a fiercely competitive environment—really is the closest precursor to the management jobs of today, whether in baseball, business, government, nonprofit, professional practice, or academia.

The first baseball managers of the 19th century were the first real managers as the job needs to be done in the 21st century.

2

Out of the Box:
Starting a New Management Mission

⚾

Sometimes you can observe a lot just by watching.
—**Yogi Berra**

Before you do anything else, when you start a new management job, you'll need to get up to speed in understanding and remaking the operations of your group.

So you just got a new management gig. Perhaps it's a promotion, and you're going to be managing people you used to work with as a peer. Perhaps you're going into a new situation where you and the group don't know each other very well. Let's start with techniques you'll need either way.

First things first: you have about three weeks to make your mark, not the imaginary "100 days" new U.S. presidents are said to have. If you don't make your mark, too much of the impression people will have of you, and more important, too much of what people will *let* you do, will be frozen. You need to deliver an image as a person who gets things done, who leads by example, who manages up for the benefit of the people below you in the hierarchy, who manages down for the benefit of those above you. You need to find a middle ground in cooperating with other departments as well as with peer managers in your department and others.

In some situations, people will try to hijack your first three weeks and fill it with their own agenda, robbing you permanently of your chance to establish yourself strongly. What kinds of situations?

- *If the organization you're working in is highly politicized.* In that case, any one of a number of managers who view you as potential competition or as someone they might fold under their arm as part of their own empire will bring "important and urgent" items for you to address right away.
- *If your predecessor was vaporized for failing to meet a specific goal* or to address a set of problems, and you were hired to accomplish that specific goal, even if there are other, more critical blocks to clear out.
- *If your organization is launching some new initiative* or direction that you had no part in crafting but you're expected to give it a big boost right away.

Some of that hijacking you can resist, especially the political kind. But if your boss has an agenda, you're going to have to be like one of the many baseball managers who land their first major-league opportunity as a mid-season replacement for a perceived failure. You've inherited the roster of 25, the 40-player extended roster, a style of play, ingrained good and bad habits. You've also got a major-league advantage: a clear view of what has been defined most recently as failure.

RULE 2.01. Make Your Mark, *any* good mark, in your first 15 days. Whatever you do, though, do *something* to establish yourself as your own person. Tell people what you're there to achieve, and what you can do for them and with them.

Racking Up Runs in the First Inning

Successful baseball managers understand that the strongest thing you can do is create "The Big Bang," results that look not just like miracle progress, but like an *instant* miracle you just whipped up out of sawdust, slag, and a 1959 Pumpsie Green baseball card. Even if you're being hijacked in ways you can't control, you must carve out time and focus for Big Bang activities.

In almost all cases, the techniques that follow should be the very first things you execute, whether you were an internal promotion or an external hire.

#1. Enlist Staff Ideas

Realize this Lou Piniella trick: just about every one of your new staff is sitting on at least one idea your predecessor either didn't have time for, couldn't absorb, didn't support, or didn't consider a high priority.

Piniella has taught himself some "turnaround" skills. Here's his first-year new manager record not counting his first management job (which was a three-year run in the Bronx working for the functionally sociopathic Yankee owner). BP is Before Piniella, and WP is With Piniella.

Before or With	Team	Year	Wins	Losses	Gain
BP	Cincinnati	1989	74	88	
WP	Cincinnati	1990	91	71	+17
BP	Seattle	1992	64	98	
WP	Seattle	1993	82	80	+18
BP	Tampa Bay	2002	55	106	
WP	Tampa Bay	2003	63	99	+7.5

It's a universal rule in baseball and beyond that a new manager tends to get better results than her predecessor (that's based on Angus's Law of Problem Evolution, a point I'll get to in chapter 4). But Piniella just has a knack for creating a successful environment for a turnaround. Like all great turnaround artists, Piniella starts by picking organizations that are not falling too short even to be a bloop single, and who realize it. Lou's uncommon approach is one I like to use myself both as a new staff manager and as a consultant.

New managers often work down the chain of command from the top to investigate what needs fixing and what needs to be left well enough alone. As Piniella understands, that's counterproductive, because management has already bought into what needs to be done and what doesn't. The problems they were able to solve are more likely to have been solved. Moreover, by the time you get to the line staff, your head is already positioned to some degree, filled with the views of the top brass whose talents have left the problems unsolved.

It's people on the line, in the trenches, generally without a position from which to force change, who have the unimplemented solutions waiting to be tapped. Managers generally ignore the ideas stored in trench dwellers' heads.

Piniella's technique is: First talk to those without a strong investment in the solution set that was the MO before you came. Then act quickly on the insights that have value. This encourages everyone in the organization who has been overlooked as a source of wisdom to come forward.

Seattle sportswriter Art Thiel's book *Out of Left Field* (Seattle: Sasquatch Books, 2004) documents Piniella's first Mariner turnaround action:

> *Upon taking the job, one of his first phone calls was to trainer Rick Griffin, seeking an assessment of personnel from the '92 team. . . .*
>
> *"I trust trainers as much or more than scouts," Piniella said. "Be honest and don't sugarcoat—nobody knows we're talking."*
>
> *In a conversation that lasted two and a half hours, Griffin spelled*

it out, saying there really was only one guy who didn't fit. A couple of days later the oft-injured, portly outfielder Kevin Mitchell was traded to Cincinnati for relief pitcher Norm Charlton, who would become vital in the Mariners' climb.

Piniella called Griffin again: "How do you like that?"

"Wow," Griffin said. "You work fast."

"From now on, we're going to work fast."

The Piniella Solution, then, is

RULE 2.02a. Start at the bottom of the org chart and solicit suggestions in the "What needs changing/improving around here?" line.

RULE 2.02b. Act quickly and publicize the change.

RULE 2.02c. Follow up quickly with more so you can accustom staff and adjacent departments to the idea that change is an ongoing process with pay-offs.

The approach is not effortless or without potential pitfalls. Many times, line workers "don't get it." Some suggestions they make will be entirely dysfunctional and not based in any reality that exists outside of old *Star Trek: Enterprise* episodes. But line staff know things others don't, and there's much ore to mine there.

Personally, I've gotten my highest quick returns in larger organizations from people who work in the mailroom. In the realm of management by walking around, they are the people who walk around the most. They see things not from a departmental perspective, but from a more integrated systemic model—the patterns that connect departments or functions.

What's the best way to put this approach into action? Start with a formal announcement that you'll be collecting positive ideas for increasing quality and quantity, trimming waste. Make one-on-one appointments with every single staff member for this specific purpose, and with managers of groups that have been working with your own group. Start at the bottom and work your way up. People at the bottom will reveal the most naïve, pure ideas, and as you move up the hierarchy, you'll discover the "why-nots" that prevented the good ones from being implemented. Just because there are established why-nots doesn't mean you shouldn't or can't use the good ideas anyway.

In scheduling these meetings, establish some firm, understandable rules:

RULE 2.03a. No complaining, just solutions. These are not vent sessions, not "things that need to be fixed, but I don't know how" descriptions. Those need to be saved for a later inning. These are for hassles the staffer has an idea about how to attack. It doesn't even have to be fully formed, but insisting that the discussion must include a hint of a solution will filter out much of the complaining-without-point that infests most big organizations.

RULE 2.03b. No personal vituperation. These are not sessions for venting disappointment, anger, or negativity about other individuals. If there are complaints about other departments that relate to behaviors or processes that specifically undermine your group's efforts, that should be open for discussion, but discourage complaints that sit on top of personality, and focus on specific processes that will break through the blockage.

RULE 2.03c. Share credit. Do it publicly for ideas that get implemented; explain you'll showcase staffers. This is an old Sparky Anderson trick—in giving all the credit to and talking up the individual contributors, Anderson won loyalty and trust. He also became less of a lightning rod because observers (the press, his bosses) slowly came to perceive the work as a team effort and, when things didn't work out, realized it was not the result of the failure of a single individual. When you deliver on this credit-sharing promise, you'll generate more incoming ideas. You'll get for free what consultants might miss but for which they'd charge you an amount that would outweigh Jason Giambi reporting to spring training.

RULE 2.03d. Demand realism. Ideas have to be within the realm of what you might be able to do. Staffers need to know you won't be fielding suggestions to make over the whole organization. Action should be within the span of your control, or within an adjacent department that directly affects your group's effectiveness. Discussions that cross that border are still appropriate, perhaps with the whole group over coffee or a couple of beers, but not in these sessions.

RULE 2.03e. Prior rejection is no barrier. Ideas can be ones already rejected by your predecessor. Just because your predecessor thought an idea was bad doesn't mean it won't work. In fact, the longer she was in the job, the more likely it really is a good idea. As you'll see when we get to the Law of Problem Evolution in chapter 4, the more problems a manager solves, the higher the percentage of those that remain are unsolvable by that manager.

RULE 2.03f. Implement with experiments. Experiment actively but start small with the ones that seem most risky. It's true I've had what I consider my most extreme failures while experimenting early on, but I've never been able to get as much forgiveness as I have then. I always make experiments mandatory. If a solution had not required experimentation, my predecessor would have solved the problem already.

If you were promoted from within the group, the techniques just described are even better, because you've been observing the group's workings and keeping a mental to-do list noting easy-but-high-return fixes.

Earl Weaver kept that list as a struggling second baseman on a struggling Knoxville minor-league team. When the manager was fired, Weaver got the job and responded with quick changes based on what he already knew about the team.[4] The very first thing he did was replace himself on the field with a younger prospect with higher potential. Then he killed the late-night-till-early-morning poker party the players held after road games. He enjoyed playing in it, but as manager, he saw that it cost the team an edge in lost rest.

The legendary "First 100 Days" are busy, but you'll never have as much latitude to act decisively as you will when you start a new management position. As in baseball, if you run up the score early, it's very difficult to fail. When a major-league team scores a couple of runs in the first inning, it goes on to win more than 68 percent of the time.

RULE 2.04a. Change some things for the better. Provide tangible benefits your bosses and staff and peer managers care about right away.

#2. Management by Taking Exception (MBTE)

Whatever you do, don't let your experimental intensity be limited by your predecessor's conception of who on your staff can do what well.

I learned this from Joe McCarthy—the most successful baseball manager ever, not the most demented U.S. senator ever. McCarthy managed three teams over 24 seasons and never had a losing season. Never. Each team improved big-time in his first year: the Cubs by 14 wins, the Yankees by eight, the Red Sox by 12. How did he do it? By examining the environment, relentlessly seeking out and unceasingly fixing current weaknesses, giving people previously considered failures a chance to succeed in a different environment, delegating responsibility, and experimenting.

With the power-needy Cubs, he picked up outfielder Hack Wilson, a reputed alcoholic dumped by the Giants. In the five years Wilson played for McCarthy, he led the NL in homers four times. In 1930 he set one of the two records most likely to remain unbroken: he had 191 RBI. And McCarthy experimented; he was one of the first managers to use dedicated relief pitchers when other managers used failed or day-off starters to pick up for tapped-out starters.

Importantly, whatever environment McCarthy was in, he adapted to it. He didn't bring a one-size-fits-all plan and try to force it, a common management error. Entire contemporary industries, like big-time consulting, are based on, more than anything else, trying to develop a viable solution for one client and then selling it over and over again, cloning the execution, maximizing the return on effort in a way that underperforms because it ignores environments. Be McCarthy. Observe, experiment, be responsive to the new environment, listen to staff. Get off to a killer start. Use what I call the McCarthy Redeployment Tool: Talk privately with each of your staff and find out what they know how to do that's not in their current list of duties, what jobs they've been cross-trained for, what they minored in if they went to college. Find out what each has always wanted to do but hasn't had a chance to do yet.

Keep the list at hand. Use it to assign help to an overworked or underqualified staffer, add a new perspective to a small team that's stuck, or remake job duties within your group to squeeze out more work with the same effort. Blend them in carefully. Don't assume an employee with college credit or even experience at a particular task does it well. Don't assume that an employee who hasn't done the task before must not be good at it.

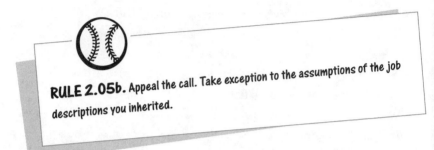

RULE 2.05b. Appeal the call. Take exception to the assumptions of the job descriptions you inherited.

Paul Richards built strong teams for the Chicago White Sox (1951–54). He was responsible for triggering the structured management approach used with such great success by the Baltimore Orioles and managed them from 1955 to 1961. He argued that his quickest and clearest ideas of how to succeed were from tracking others' mistakes or omissions. He built his teams by doing those things correctly, deriving theories of what should work by subtracting all the consistent failures from all the possible paths to success.

You'll benefit from what I call the Richards Counter-disciple Tool: Make another list of every boss you had long enough to understand at least a little. For each, write down every operational decision that was clearly a failure from the start and that was important enough to affect the work. Write down everything they didn't do (omissions) that would have made a difference—just the ones that were difference makers. Now put them all together in one master list of failures and omissions.

On the master list, put an X next to any item that made (or could have made) a lot of difference to the outcome. Put a check mark next to any item that looks like it might be relevant to the situation you're in right now. For each of those, choose an alternative approach that's not necessarily the opposite.

Start by quickly implementing the items that have both an X and a check mark, then the ones with either. Keep the counter-disciple fixes coming, slowing only if staff are confused or getting overwhelmed by change. It's critical to train at this point, to coach, to set things up so people are used to the fact that the team is active and that you're working together with them, not just shoving them around on a chessboard.

This doesn't mean you're asking permission: you're not; you're enlisting. And when you slow the implementation of new methods, processes, actions, make it clear that the slowing is only temporary, that you're not stopping. You're only giving people time to internalize the changes you've already given them; there are definitely more on the way.

#3. Management by Imitation

I mention Management by Imitation—following the lessons of other managers you've worked for—*after* MBTE because I think it's more obvious. Most managers come to this approach naturally, many of them unconsciously.

When they get their first chance to manage, some people just create a template of a past manager. It's not necessarily a bad idea, but if you do take that approach, don't get too comfortable and allow that to be a rut. It's almost a sure thing that you're different, the staff is different, and the decision environment is different, so that template will need at least some tuning.

Consider each manager you worked for as having a tool kit, a set of ways of making things happen, some of which are worth picking up and using for this job. When you move into a new position, you can browse through each manager's tool kit, through each of their tools, and pick out various ones to use.

Dick Williams did this when he started his first major-league assignment. He remembered Branch Rickey's rigorous spring-training-camp drills for instilling fundamentals in the Brooklyn Dodgers. "The first key to surviving this camp was . . . realizing that fundamentals were the most important tools a player can possess," Williams wrote. "By the time camp ended after six weeks, you had either quit or were so fundamentally sound that the majority of mistakes you made that year involved bad hops."

This was conscious imitation. "The best thing for me about those training methods was that I stole them shamelessly when I became a manager." You can emulate Williams and cherry-pick pieces of management skills from previous bosses, as long as you think about whether the pieces fit in your current situation. And be vigilant that you're not imitating unconsciously, simply cloning something ordinary or even very flawed just because you don't know any other way.

You see a lot of unconscious imitation in decision-making approaches. A manager who's had but one boss will often be unaware that there are many approaches, and will follow whatever she experienced before without questioning it.

There are certain patterns that just plain work. All else being equal, it's easier to advance a runner from first base to third base on a single to right field than on a single to left field, so it makes sense to try to hit it to right field. But even in baseball, most situations are not so clear-cut. Conscious, examined imitation is a powerful way to pick out successful approaches from past experience.

The Decline of the Player-Manager

When I manage a group, I take on a share of the work myself to stay involved on a daily basis in some element of the job that gives me feedback about what's going on in the group at a molecular level. I also take on tasks that reinforce my awareness of the big picture. When I advise clients, I usually advise them to do the same.

How much line work (work that's got no management content in it) should you try to do as a manager? Should you just manage, or should you take on actual production work, too? I'm going to tell you why taking on some work is problematic and why you should do it anyway.

When the National Association started with a formal schedule and set of teams in 1871, all the "managers" were players doing double duty. There hasn't been a single major-league team managed by a player on the roster in the 21st century; the last, Pete Rose, did his double duty in 1986. What's changed? For one thing, the economics. Early professional baseball had small rosters, specialization was spotty, and finances were tight, but more than anything else, the job wasn't seen as critical. The manager of a team in early baseball was more like a team captain.

But the game got professional in the 1870s. After a while there was a cadre of retired pros who liked the game, and it started making sense to allow some of them to stay involved, mentor, and share their lessons learned.

As you can see from the table, the number of player-managers fluctuated, rose in the first decade of "modern" baseball, and declined consistently,

Decade	% of Player-Managers	Decade	% of Player-Managers
1870s	68	1940s	19
1880s	41	1950s	7
1890s	50	1960s	4
1900s	57	1970s	2
1910s	44	1980s	1
1920s	24	1990s	0
1930s	32		

Source: *The Bill James Guide to Baseball Managers*

with the exception of the decade of Herbert Hoover's Great Depression, which put pressure on baseball costs, making it more appealing to have a player do double duty as manager.

There are always structural challenges for baseball's player-managers. You have to divide attention between managing and your play. It's physically possible to be a base runner on first and signal to the third-base coach to tell the batter you want him to lay off the next pitch because you're going to try to steal, but functionally, this has overhead that diminishes its effectiveness. Extra signals mean extra chances for misinterpretation or sign theft, and the manager has to focus on that particular play, not on the sequence that must follow. Also, you have to give orders to people who are, in one sense, your peers, and this creates social friction. ("Hey, you're just a third baseman, who are you to be telling me what to do?") Players are unionized now; a player-manager can join, and compromise his position with ownership, or not join, and compromise his position with his fellow players.

Finally, you will rarely get compensated for the sum of what you do on the two jobs together. When I say compensated, I mean in money or honor or respect or in any of the most common currencies you might value. The average baseball manager's salary today is probably one-fourth the average ballplayer's. So the three reasons together inspire both prospective player-managers and front offices to back off the arrangement.

Beyond baseball, those three reasons hold sway, too. In most organizations, politics and false assumptions pressure managers to attend meeting after meeting, talking about work. In many shops, being absent from a meeting means being punished with random tasks your department will have slathered on it like pump cheese on ballpark nachos, or causing a weakened sense of your group's importance among peers. In most shops, doing line work, the everyday tasks in your staffers' job descriptions, diminishes the focus you can put on your management tasks and vice versa.

And if you choose to roll up your sleeves and do line work, some types of staff members will view you with less respect. There are some people who see the world as divided between lords and serfs, and if you're not acting like a lord, they assume you are, or want to be, a serf, and this can undermine your authority.

Those are all good reasons not to do line work. But if you're in an organization that is not extremely unhealthy, the balance is in favor of being a player-manager. It's easier to get a fine-tuned view of individual employees' strengths and weaknesses when you're working alongside them or actively helping them. You get a clearer perception of how things are going, what support systems are creating wind drag, what regulations are wasteful, where you should add quality-control steps. Moreover, if the manager is cross-trained to get line work done, she's available in emergencies.

All groups face frustrations. When you've experienced them firsthand, you may generate the energy to fix them, or you may find them trifling and be in a better position to ask your staff to take them in stride (they'll have reason to believe you).

Close-up observation and working alongside your staff push efforts across the finish line, ones that might not make it otherwise, and can win the loyalty of employees who, under pressure, see that you're there for them. If you do particularly good work, you get the added benefit of having them respect you for being good at what they do well, and then they will find it easier to take coaching from you.

When I ran the InfoWorld Test Center, a group that tested and reviewed computer-related products for a weekly publication, I was the tester of last resort. All the problems that couldn't be solved by the specialists or their more experienced supervisors ended up on my desk. I happen to be better than average at solving those problems, even though I always knew less about any single product than the specialist's supervisor did. But even if I hadn't been good at it, I was still gaining the insight I needed to help staff break through the problems. In addition, it made me better prepared to answer questions like "How should I structure the work?" and "Do we have the right personnel and equipment?"

A consultant friend once called on me to help him with clients, a couple who had expanded their successful specialty retail store into a small local chain that had both retail and wholesale customers. As they prepared a franchise scheme to expand, they noticed profitability flagging, sales off a little, and theft up a lot—the worst thing that could happen for the window dressing required to either borrow or sell equity for expansion. The consultant friend had beaten his brains out using his full tool kit trying to locate the failure. He'd helped them buy security systems, devised a product-tagging scheme, analyzed marketing—the works.

I couldn't find anything either. So we met with the clients, and I got the couple to detail what they had been doing month by month. When I mapped it back against their problems, I saw that their slump began when the wife started doing the books from home so she could care for a child while the husband was tied up off-site with the financial efforts for the expansion.

I still didn't know what was wrong, but I bet myself *they* would know if they spent two weeks on the floors. Acting on my advice, each of the co-owners went back to a storefront (she to the largest, he to the smallest) as a floater (a stocking clerk–cashier–customer–assistance person). It took her two days to find the problem.

Their new computerized inventory system needed to maintain a single inventory that kept the wholesale business and the retail business conceptually separate. There were configuration problems; the system wasn't registering any small-quantity wholesale purchases as sales. The sales were made, but because the system didn't know about them, when the stock was scanned, the disparity between what had been registered as sales and the store inventory made it look like stock had "disappeared" (been stolen). Also, because the system was set up to trigger reorders, and it was not tracking items that had sold, the shelves weren't properly stocked and they were losing sales opportunities, ergo the lagging sales. Because she was an old-fashioned kind of manager, she printed out tapes and resolved them against the inventory system at the end of each day to get a feel for the small details. Everyone else had simply trusted the electronic system because the couple had assumed it was trustworthy. Nobody else had the molecular feel for the shops that the owner-managers had, and they could spot almost instantly the flaw that others couldn't.

Hands-on work provides a level of detail that informs the management decision-making process. I'm all in favor of being a player-manager. But let me warn you of two wrongheaded seductions that motivate people to be player-managers. Avoid these.

A common one is the inability to let go of the relative ease of line work. Some people, promoted from within or insecure in their management ability but secure in their ability to do their old job, escape into line work. It can be a security blanket. They get to feel good about themselves, like they're really making something happen no matter how badly the management work is going.

Another seduction is the "If it's gonna get done correctly, I have to do it myself" neurosis. It may be totally wrong, it may be totally correct; but either way, the group doesn't function if you don't delegate and train. If you can't make another worker close enough to "as good" as you are, you're probably not management material.

If you can be a player-manager and not be doing it for the wrong reasons, experiment with it. You'll stay in touch with details that few managers have access to.

Establishing a Reputation, Dick Williams Style

When you start a management position in a new company or in a group that doesn't know you well, there will be staffers who don't want it to be too easy for you.

One or two of them might have been angling for your job themselves. Many males compete by a zero-sum equation; they re-create frat boys' hazing rituals, behaving as though you have to earn their compliance. Similarly, many females manage their environment by manipulation, testing your resolve and determination.

You're going to have to establish a reputation that has a full spectrum of possibilities, because different people are best managed with different incentives and approaches. If you're a natural hard-ass, you'll need to learn to establish a reputation as a cooperator. If you're a nice guy, you'll need to show your assertiveness.

And once established, you'll need to reinforce your reputation with consistent "marketing," that is, presenting yourself in a certain way. But you may equally need to alter your reputation in response to group needs or events.

Dick Williams was hired by Charlie O. Finley to take the Oakland A's to a new level. The team had built a roster very wisely in the late 1960s and had two second-place finishes in a row (1969 and 1970) with aloof, businesslike managers Hank Bauer and John McNamara. Finley understood that a different style can frequently bring out new strengths without losing strengths already internalized.

Williams was more a one-of-the-guys manager, but when he got to the A's, they were already swaggering, feeling like champs, and had three clubhouse leaders, according to Williams. There was Reggie Jackson, the vocal one; Sal Bando, the quiet clubhouse emissary; and Catfish Hunter, the ace pitcher and campus clown who kept everyone loose. As Williams wrote in his book *No More Mister Nice Guy:*

> *I'll let players lead themselves, particularly veterans like Catfish, as long as they recognize and respect the ultimate authority. Me.*
>
> *. . . We had opened that first A's season by losing four of our first six games. . . . I was a little worried about a pitching staff that had allowed 40 runs in those games. Then I became more worried after Charlie called me and pitching coach Bill Posedel to his apartment and asked what the hell I was going to do about it.*
>
> *By the time the plane landed in Milwaukee to begin the trip, I had advanced from worried to angry.*

His players were loose, but in a bad, unproductive way, and they were not listening to their manager. Williams knew he needed to change the established shape of the manager-player relationship in a way that asserted his dominance, but not in some hysterical Captain Queeg out-of-context rant. Fate handed him an opportunity right that minute in Milwaukee.

The players got off the plane and boarded their bus. A flight attendant came running out to the bus, jumped on it, and explained that someone had stolen a megaphone from the plane and he had to return it.

"I sucked in my breath," Williams said. "It was time to stop staring in awe at my Athletics and start shoving them." He stood up in the aisle and announced he was going to stand there until they coughed up that megaphone. Silence, jostling and nudging, snickers.

"I don't know if you guys know this, but we aren't exactly burning up the damn league." More silence, more snickers. "I know some of you think you can be assholes. . . . Well, I can be the biggest asshole of them all. And if you have a problem with that, just call Charlie . . . but he ain't here now and I am, and you'd better learn to live with—." Clunk. The megaphone was returned.

It turned out it was ace pitcher Catfish Hunter who'd stolen the megaphone.

"I knew and the team knew but I never did anything about it. As it turned out, I should have given him a bonus for feeding me the slow curve that enabled this team to feel my swing. I was never told how they reacted to it, but then I didn't need to be told; I saw. We won 12 of our next 13 games. Six days after my meltdown, we went into first place and were never caught."

Sometimes a tantrum is just what's needed. Usually it's something else. But you have to wait for the right opportunity, because if it's out of context or feels staged, it will actually degrade your authority. Be prepared as a new manager to broaden your normal public responses to difficult situations and challenging people, especially in the first three weeks of your tenure.

Exploding out of the Batter's Box

Starting a new management gig is exciting, especially if you make the most of it. Even if it's your first time as a manager, there are things you can do to establish yourself with your staff and with your executives and harvest quick returns. Just follow the examples of great baseball managers like Joe McCarthy.

But managing ongoing operational tasks is different after you're established. To be effective at managing over a long season with a stable rule book but ever-changing environments and situations requires deftly working with the three elements that make the key difference between adequacy and running up big scores. In chapter 3, we'll cover those three elements.

3

Executing the Fundamentals: Marshaling Time, Humans, & Knowledge

To get the most from the people you manage,
you must put them in the right spot at the right time.
—Joe Torre

Once you've established yourself, scouted out your new situation, and hammered out some hits, you will face the equivalent of a long baseball season, the daily chance to prove yourself, to succeed, to fail, to learn from both and come back the next day and start again.

If you don't focus on keeping your operational management very sharp, you're likely to lose effectiveness. There's nothing sadder than seeing a team that's 12–21 struggle through the rest of its season, straining to find the juice just to crawl to .500. On the other hand, teams that are competitive every day, that are playing the fundamentals well and know they're producing face every new day with higher enthusiasm, win or lose.

The core of those operational-management fundamentals is the management of time, humans, and knowledge. If you master all three and nothing else, you'll be better than 65 percent of managers, who, in my experience, never get to first base safely.

Time: A Friend or the Grim Reaper

Marshaling time may be the hardest challenge to master among this trio. That's because unlike managing humans and knowledge, the ability to deal with time is mostly innate—like hitting a knuckleball, it's a gift that some have and some don't, and it really can't be learned.

Baseball is the only sport where the final outcome of games is unattached to a clock. As significant a philosopher as George Carlin has argued that this fact alone makes the National Pastime morally superior to other sports. But time is as essential to baseball as it is to any other profession, and successful baseball managers need to be as sensitive to time as managers in any other endeavor.

Scientists frequently describe time as "the fourth dimension." For the good managers I've worked with, time really is a dimension, like height or width. I've found that people with a strong aptitude for realistic schedule making also know, for example, how to pack a moving van. Those who see time spatially can manipulate their own use of it, as if it were any other dimension. Of those people, I say, "Time is their friend."

But I've yet to meet anyone who got training that took him from low to high performance in marshaling time—knowing how to plan a project, how to sequence tasks, which event to set in motion today even though it won't deliver results for weeks, and how many additional employees the project needs to shorten delivery by a month. There are formal tools like project-management theory (combined with either paper 'n' pencil or software). Training can act as a crutch for a person with a broken leg—it alleviates the injury but can't make the injury whole. The clearest sign you'll ever get that a person is controlled by time and can't marshal it himself is if he utters the fantasy phrase "do more with less." For those people, time is the Grim Reaper (Latin motto: "No one gets out alive") closing in on them inevitably while they try to bargain with it.

Because the majority of managers don't manage time well, they can't manage "slack," work hours not assigned to a scheduled task. When managers don't know how much slack their team has, some throw up their hands and leave too much. Most do worse, leaving no slack in any effort, so everyone is always an ångstrom away from snapping, without a minute for introspection, quality control, or process tuning. The ideal to aim for is more than enough slack, but with the manager providing lower-urgency, high-value assignments for everyone to work on during slack times.

Time: Pie Traynor's 1938 No-Slack Pirate Burnout

Failure to allow slack puts your team in the position of having no margin for error. Recognize that slumps happen even to the best, and without slack, a manager has no resources to pile on against a slump. Hall of Famer Pie Traynor taught us this the hard way with his management of the 1938 Pirates, famous for losing the pennant on Cubs' slugger Gabby Hartnett's "Homer in the Gloaming."

The Bucs had a great season: by August 9, they were 62–35, scoring about 4.9 runs per game, 6½ games ahead of the second-place Giants and eight games ahead of the Cubs. If the season had ended at the two-thirds mark, the Pirates would have won the flag by five games, their glory assured.

That's also true of projects outside of baseball at the two-thirds mark, and too many fail even after getting off to a good start. Most projects that fold after a good start have had project managers who were pressured to overcommit resources so there was nothing set aside, pushing people to their limit while allowing no reserve for change of direction. Even the need for a moderate midterm tweak will blow this puppy off the tracks like a British commuter-rail disaster. The incongruous result is that a manager who's blown a project off deadline by making this error before is most likely in her next project to try to drive people harder and trim *more* slack out of schedules.

At September 1, with a month to go, the Cubs were still seven games back. The Pirates continued to play tepid ball, their offense scoring 17 percent fewer runs per game (4.1) from August 9 on, finishing the season with a 12–16 month and finally being surpassed in a head-to-head contest with the Cubs on September 28, when Hartnett, the best all-around catcher in the majors at the time, hit his legendary homer.

It was, as they say in the circus, "cherry pie time." Traynor had fallen in love with his starters, resting almost no one. According to Bill James: "Like Leo Durocher in 1969 and Don Zimmer in 1977, Traynor rode his starting lineup into the ground. All of his regulars except the catcher had more than 600 plate appearances, and all played more than 90% of the team's games." [5]

James adds that the exception, Al Todd the catcher (motto: "Not quite good enough to be mediocre"), caught more games than any other catcher in the majors. This was a classic blunder, what I call "strip-mining," which is all about achieving in the moment, and nothing about sustaining a winning effort over time.

Baseball is more accountable than other lines of work. After Traynor had an off season the following year, he never managed in the majors again. Sadly, managers who do this in other lines of work sometimes escape reckoning for a while. You know the types I'm talking about: the little martinet who has a newborn at home and fabricates excuses not to have to leave work, the spineless yes-manager who transceives the ignorant urgency of her executive team and merely rebroadcasts it to the staff, the adrenaline junkie who loves the jolt of the 70-hour week and fluffs himself up with the delusion that the new shrink-wrap roller project carries the import of holding the Allied flank at Sword Beach on D–Day.

A manager needs real slack in the schedule. For the "I'll do it later" denier, there *never* is a good time. "We're ahead, let's stay ahead." "We're right on target, let's not take a chance." "How can I give you time off for that vacation you earned? We're behind."

People can be driven very hard, harder with the right balance of morale and compensation. But even ambitious and happy contributors will hit a point where their contributions will start failing in quantity, quality, or both. Studies I've done indicate that about 77 percent of people lose *at least half* of their effectiveness after 52 hours a week compared to what they produced over the first 52 hours. Strip-mining managers waste their group's effectiveness, pimping quality for the joy (sometimes illusory) of instant quantity, and end up suppressing both quality and quantity over the long haul.

The tough part of managing slack if you're not already good at it is that it's almost impossible for those who have the knack to come up with crutches for the ones who don't. Here's a tool I use for managers who are not naturals at managing time. It works for about half of them.

RULE 3.01a. Stop-loss. Never schedule anyone for more than 52 hours a week.

RULE 3.01b. Reserve slack for your productive contributors, an amount of time in their week without preassigned work. If your project/work staff has more than five people, the percentage of the workweek you set aside for slack should be around 1 divided by (the number of people on your staff + 1), so if you have six people, you'd set aside $1/(6 + 1)$, which is $1/7$ of the time for slack, which is about 1.1 hours per day. So when you schedule a productive individual's time, leave out assignments for 1.1 hours a day. This is a reserve you can throw at other things that come up.

RULE 3.01c. Experiment with your nonproductive staff. Start by scheduling the nonproductive full-time (no slack). Track their production on a daily or at least weekly basis. Then start introducing slack into their schedules, trying out different activities and different amounts of time each week and continuing to monitor production quantity and quality. After about seven weeks, go back and look at your collected data. Do individuals have unique patterns? Do certain people perform their work better when their slack activity is something specific? You may find people who cannot be productive. Try being creative and getting other staffers' ideas before you give up, because you'll always be carrying the stigma of your failure, a failed staffer.

If you can't find a way to make unproductive staffers reasonably productive, you're the wrong manager for them and you should be looking for a way to move them from your department, with one exception (see "The Résumé Is Not the Person? Hiring Doug Glanvilles and Tony Phillipses," in chapter 5).

Time: Branch Rickey's Model for Managing Meetings

I won't understate the problem of *too much* slack. When Branch Rickey, then general manager of the Brooklyn Dodgers, opened the first structured spring-training facility at Vero Beach, Florida, he attacked what had been a leaguewide pandemic of too much slack. In the model he inherited, equipment was meager, drills were desultory, training was absent. Rickey not only created and scheduled structured drills for hitting, pitching, and infield execution; he devised mechanical aids, such as a physical "strike zone" for pitchers to throw to and a special sliding pit so players could practice that art repeatedly with a low risk of injury.

Another thing Rickey was fanatical about was the amount of time spent in meetings—yes, in baseball they have that problem, too. These are his words to a hall of players at Vero Beach early one spring training:

> We have 140 men here, and there will be another 35 here in a few days, making 175 altogether. One man comes in late which takes the time of at least 150 men which is 150 minutes, which would make him two and a half hours late. There will be men late and sometimes unavoidably so. Rather than stay outside, they come in ten minutes late, if necessary. That's 1,500 minutes or 250 hours. On the field, when you're called, don't just walk over, come double-time, get there fast. Men are waiting until you do.[6]

It's been my experience that in most organizations, white-collar employees spend about 16–22 percent of their work time in meetings (the women as well as the men, Mr. Rickey). I know this because I make them use a log to keep track of their time (more on that tool later . . . it's one you can use to great advantage). The higher people are in the hierarchy, the more their time is allegedly worth, but the more time they spend in meetings. I'm not opposed to meetings, but given the vast resources most organizations throw at them, they'd better be as effective as possible.

Many formal meetings follow Robert's Rules of Order, but I always try to apply Rickey's Rules. I have two rules of my own I like to add to Rickey's. First, and this is especially useful if you make a point of starting meetings on time, try to deal right away with one or a few uncontroversial or small issues that you can knock out of the box one right after another. Most planned meetings start way out in the bleachers away from the action, either with a reading of minutes (make sure whoever's responsible sends minutes around before the meeting so people can read them at their own pace) or a bit of comforting social time. But going straight to the mission, providing current information and making decisions based on that, not only sets a fantastic tone, but pressures the chronically late to be

RULE 3.02a. Start on time. If the meetings are worth having, start 'em on time. If there are twelve people attending and it starts five minutes late, that's (12 x 5) an hour torched.

RULE 3.02b. Start on time no matter what. If the person who usually dominates or runs the meeting is late, start without her. In most cases, supervisors are chronically late because of (a) insensitivity or (b) a neurotic control/dominance assertion. If it's (a), there's some hope; many executives can be trained to be sensitive to time when you run the Rickey math of wasted time and explain it to them. If it's (b) and they're coming late to prove they are important, starting on time sets off two possible outcomes. The productive neurotic will start coming on time so she can stay in control. The destructive neurotic will out herself by being publicly petulant, and out herself with nowhere to hide, undermining her support.

RULE 3.02c. Don't fill time. If you have objectives for the meeting, don't act like you have to fill the time. If you finish early, break early and make something positive happen with that time. Once you're in the habit of finishing early, it'll benefit you to plan in advance what to get done with the extra time.

RULE 3.02d. Start moving quickly. Knock out some small, tractable issues first to get on a roll. It sets a winning tone and pressures the late to arrive on time.

RULE 3.02e. Rotate scut work to focus attention. Everyone should have to maintain minutes once in a while.

on time. Some actually improve their on-time attendance. But even when they don't, things move along, and the attendees get an early sense of progress, like scoring a run or two in each of the first couple of innings.

Second, I like to rotate note-taking responsibility among all attendees regardless of status. This forces everyone to pay full attention at least once in a while. And as I mentioned earlier, minutes should go out in paper or e-mail long enough before the scheduled meeting that people can absorb them at their own pace and not slow down everyone else, like a late Dodger to one of those Vero Beach confabs.

Gaining control of time doesn't always require trimming. Sometimes you just shift time from one function to others. But most organizations, while they might be able to *guess,* couldn't tell you with any degree of accuracy how they actually invest their time. That information is invaluable. For example, if you knew how much time your nurses spent filling out redundant information on forms, you might refine the processes to prevent these time wasters in the first place.

The main benefit of tracking time stats is parallel to a ball club tracking its stats to squeeze more advantage out of its roster: you can create slack time by finding activities to cut back or eliminate to free up time for important ones. There's a nimble technique you can use in most organizations to get that information. In my work, I frequently get managers and staff to log their time in tenths of hours. I have my own system, somewhat like the Dewey decimal system, but for categorizing white-collar work. I call it the WCS (Work Category System). WCS is a simpler, lower-overhead version of a system big organizations use called Work Breakdown Structure (WBS).

In WCS, you have overarching categories that describe kinds of work people in a work group do. Then you break that work into the tasks that make it up, and if you're really ambitious, divide those smaller pieces into subcategories (more categories aren't necessarily better . . . and can be worse). At the Tools page on the *Management by Baseball* Web site (www.ManagementByBaseball.Com), you can download a sample file you can tune to your own requirements, and find instructions for designing and using your own WCS. I strongly urge you to try it out; it's one of the most powerful tools you'll have.

The decisions powered by analysis of WCS results will vary between organization. The kinds of reshaping tactics that are almost universal include prescribing stricter limits on meeting times, correcting excessive investments in lower-value efforts, redirecting time to higher-value efforts, and tuning of job descriptions to distribute work more efficiently.

You'll find links to decent books on using WBS at the same *Management by Baseball* Web site page. While books tend to prescribe methods that are overkill for most organizations, don't allow yourself to be intimidated by their formality—remember, the WCS is a simpler system and only needs to be precise enough to give you the information you need. Branch Rickey knew about WBS, but when the time came to make spring training effective, he didn't mess with the full system. He created a simplified variant that turned his teams into competitive monsters.

Time: Earl Weaver's Model for Pacing

For Rickey's minions, spring training was like drinking out of a fire hose. Almost three decades later, Earl Weaver tweaked that model in a brilliant example of managing time. Knowing that most players wouldn't start spring in playing shape, he began training with a mandate to start slowly, to get players through the first few weeks uninjured. Like Rickey, Weaver didn't believe in downtime, but he understood that life is a marathon, not a sprint.

"I'm trying to keep standing around to a minimum," Weaver said. "The worst type of spring training is a camp where nothing happens. You've got to make sure everybody's busy every minute they're on the field. The players get bored and feel like they're not doing anything." He added, "You can always have drills to keep people moving."

Weaver never advocated busywork. Drills are skills-building exercises, like focused training. For your group, maintain a list of index cards with actions you need to take but never seem to have time or resources for.[7]

RULE 3.03. No busywork. In nonbaseball settings, the drills to keep people moving should *never* be busywork; they're that pile of Important-but-not-Urgent tasks sitting on everyone's back burner. If you build in the right amount of slack, there are times when people have no direct project work due. But if we give everyone the important-but-not-urgent tasks and make clear that we expect them to work on them during slack times, the good contributors are happy to get something valuable done.

Time: Dick Williams's Applied Fun Gambit

If your own team is both stressed and has extra slack—lots of postmodern American organizations garner that dubious achievement—you can even make the work notably fun, as long as you get some actual production out of it. Dick Williams devised a different downtime devastator when he was a rookie manager with the 1967 Boston Red Sox. He decided to replace the universal time-filler for pitchers (time spent desultorily shagging batting practice fly balls) with a drill that had an element of fun. He scheduled pitchers for volleyball games, working vertical movement eye-hand skills and quick feet skills, neither of which are an enjoyable part of the pitchers' spring training regimen. So it was a drill, but it was a game, naturally fun for active people. Plus, the winning team won a prize— the right to run only half the postworkout sprints.

Find something competitive and fun to use as a idleness eraser. Rookie manager Williams took that team, in ninth place the previous year, to the World Series, in part because from the start they were striving relentlessly *and* having fun.

Humans: The Talent *Is* the Product

Managing time requires a mixture of the concrete and the intuitive, but managing the people who work within your group is more of a challenge. The insights in this chapter are not for understanding individuals—those are second-base skills—but for getting the most out of their time and skills, and setting up the environment for them to succeed so the team can succeed. There are two polar-opposite views of people as resources in operational management, and both are illusions. The first is the mechanistic view, that people are interchangeable machines, or should aspire to be. The other is that people's humanity is violated and they're being manipulated if we're shaping the environment to squeeze more effectiveness out of them.

People are the irreplaceable ingredient in valuable work. Just as you invest effort in keeping office temperatures in a zone where people are effective, you should invest in making effective teams by blending talent on projects and by keeping job descriptions tuned to what the group needs and the talent can do.

Knowledge: The Indispensable Competitive Tool

Because of Michael Lewis's book *Moneyball*, awareness of sabermetrics, the craft and art of modern, research-based baseball statistics, exploded like a five-run rally. The results were typical: team owners read the book, and instructed their staffs to pay attention. Some adopted, some synthesized, and others created a counter-reformation. The backlash pushes the idea that scouting is everything, and the numbers are just vapor.

The duality is a false one, created for the political jockeying of a few insiders and to provide grist to some sportswriters who need a parade of ideas to supplement their own meager store. Even the most statistically focused baseball teams spend more money on nonstatistical player evaluation than they do on stats. Even the most scouting-focused teams pay close attention to the stats. Every baseball team applies the four core elements of knowledge management (KM): acquisition, organization, analysis, and delivery. This puts baseball way ahead of about 80 percent of all other lines of work in the ability to create and use business intelligence.

Two of the most successful practitioners of business intelligence in any field are Tony LaRussa and Mike Scioscia, both of whom publicly dis the stat-heads. Yet St. Louis Cardinal manager LaRussa was one of the first managers to use computer printouts to organize his knowledge. And Angel manager Scioscia spends hours every week poring over number-stuffed reports. He reveres the statistic that sabermetricians consider the crown jewel: on-base percentage.

Scioscia's Angels are the most successful team that runs an anti-Moneyball offense. While the Oakland A's as described in the book practice patience at the plate and passive baserunning, the Halos count on contact hitting and aggressive baserunning. Scioscia understands the A's tactics but doesn't try to re-create them, because the Angels don't have the A's personnel. He's got what he has, and he applies his tactics, free of wishful thinking or self-delusion. As he said to me: [8]

> *We hit few home runs, our slugging percentage is down near the bottom of the league. Our on-base is like .325, so how can we compete with a team that has on-base of .350? Some of those teams that have OB of .350 or .360, they can let on-base die on the vine because it's going to be there again. We've got to score runs by maximizing the on-base percentage we have. Ours is only going to be there, .325, and we'd better grasp the opportunity when we can or there's going to be stagnation.*
>
> *I think running the bases aggressively is something that should be the tendency for all teams. That aggressiveness is part of baseball whether you believe in waiting for the three-run homer or not. The Yankees, for example, do a great job of it. All teams get a lot more singles with a runner on first than they do home runs. If you can get that guy to third instead of to second that's a much better statistical position to be in.[9] You're going to have more runs on the bottom line.*

Scioscia, like every passionate sabermetrics fan, pays attention to the on-base proclivities of each batter on his roster. He even has internalized and operates off of a favorite sabermetric tool: a chart that describes the odds of a base runner scoring given the number of outs and bases occupied.[10] If you know the numbers on the chart, you know, for example, what percentage of the time you have to be safe trying to go from first base to third base on a single to make the gamble worthwhile.

The Angel manager led his team to a World Series Championship in 2002 with an offensive style that in the 21st century usually falls flatter than a month-old glass of Dr Pepper. What makes the difference is Scioscia uses the knowledge his front office gives him and he applies it intelligently.

Most organizations are way behind baseball in their collection and analysis of data designed to make everyday work processes better. In tight times, KM initiatives tend to be the first cut, perceived as optional. Baseball proves that organizations in competitive fields that use KM techniques own a strong advantage over those that don't . . . even when they're using strategies that are difficult to implement successfully.

Knowledge: The New York Mets Confront the Diseconomies of Scale

As an organization grows arithmetically in the number of employees or functions it has, the diseconomies of scale corrode efficiency. Yes, there are a few "economies of scale," such as the ability to grind down suppliers because you buy in such bulk, or running a single daily newspaper ad for a three-store burger chain costing the same as it would for a single store, or the ability to reduce per-unit production cost. Contemporary pundits with selective vision like to talk about them, but they never tell you (or perhaps haven't figured out yet) the drop-dead obvious truth: for every economy of scale, there are two or three diseconomies. And here's the collision at the plate. As organizations grow, the diseconomies' symptoms grow at a rate significantly higher than the rate of staff count growth. This is why small businesses, school classes with small numbers of students, small government agencies, and small military units tend to outproduce bigger competitors in truly competitive systems.

One of the key diseconomies of scale is knowledge. Results happen too many departments away from the decisions that shaped them. As organizations grow, knowledge becomes specialized in different areas, and organizational "wise men" become harder to find. That's why smart leaders know and protect those old hands who have institutional knowledge of an organization. The veterans who know how to work the levers and layers of a company in intimate detail prevent most embarrassing misjudgments. Getting the effortless knowledge management that's natural to the small shop working in a larger organization becomes a challenge.

Baseball has many examples of the challenge of KM in a complex organization. Over time, functions tend to get specialized, and cooking up multifunctional or multidisciplinary teams (the kind of groups that tend to produce bigger innovations or important observations) becomes much harder. Ask the New York Mets.

Starting the 2004 season after four consecutive seasons of decline, the New York Mets faced a fussy Gotham market for the team, and knew that what they were doing hadn't been working. The most significant move they made was to pluck the extraordinary knowledge management practitioner and accomplished pitching coach of the Oakland A's and bring him back to the East Coast.

Rick Peterson and his KM wizardry were the foundation of the success of the A's pitching staffs that had brought the team four straight seasons of playoff appearances. As with all top achievers, his toolbox isn't limited to the standard tools. Some sabermetrics aficionados appreciate his famous motto, "In God we trust: all others must have data." But while his approach requires the pitching staff to collaborate with him in a relentless analysis of the data (for example, a pitcher needs to know and act on the fact that a specific batter will swing 75 percent of the time at an 0–0 pitch that's inside or that the batting average of inside 0–0 fastballs put into play against him is .450), his approach extends far beyond unusually wonky printouts.

He's also renowned for dragging his pitchers to a cutting-edge biomechanical lab in Alabama to get their deliveries analyzed by a 500-frame per second, 3-D motion tracking system. The analysis provides information the coach can use to help a hurler refine deliveries to increase speed or to diminish the likelihood of stress injuries.

But a core collection of the knowledge Peterson needs to work his method transcends hard science. It's understanding each individual pitcher's emotional style and staying current with their emotional state. Blending the insights emotional intelligence delivers with data and technology is the essence of successful knowledge management.

The Mets committed to a KM strategy when they recruited Peterson and installed him as the knowledge hub for a vast swath of their baseball operations.

According to a *New York Post* article,[11] the Mets trusted Peterson's KM model and opinion so much, that they changed the way a pitching coach would interact with the rest of the organization.

He campaigned for and won the right to look at tapes of potential draft choices so that he could help recruit the candidates who could best succeed in his system. And Peterson instituted another KM initiative, pooling knowledge about techniques and then diffusing a parallel approach up and down the chain from the bottom of the farm system up to the big club.

I had presumed this would be a standard practice, but when I asked Peterson why the Mets were so slow to join the KM club, he enlightened me—the Mets aren't slow, they are among the vanguard. He explained that in the majors today, this KM practice is an exception, not the rule. Branch Rickey's Dodgers and Paul Richards's Orioles did this 50 years ago. The economics of the game have changed over time, and with it, some KM practices.

The Mets have attacked the diseconomies of scale by letting the intense and visionary coach loose on the problem. It's pretty obvious there's no one better positioned to observe micro and macro trends in major-league hitting and pitching than the big club's pitching coach. He doesn't have to distribute his attention among the myriad of occupations the manager does, has half the personalities (just the pitchers and catchers) to deal with, and is more an observer than a decision maker on in-game decisions. The pitching coach's rôle leaves more energy to devote to basic observation and applied research.

While engaging the pitching coach in scouting decisions may be new to the Mets organization, it's not unprecedented in baseball. In the middle 1950s, Paul Richards laid the foundation for the Baltimore Orioles' two decades of pitching dominance. It was built on multifunctional teams, cross-pollination of observations, and feedback loops designed to get the knowledge of what was going on in the big club's ballparks into a medium that the scouts and minor-league coaching staffs could absorb and turn into action.

Beyond baseball, the model the New York Mets just replaced is the more typical one. When the whole organization fits into a pair of connected rooms, (most always) everyone knows everything important that everyone else knows. It's an extraordinary small organization that doesn't. As you add people, office space, more specialized job descriptions, this starts to come apart in all directions simultaneously, that is, quaquaversally. The natural reaction is to throw meetings or memos at it, both of which, even when they work, attach a ton of overhead to that which was effortless at a more appropriate scale. If you outsource functions, knowledge flow is less efficient, yet you have to create organizational plumbing to connect internal with external groups. If you offshore, you bleed more overhead to add varying degrees of cultural plumbing. Plus, the lack of proximity stresses the convenience of knowledge sharing when an environment might span six time zones (perhaps three hours a day of shared work time if you stretch it). Every time zone you add after six exacerbates the losses.

In the practice of KM we try to address these problems by throwing procedures and sometimes technology at them, and if the organization is both willing and capable of being healthy, we can achieve significant gains, though never (yet) with the magical overhead-less smoothness of the small organization. One of the things you can always do is formally cross-pollinate knowledge.

If you have problems, consider Peterson's initiative for the New York Mets, and use it as a pattern:

- ⑩ Pick out your most irritating problems.
- ⑩ Checkmark the ones most amplified by lack of uniform knowledge across departments or the whole organization.
- ⑩ Build a cross-disciplinary connection between what's really going on (operational people; in the Mets' case, the pitching coach) and the strategic or other upstream departments (in the Mets' case, the scouting/drafting function).
- ⑩ Give the participants incentive to succeed.

Add technological support (such as databases, internal radio broadcasts, bulletin boards, newsletters, video recordings), but only if you need to. This approach, if you execute it properly (it will be different in each individual organization), will always have some returns. It won't solve every problem, but you'll better define its roots and, therefore, have a better chance to beat it.

The Mets are in a great position. With the New York market to tap into if they succeed, they have tons of incentive to be successful, and before Peterson came they had a poor recent track record. Given that combination, it's harder for entrenched specialists to stand in the way of an initiative like this. But even if you have entrenched opposition, it's time to channel Sal "The Barber" Maglie or his kinder/gentler descendant Pedro Martínez, and throw the brushback pitch to reclaim home plate.

Use the tools in this Chapter to understand the possibilities of what you can do. Like a catcher deciding which pitch to call, once you've gone through the options, you still have to call a pitch or the umpire will call an automatic ball. Options are great, but the real currency of management is decisions, which is what we'll check out in chapter 4.

4

Calling for the Hit-and-Run:
Making Decisions

⚾

A weak man has doubts before a decision;
a strong man has them afterwards.
—Karl "The Bohemian Bomber" Kraus

Mike Scioscia, manager of the 2002 World Champion Anaheim Angels, once suggested that a skipper was confronted with hundreds of decisions per game. And he wasn't including the decisions managers consider before the umpire ever says "Play ball." Not all of those hundreds are decisions for tactics put into action—many are what-ifs for situations that might or might not happen, but deciding not to do something is a decision in itself, as is deciding not to make a decision at all.

What will I do *if* this batter gets on base? Should I warm up a reliever *if* my starter can't get his breaking ball over? Should I use a pinch hitter, and *if* I do, which one? When you roll these contingency situations into the count, Scioscia's measure is reasonable. While your rôle may not be quite as demanding as a baseball manager's, most managers face dozens of considerations or decisions per hour throughout the day.

Decisions are the most obvious artifacts a manager produces—and the evidence on which she's most often judged. A good decision maker exercises balance along simple, two-ended scales: balance between past precedent and the current situation, between caution and aggression, purity and compromise. She also balances scales that work in multiple dimensions: benefits against costs, short-term benefits against longer-term ones, individuals' needs against organizational ones.

And while every decision requires taking these balances into account, not every decision *should* reflect balance. Like a base runner getting hung up between bases and tagged out because he can't decide whether to go back or commit to taking the next one, some halfway decisions are doomed to failure in ways decisive choices of either extreme aren't.

Balancing the Past & the Present, Emotions and Rational Thought

The past, as Shakespeare has the Duke of Milan say, is merely prologue; the present is what we make happen in response to it. Alvin Dark, a controversial manager of the Giants, Athletics (twice), Indians, and Padres, waxed more poetic on the subject than the Bard: "There's no such thing as taking a pitcher out. There's only bringing another pitcher in."

Leonard Koppett's elaboration of the truth of Dark's discernment is right over the plate: "It sums up the central facet of effective management in all aspects of life. The only thing that matters is the next pitch. Whatever has happened has already happened and cannot be undone. When you decide to take a pitcher out, it's not as retribution for the hit he gave up, but an attempt to get the next man out. If you don't think the man you bring in has a better chance to get that out than the man already on the mound, don't make the change, no matter how it looks to anyone else."

And Koppett homes in on the key lesson: "The whole purpose of every decision is to maximize your chances—in your own opinion—of making the next thing succeed." [12]

Scioscia is unusually talented at compartmentalizing his emotions from his rational thoughts. He doesn't discard emotion when he's managing; he uses it as a tiebreaker, apparently. He understands fully that his players are human and incorporates that into his decision making, but what he chooses to do in a game is not about his feelings or theirs; it's about creating the best opportunities for winning the game.

One of the managers who influenced him was Monty Basgall, the bench coach for the Los Angeles Dodger teams he had played for. While the manager, Tom Lasorda, fizzed and flamed like an extra-jumbo box of July 4 fireworks onto which a tiki torch had just toppled, Basgall sat next to him, the ever-still, calm sidekick. While the extroverted Lasorda gave his highest priority to dealing with people and personalities, Basgall, an introvert at least during games, was all about tactics and decisions.

"Monty would just 'think the game,' " Scioscia said; he would sift through possibilities, watch for insights, look for opportunities. The Dodger catcher started "thinking the game" along with Basgall, and when Scioscia became a manager, he started emulating Basgall's dugout style. It's not Mike the Human Being, it's Mike the Manager who compartmentalizes his emotions and calculates coldly and clearly. If you meet Scioscia outside of the time his rôle is to think the game, he's personable and very human. If you watch him during a game, or catch him in the clubhouse when he's making out his lineup or other thinking-the-game managerial work, you're facing the relentless, unflappable decision maker, deliberately and intuitively going over possibilities, trying to find edges, balancing costs and possible rewards.

It's not easy for most people to do, but you cannot do better than emulating Scioscia. Good judgment requires disengaging your emotions about people and situations. If you can't do that completely, at least understand how your emotions are coloring the decision in progress and adjust for it.

Most mature adults, if they "count to ten," can make a decision that's not just a rash response. Most managers don't yank a pitcher because of a couple of bad pitches. Some do adhere too closely to the batter-versus-pitcher records and make automatic decisions based on only the historical trend. But in baseball, you rarely see a manager storm out to the mound and send a guy to the showers in a fit of pique. I wish that kind of irrationality was as rare outside of baseball.

RULE 4.01. Calling a brain delay. If you know you're capable of responding petulantly in your rôle as a manager, the fix is easy. Stall, and hold off a decision until the tantrum blows over. I say "easy" because it's a straightforward make-or-break skill for a manager—if you don't have at least enough self-control to take that course of action, you shouldn't be a manager any more than a convicted sex offender should be a child-care professional.

Loyalty is the emotional opposite of blame—and it's harder to manage. The past should color the manager's view of the present—why collect all that data if you're not going to use it?—but often you need to balance the intelligence in the historical record against what's going on right now.

One manager who didn't was Jim Fregosi, who led the Philadelphia Phillies to the 1993 National League pennant. But the team lost the World Series to the Toronto Blue Jays largely because Fregosi ignored Dark's Dictum.

His prize reliever that season was Mitch "Wild Thing" Williams, who looked and acted like he was half Hell's Angel, half unmade bed. Williams racked up 43 saves, in spite of walking a ton of guys during the season, anathema to a closer. Fregosi, rightly, thought of him as a main constituent of the team's success. In the playoffs that got them to the Series, Wild Thing was more erratic than usual, but the Phillies' offense put them over the top anyway.

In the Series, Wild Thing was shaky in Game 2. He had a complete meltdown in Game 4. In Game 6, with just one victory between the Jays and the title, the Phils took a one-run lead into the bottom of the ninth. Fregosi called on Wild Thing to protect it. Williams walked the first batter he faced, putting the potential tying run on first. Fregosi left him in. The next batter flied out, but the following one singled, putting the winning run on base. The next Blue Jay was Joe Carter, a dangerous power hitter having a respectable Series.

Fregosi had a decision to make. Wild Thing had been a key cog in the machine during the season. He'd been shaky or just plain bad in the playoffs and Series. He was left-handed and Carter right-handed, not only an advantage to the hitter, but a ready-made face-saver. Fregosi could have told Williams he was putting a right-hander in there to make the matchup tougher for Carter.

Fregosi, in Dark's words, worried about taking the pitcher out instead of bringing a pitcher in. Looking to the past, he left Wild Thing in. On a 2-2 count, Carter nailed the Series for the Jays, blasting one of the more memorable homers in baseball history, and capping it with a postgame statement that actually used the word "ironic" properly.

Fregosi defended Wild Thing, he of the Series ERA of 20.25: "He's the one who got us here." This was a statement about the past, not the present. Even having made a decision that clearly just caused his team to fail spectacularly, Fregosi was unable to convert feedback into insight.

Follow Alvin Dark. Don't be angry about your charges' current troubles, and if you honestly think an incumbent contributor has the best chance of completing the task successfully, don't remove that contributor. But equally, don't let the positive emotions attached to that individual's past heroics—or your own fear of seeming to be indecisive by not sticking with your prior decision—stand in the way of a move for a change. And in a critical moment, you can't let your concern for the individual's feelings undermine the opportunity for your whole team to succeed. Obviously, you can do the equivalent of what effective baseball managers do—occasionally decide to leave a hurler in as an experimental move if it doesn't matter much.

There are times and places for emotional decisions. The bottom of the ninth in a close World Series game and crucial moments in your organization's ongoing efforts to capture advantages are not those times.

"The Book"—a Balance, Neither Rigid nor Random

Most organizations are not as rigorous about keeping a historical record of accomplishments as baseball, but they tend to be either too rigorous or not rigorous enough about applying rules or procedures for making decisions. Baseball knocks the stuffing out of most large organizations' decision-making patterns because it often goes by "The Book"—a set of guidelines it applies in a way that's informed by collected wisdom, but designed to be flexible in patterned ways. There is no physical book; The Book is collected knowledge passed from manager to any interested player a little at a time during a game, or practice, or over drinks after work. Watch wildly different teams, even in different leagues, and you'll be surprised at how uniform yet flexible the unwritten guidelines are.

Take the most absolute injunction in The Book: "Never make the first or last out at third base."

You never want to make the first out at third base, because with a runner safely on second and no outs, the team is projected to score an average of 1.14 runs for the rest of the inning, while the average runs the team will score if the runner is at third with no outs is 1.51, merely 0.37 runs more. A runner getting thrown out trying to get from second to third base drops the average score for the rest of the inning to 0.28 runs, a diminished potential of 0.86 runs. He's risking the average of 0.86 runs to gain 0.37.

The last-out rule is simpler. You never want to make the last out at third base, because the odds for scoring with two outs from third base are only 5 percent better than they are from second base. Events that'll score a run from third with two outs score that same runner from second base 95 percent of the time, so the risk of getting thrown out is almost inevitably greater than the microscopic reward.[13]

Even though the rule says "never," baseball managers understand that in any individual case, it's not an automatic "don't go for it" decision or even a "don't go for it unless your chances are better than 85 percent" decision. The opponents understand the same metrics you do. You have to go for it sometimes when they don't expect you to.

Why? Going once in a while when the chances are below breakeven actually changes the chances. Nothing that involves life forms or post-1990 computers is predictable, and if you insist on reproducing the same decisions autonomically, you give all your competitors a free pass. The slow runner who violates the book by trying for third base with no outs may surprise the defense and succeed or just get ignominiously gunned out, but that act will force the defense to invest effort in eternal vigilance, expending energy on consideration of what you might do, an investment that's not without costs. That's why slow-footed sluggers like Todd Helton or Travis Hafner will occasionally try to steal a base, or why occasionally someone who should "know better" will make the first out at third.

Once you have a reputation for going against The Book, you create overhead for competitors, a potential advantage for you. In the 2005 World Series, White Sox manager Ozzie Guillen used the press to inform the Astros that he would be stealing bases when Roger Clemens was pitching, planting an idea that then added to the opponent's processing requirements—whether Guillen tried it or not.

Baseball's guidelines can also change over time in small or large ways. Ron Fairly, a former outfielder, now a broadcaster, noted that, on average, right fielders no longer have throwing arms as strong as they did when he played. I agree with him. During his playing time, lots of players prided themselves on their ability to throw out a runner trying to advance from first to third base on a single—stars like Roberto Clemente and Reggie Smith and even, to a lesser degree, Reggie Jackson. In early-21st-century baseball, most right fielders throw more often to the cutoff man, conceding the extra base. This has changed the benefit/cost ratio of trying to take the base, so The Book, while the same, guides a little differently.

So baseball's Book is far superior to almost every business or medical or government operations protocol ever developed.

When I worked for a few years at Microsoft Corporation in the early '80s, the company had no decision-making rules whatsoever. Almost none of its managers had management training, and few had even a shred of management aptitude. When it came to what looked like less important decisions, most just guessed. When it came to the more important ones, they typically tried to model their choices on powerful people above them in the hierarchy. Almost nothing operational was written down. The place was really what I call a futility factory, cranking out waste at the same prolific rate today's Red Chinese prison factories crank out cruddy, fragile home electronics for export to North America. The tragedy wasn't that so many poor decisions got made—as a functional monopoly, Microsoft had the cash flow to insulate itself from the most severe consequences—but that no one cared to track and codify past failures as a way to help managers create guidelines of paths to follow and avoid.

My next gig was with Boeing Company. It was the polar opposite. Every department had Brobdingnagian procedure manuals consisting of thousands of pages of specifications for behaviors and decisions, all supported by dozens of people responsible for codifying and updating everyone's Books by the Foot rendition of management diktat. Exhaustingly detailed prescriptions like these often fail, sometimes more often than not. But managers are nonetheless forced to follow them. Even when a clever practitioner figures out how to skirt the diktat, she still uses up energy to evade and cover for it, robbing energy from actual torque.

In chapter 1, I described how all standard corporate management is an imitation of government management design, for good and ill. From a management practice perspective, Boeing is a clone of its main government customer, the Pentagon. Skeptical? Here's a bit of synchronistic black humor for you, with a little detour through the Gulf Coast. In late 2005, when Hurricane Katrina swept over recently drained wetlands to inundate hundreds of miles of land along the Gulf Coast from Alabama to Louisiana, the U.S. Army immediately mobilized to aid tens of thousands of stranded victims and evacuees. It immediately prepared the supplies and planned the logistics, according to an interview with the commanding First Army general in a September 5, 2005, Newhouse News Service report by Davis Wood. But then everything went on hold while the Army awaited permission and paperwork from six sources. Here's how Homeland Security designed the work flow.

The Department of Homeland Security agent first has to fill out a request with specifics for each individual item, say drinking-water delivery for 1,000 people a day (step 1). It has to come through a defense coordinating officer in Baton Rouge or Jackson (step 2). The DCO then forwards it to the operations center at Camp Shelby, which ensures that the military can meet it (step 3). The center forwards it to an Air Force base in Colorado Springs, where Northern Command assigns the work to specific units (step 4). The item or package of items finally goes to the Pentagon to await the signature of whoever is defense secretary (step 5). Then the order goes out to deploy the unit and gather the resources (step 6), whether they're drinking water for 1,000 or a dump truck.

Apparently, Homeland Security didn't initiate any requests, and apparently no one in the First Army either was close enough to retirement or had the huevos to sacrifice his career to save a few hundred lives. There were exceptions. According to the story, the air officers of the USS *Truman,* stationed in the Gulf, ignored orders and permitted helicopters transporting the rescued victims to land even though the pilots weren't properly certified to land on an aircraft carrier.

Here's the synchronicity. Boeing used the same procedure with the same number of steps and different departments minus just one, the C-level signature, for ordering a nonstandard personal computer. Our group was developing a desktop publishing system to save the company about $95,000 a year, and to produce higher-quality publications more quickly, but it required a few features neither of the standard computers had. The computers we wanted cost less and had more features than the standards. It took only four months and six meetings with four different groups that had authority and paperwork responsibility in three different locations (one gave another its proxy) for the requisition of the two PCs. That was 1986, and there was no Department of Homeland Security involvement in the airplane manufacturer's processes as there is now. There may be more steps today.

So when some pundit asks, "Why can't government be more like business?" just say, "It already *is*."

All of us who have been in the Army or those who've invested some of their life working at a corporation like Boeing recognize protocols like this as unextraordinary. No matter how useful they are as general processes to follow, the organization that creates them becomes dysfunctional when it refuses to recognize that circumstances require variations. It's management's black-and-white adherence to all-or-none rules that makes decisions brittle and low-torque (or in the case of the Katrina efforts, fatal). Baseball proffers the superior model.

Baseball's decisions are stochastic. The Book is designed around stochastic guidelines, neither rigid nor random. Yours should be, too. Stochastic means choosing from the palette of most-common past successes most often, the less-obvious ones less frequently (but not ignoring them), and the least likely the least often. Stochastic is neither random (drawing an equal amount from every possibility no matter how likely or unlikely) nor deterministic (always choosing the same decision with the single highest probability of historical success). Life itself is stochastic.

Stochastic decision making keeps you and your team fresh and alert, your competitors and rivals off guard and using up resources trying to interpret your intent. It gives you insights into how alternatives work (and don't) and may give you early feedback on how change is tweaking your environment in ways you have to understand. You'll need those insights to get to home plate in the *Management by Baseball* model (see part 4).

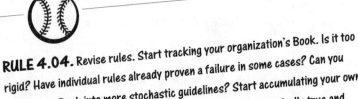

RULE 4.04. Revise rules. Start tracking your organization's Book. Is it too rigid? Have individual rules already proven a failure in some cases? Can you tweak your Book into more stochastic guidelines? Start accumulating your own guidelines. Can you make general rules of thumb that are basically true and contained in explanations short enough that any interested protégé could remember them?

The Law of Problem Evolution

Decisions require more than balance. To be successful, you have to over-come the Law of Problem Evolution. The Law exerts a massive force that makes your every successful streak of management decision making something that's likely to lead to lower yields in the future. Unintuitive? Let's look at a great recent baseball example.

The 2004 Houston Astros will be our case. Like a trinary star's solar system, they'd been built around three forces: young, skilled starting pitching; a nucleus of players in their prime (like Lance Berkman); and the old smoothie class-act guys, Jeff Bagwell and Craig Biggio.

In the recent past, this seemed like a solid-citizen team, perhaps even a bit hypothyroid, very unlike the city it calls home. The Astros started 2004 with a quiet tactician type as manager, Jimy "Beyond the Valley of the Bland" Williams. As usual, they looked like an even-keeled, serious competitor, neither a dominant team nor one you'd write off. But before their season started, something happened. Perhaps their acquisitions of the anger-management-challenged Roger Clemens, the fussbudget scold

Jeff Kent, and the quiet but gritty Andy Pettitte affected the chemical balance of the team. Or perhaps it was the Roller Derby of the Mind race for the title—every team but the Pirates held first place in the division during the year—that set them off-kilter.

Whatever it was, it was a strange trip. The Astros started the season 21–11, enough to put them in first place, though not by a lot.

CENTRAL	W	L	PCT	GB
Houston	21	11	.656	–
Chicago	18	14	.563	3.0
Cincinnati	17	15	.531	4.0
St. Louis	17	16	.515	4.5
Milwaukee	16	16	.500	5.0
Pittsburgh	13	17	.433	7.0

For the next 36 games they were doing the butterfly stroke in molasses (14–22), not exactly drowning, but flailing around making little progress, and the Cardinals started a run of excellence. Worse, the other teams in the division were playing roughly the same kind of .500-ish ball they had been earlier. While the Astros weren't buried, by June 20, they *looked* buried under the weight of competitors. Williams steadily kept his focus, using his historically successful management techniques, keeping the team on course, not blowing his cool, managing them professionally and quietly.

By July 14, the team was playing merely .500 ball (44–44) but it had acquired all-star-caliber contributor Carlos Beltrán, which improved the defense in a key position. Yet the Astros were stuck in fifth, and the Cards had buried the whole division. Williams hadn't turned the situation around, and the front office felt he wasn't going to be able to, either.

Given the city of Houston's traditionally close ties with France, the front office carefully chose Bastille Day to change managers, switching

CENTRAL	W	L	PCT	GB
St. Louis	41	28	.594	–
Chicago	39	30	.565	2.0
Cincinnati	38	31	.551	3.0
Milwaukee	35	31	.530	4.5
Houston	35	33	.515	5.5
Pittsburgh	26	39	.400	13.0

from Williams to his elemental opposite, Phil "Scrap Iron" Garner (lifetime managerial record, 708–802). Where Jimy is phlegmatic, Phil is fiery. Where Jimy manages based on history and best practice, Phil tries to eviscerate opponents with improvised aggression and derring-do.

The immediate results of adding Garner's kick-ax fire to the mix were scary. Bad scary. The team started losing more. Feuding, exploding heads, pitcher fu, a Joe Bob Briggs five-star horror movie. Third-base coach Gene Lamont was a Williams advocate and saw things quite differently from Garner, and they gave off a lot of sparks around each other. Garner installed a young player Williams didn't like, Morgan Ensberg, at third base, and both he and young shortstop Adam Everett found fellow infielder Kent's hectoring barely tolerable. And then, they "simply" came together and started winning. Bad chemicals and a Beltrán hot streak made for Reanimator moments.

Starting August 20, when they were 60–61, they ran off a 15–2 streak, and they finished the season 91–71, earning them a wild-card entry into the playoffs, where they beat the Atlanta Braves and then went the distance before losing the pennant to St. Louis.

It wasn't that Garner is intrinsically a better manager than Williams. Each piloted the team to a pair of second-place finishes in his first two years at the helm. It's just that the Law of Problem Evolution guaranteed that Garner could get better results in that short, happy span of 2004.

Here's how: Any manager with a shred of ability will solve *some* kinds of problems, and no matter how good, will leave *some* problems unsolved. The manager, as a human being, has strengths and weaknesses, high aptitudes and black holes of incapability from which no wisdom escapes. Over time, the problems within an organization that a manager can solve get solved, and the ones he's not good at solving fester and become an ever-greater proportion of the remaining problems. For most managers, this plaque of unsolved problems usually saps their effectiveness. And for the manager who follows, there's a much better chance that the residue of unsolved problems will consist of ones the newbie *can* solve. For Williams, the tactical problems that he could solve stayed solved, but the ones at which he didn't do well festered. They became predictable gaps that an increasing number of competitors could predict and sometimes exploit.

The pattern tends to repeat itself. Fans and media start harping on the incumbent's repeated shortcomings in the same decision zones. The front office feels a crisis bubbling. Roll in a losing streak (or in the 2004 Astros' case, a winning period that wasn't good enough to achieve preseason goals) and you have a Flipping Point. As I mentioned in chapter 1, there is a solution so common it's almost knee-jerk: replace a manager who is having problems with a successor who has the opposite style, and the opposite is likely to be able to solve problems the predecessor couldn't. Sayonara, Mr. Williams, here comes Mr. Garner.

Will he too face the consequences of the Law of Problem Evolution? Almost certainly. Every team Scrap Iron has helmed has improved in the first year, reacting to his management—the Brewers by nine games from their previous season, the Tigers by 10 games. After that, they don't improve much. It's a small sample (three teams now), but there's only so much you can do with the chemistry of raw aggression. It seems the tools Garner deploys are enough for specific moments, but not enough for the evolving set of circumstances that managers, in and beyond baseball, face.

As managers, we all have a specific set of tools in our tool chest. If we're successful, we tend to go back to them again and again. You don't throw away the tools with which you crafted success, but it's critical not to pretend you're immune from the Law of Problem Evolution. Not even the best tool works in all situations.

We all have chances to improve on our past managerial performances, if we can bottle and reuse the techniques that we have had success with while adding new ones that work in the current situation. I always advise managers to track their decisions for patterns of success and failure and stay alert to opportunities to improve on their weaker areas. Once you've spotted your own patterns in areas where your natural abilities don't achieve star quality, consider getting training (which is getting someone else's standard tool set) if that option is available.

Consider consulting with staff or fellow managers who seem to be effective at the skills you're looking to develop. You can always swap coaching lessons if you work in a healthy organization (and if you're not in a healthy organization, get out of your current one as soon as you can).

The Final, Most Important Fact About Decisions

Before we move on, I want to remind you of the most important fact about decisions. I'll let a baseball lesson I call "Defoliating a Victory Gardenhire" explain it.

In the 2004 American League playoffs, the Minnesota Twins and their very capable manager Ron Gardenhire were pitted against the favored New York Yankees. In Game 2, Gardenhire defoliated himself, turning a potential coup de grâce into a turning point that buried his team. This was a five-game series; in such a short series, you are never in a position of being able to finesse one game (take a loss) to preserve or increase your chances to win a later one. Decision making has to be significantly more aggressive.

Here's the specific situation. It's tied at 5–5, it's the bottom of the 10th inning, and that's a vast advantage to the home team, in this case the Yankees, because home teams are always at a vast tactical advantage in extra-inning games. Gardenhire brings in his best reliever and closer, Joe Nathan, at the start of the inning to protect the team's chances. He's already used two of his lesser relievers. Nathan had pitched an inning the night before.

Nathan's perfect in the 10th. The Twins can't score in their half of the 11th. Nathan comes back for the 11th. He's perfect again. He's faced six batters, the most he's faced since April, when he faced seven while getting hammered. He's moving into what is, for him, terra incognita.

The Twins score a lone run in the top of the 12th on Torii Hunter's homer. The Twins' manager has an easy decision to make here. On the side of taking his pitcher out, Nathan's not pitched more than two innings in relief this season, plus he'd pitched a (short, uneventful) inning the night before. There's basically nothing in favor of rolling him out again, except Nathan's general skill when he *hasn't* already pitched to six batters, and the fact the following day is a sorta day off, a travel day, so he can get some recharge.

Gardenhire makes no move, and Nathan goes out to the mound for the bottom of the 12th to defend a lead that would produce a victory that would put the Yankees at death's door. The manager doesn't use any of his surplus starters or his remaining fresh relievers. Here's what follows (my comments in italics):

NY YANKEES 12TH

J. Olerud strikes out swinging.

[*OKAY. Nathan's faced seven hitters.*]

M. Cairo walks.

[*OWW-OOH-GUH. DANGER WILL ROBINSON. Miguel Cairo, the least effective hitter in the Yankee lineup. While he had a good September, he was only getting on base at a .330 clip against right-handed pitchers. Cairo is absolutely* not *a guy you pitch around, and you certainly never want to put the winning run at the plate, as Nathan has just done. He's clearly shaky. Probably time to take a chance on a fresher arm even if it's a lesser one. Gardenhire dithers indecisively, and stands by his toast.*]

D. Jeter walks, M. Cairo to second.

[*DOH. Okay, dude, winning run on first, tying run in scoring position. No slack left. Time to act. Really. Nathan's faced eight hitters, and the last time he faced nine in the same game was a fiasco against the Rockies in May 2003 where he relieved in an already-lost cause and took one for the team, absorbing a beating like one of Buddy Rich's snare drums so his manager could retain the freshness of his other relievers. Oh yeah, the next batter is Alex Rodriguez, the $252 million Eddie Haskell who's 5-for-8 so far in this series. The TV image of Gardenhire reveals no gears turning; the manager fails to act and therefore allows events to happen without acting upon them.*]

A. Rodriguez hits a ground-rule double to deep center; M. Cairo scores, D. Jeter to third.

[*Game tied, winning run on third. Nathan is now a crispy critter, moundkill.*]

G. Sheffield is intentionally walked.

[*Finally, an actual Gardenhire decision.*]

J. Romero relieves J. Nathan.

H. Matsui hits sacrifice fly to right; D. Jeter scores.

2 runs, 1 hit, 0 errors.

Minnesota 6, NY Yankees 7

Game over, series probabilistically over. Gardenhire is a fine manager, and he knows better; he just froze. In baseball, you can *never* fall into the pattern of not making a decision.

Not making a decision, as the father of American psychology and noted fan of the National League's miserable Boston Beaneaters William

James said, "is itself a passional decision—just like deciding yes or no—and is attended with the same risk." Even in the best case, managers who dither out of fear of making a mistake miss out on opportunities to beat schedules or quality targets. The best outcome their teams can hope for is mere adequacy, and even to achieve that limited outcome there'd better be a lot of other skill or slack or brute luck to get it there.

Listen. I'm not arguing that you always have to make a decision *yourself*. There are rare decisions where all the possible outcomes are roughly equal. You can delegate that to someone to test his methods (discussed further in chapter 6). In many cases, wise managers hesitate to commit to a decision because they simply don't know enough about the subject to do it decently. You can delegate a decision like that when someone on your staff has a stronger grip on the details, or you can do more research, as long as you don't crash the deadline for the decision (because then you *have* made a decision . . . to do nothing).

Baseball, the perfect test lab for management in competitive organizations, proves that you can't succeed by merely avoiding mistakes. Can you imagine a game starting and the manager waiting passively for things to happen? No way. You have to fill out a lineup, you have to make game calls, you have to assign resources, make mid- and long-term planning decisions. If we take Mike Scioscia's hundreds of decisions per game as a guideline, it's obvious that no field manager in baseball who dithers in the hope of avoiding making a mistake can hold on to the job for more than a game or two. If dithering, allowing fate to just happen as the usual decision, can't be made to work in baseball, you'd better have a compelling argument why you think it might be able to work in any other competitive environment.

Beyond baseball, roughly 38 percent of managers dither decisions regularly as a standard approach, feeling that if they just wait long enough to close on a decision, it will go away or magically resolve itself. They are mistaken. Baseball proves that just avoiding mistakes is not management, it's a perfect formula for defoliating a Gardenhire.

. . .

It helps if you usually make the right decisions, but the factor that makes it possible to have them succeed is the makeup of your roster. Managing people, second base in the *Management by Baseball* model, is the set of skills which assures that you and your organization get the most effective performance out of your team. Part 2 explains some of the essential baseball wisdom for picking a roster, forging a team, and making it effective through the ups and downs of a long season.

Part Two

Stealing Second Base—
the Players *Are* the Product

With very few exceptions, successful modern organizations understand that in noncommodity endeavors, the players *are* the product. And if the organization doesn't already understand that, its success is likely on the endangered list.

Baseball is a wonderful example of an endeavor where this is crystal clear. If you could wave a magic Louisville Slugger and remake the game, keeping the uniforms and stadia and announcers and concessions the same but removing the major leaguers and replacing them with skilled recreation-league players, game attendance (and people tuned in over radio and TV) would plummet to perhaps 25 percent of what it is now, and it'd be that popular only if it wasn't up against something as compelling as University of Chicago Economics Professor Beach Volleyball (you'd agree with me if you'd ever seen Milton Friedman in a Speedo).

The talent is the product. Beyond baseball, the apparent benefits of offshoring blue-collar and white-collar work have been reaped, tapped, sucked close to dry. The point of diminishing returns occurred several home stands ago. The benefits that are left from amplifying past tactics to achieve an ever-declining yield on them is called "intensification." The repercussions of intensifying outsourcing are just starting to be understood on a global level. Some trends are clear now. One is this: for the foreseeable future, organizations in competitive lines of work that expect to succeed cannot do it through technologies alone or creative accounting leadership alone or market share alone. The only single difference-maker is the skill, determination, and commitment of the talent you hire for your roster and how well you shape and build it for your survival.

The talent is the product. With the right people, given the correct incentives, encouraged and driven to their highest individual accomplishments, blended into a balanced and adaptive team, winnowed when they can't succeed, you will adapt to most competitive challenges. You will weather more rain delays, bad ump calls, flat beer in the concessions, and all the other routine disasters of the zero-sum standings table most organizations are facing. Management puts the right roster in place and the contributors manufacture whatever refinements, innovations, or survival tactics you need to win. The talent is the product. Baseball learned this over a century ago and has thrived with this reality. Few other lines of work have even a decade of experience with it, and most of them resist it, pointlessly hoping they can get around the inevitable truth. The most refined and practical methods for thriving in the current global economy are contained in baseball. Baseball knows.

The talent *is* the product. Baseball's openness makes the organizational and management effects easier to decode and track. Methods that work in baseball work in all competitive workplaces. The ones that failed in baseball and are still being used elsewhere are failures. If you examine baseball hiring and personnel and career-development and general people-management arrangements, you'll have an almost perfect how-to for guiding practices, a scorecard showing what wins and what loses, and how and why.

5

Scouting & Signing Your Players: Hiring

⚾

Labor, therefore, is the real measure of the
exchangeable value of all commodities.
—**Adam Smith**

The First Step Is the Most Important Step—
the Unrivaled Importance of Hiring

No single managerial skill you have can ever be as valuable as knowing how to hire the right people. I can't stress this point highly enough. That's true in the immediate torque you get from the right contributor. More vitally, it pays daily dividends for as long as you can keep that contributor from being demotivated.

More than anything else, the people you have working for you and with you define your ability to achieve as an organization. Measurements I've taken in several lines of work indicate that excellent performers produce at least 20 percent more usable work than average contributors. That's like getting an extra 10 hours a week. The hiring decision that may take 10 to 60 hours of time up front will pay for itself in the first few weeks of work. After that, it's all phat dividends.

You can be brilliant, but if you don't have the right players on the roster, nothing less than extraordinary luck (and extraordinarily bad luck for your rivals) can leave you even a narrow chance to succeed. Here's the extreme example, the breathtakingly awful 1993–2004 Milwaukee Brewers, a team depopulated of any excellence by its owner's apparently deliberate strategy to create a low-payroll team that could cash in on an odd internal-to-baseball tax scheme he had helped shepherd through MLB acceptance. How would you like to have as your first chance to manage in the majors a team that had just one winning campaign in its last 16 seasons; a team packaged to sell by lowering costs and stripping assets, and eventually being manipulated to harvest tax breaks—tax breaks that are easier to harvest if the team roster remains significantly inferior to its competitors?

Take Dave Lopes. He'd played on four Los Angeles Dodger teams that went to the World Series. That probably made worse his two years of existential travail as the manager of the Brewers during that era. "If you don't have the horses, you're not going to get into the playoffs," he observed. And Lopes had mostly what amounted to pack mules.

Presume you have a roster like Lopes's: a few promising young players who are not yet proven successes or failures, a drizzle of two-dimensional veterans who can contribute in some ways, and a big helping of players who are "replacement level," that is, those for whom, if you lost them to free agency or between connecting flights at O'Hare, you could easily pick up replacements. You can manage all you want, tweak job descriptions, inspire, squeeze out every drop of value, make all the right calls, but the likelihood of serious success is minimal.

You have one advantage over Dave Lopes: while you may inherit a roster lacking in skill, you can force yourself into the hiring process more easily than a baseball manager can. In a business or government organization, the average manager comes into the process too late, after HR has filtered the piles of candidates he gets to see. Usually, it's not because the manager isn't allowed to participate; it's that he delegates the task or allows it to get delegated. Terrible idea.

If you are not involved with the criteria by which HR sends you candidates, you are likely to get a normal distribution of candidates from which to choose, a normal distribution that conforms to Angus's First Law: In any job category, 5 percent are excellent, 10 percent are utilitarian/A-okay/just fine, and the rest have room for significant improvement.

Look around you. Is your organization a talent ghetto, packed with high achievers who are easy to manage? If it's not, and the norm in your shop is to allow HR to filter incoming résumés and applications, HR's process is probably acting as the gateway to nonexcellence. There are creative and effective HR departments that have enough mojo to infuse organizations with lots of winners, just not many, conforming to Angus's First Law. And recent regulatory trends have tied down HR departments in defensive, fear-based initiatives designed more to avoid being sued or having nonconforming records than to actively pursue excellence.

RULE 5.01. Engage and direct recruiting. Try to engage HR in clear and early discussions about new hires. If you can get HR to team up with you in the effort to recruit the kinds of people you find outstanding, it frees you up for other activities. Explain your objectives and engage HR in a structured conversation about how to get the kinds of contributors you're looking for. And good HR people bring insights to the table that you don't already have.

As in baseball, no single recruiting model works for everyone. In fact, standard models evolve to punish those who use them, so rejecting traditional hiring models is the only sane approach.

Assembling a Roster: "Best Sourcing," Joe Cambria, Tom Peters, or the Major League Scouting Bureau

Contemporary organizations that will survive the coming economic shocks follow a single common thread: they know and act on the idea that talent *is* the product. Thanks to decades of competition to acquire talent, baseball is way ahead of other kinds of organizations. And since that competition is so visible and public, it holds great lessons for managers in all kinds of work who are looking for an edge.

Tom Peters is one of the rare management thinkers who came to this before it became obvious. He developed an idea called "Best Sourcing," which is exactly the model baseball front offices understand and that most nonbaseball organizations should be following. I'll get back to Peters, but first let me explain how it works in baseball as a model to follow.

Baseball teams have to scout hundreds of potential prospects to find a handful in whom to invest resources. Only a small percentage of those will actually contribute in the major leagues (see sidebar, "Making It to the Majors"). In such a challenging, winnowing model, small errors in judgment have devastating effects. For example, the Brooklyn Dodgers gave up on Roberto Clemente, one of the 100 best outfielders of all time. Rather than protecting the 19-year-old in the Rule 5 draft (which allows other teams to pick up unprotected players for a tiny sum), they favored instead nearly a dozen players who never were able to contribute to the major-league team.

There are dozens of notorious examples. A recent one is the Boston Red Sox' David Ortiz, left-handed slugger extraordinare and probably the Bosox' most valuable player in their run for the 2004 and 2005 titles. In 1996, desperate for left-handed power, the Seattle Mariners coughed up Ortiz, opting for 28 games of Dave Hollins, a Minnesota Twins third baseman who gave the M's a wonderful contribution in a not-quite-good-enough stretch drive.

Making It to the Majors

When the talent is the product, when almost all success is based on merit and not office politics, excellence is proven to be pretty rare. Only a few survive the winnowing process, and there's room at the top for only a few cronies and nepotism beneficiaries. One rigorous study by *Baseball America*'s editor, Allan Simpson, on making it to the majors dates from the early '90s.[14] With expansion and changing economics, today's numbers are a little different, but these are close. This table shows the percentage of all players signed who make it to that level.

Level	Percentage
Signed	100%
Class A	86%
Class AAA	46%
Majors	11%

This ladder of promotion, based largely on merit, makes each level more skilled than the previous one. In baseball, the ultimate talent-*is*-the-product industry, few people get to play in the majors before they're proven at a lower level. In nonbaseball organizations, employers tend to try to short-circuit that, hiding their heads in the sand, pretending that fresh-faced MBAs or other organizations' failures and mediocrities or intelligent but unenculturated people in third world sweatshops getting $9 a day are capable of the high achievement the organization needs to succeed.

Does your organization have a baseball-style organization that trains less experienced talent on less important or lower-pressure projects and work, promoting them to tougher and more important projects as they learn and prove their potential? If not, why not? Can you imagine what a major-league baseball team's talent would look like if it followed the way *your* organization chooses talent for key projects?

In any competitive endeavor, talent acquisition is the single most important area that determines success or failure. Before free agency forced teams to become hypercompetitive, teams had blind spots about talent acquisition. They looked for players everywhere in the U.S., sure, but they typically centered their efforts around one or two techniques. Talent tended to cluster around the efforts of a small handful of regional scouts.

Scout Joe Cambria, for example, acquired a lot of the second-line talent for the old Washington Senators. Struggling with a small budget, the team hired Cambria to scour Cuba for cheap prospects. Cambria had little competition and he was good, so fishing in that secret (for a while) pond made him effective. Other teams later focused on Puerto Rico or the Dominican Republic. Some, like the Dodgers, were more aggressive in combing Japan and Korea. But when the sudden death of the reserve clause escalated competition, baseball got serious about the Major League Scouting Bureau, a cooperative venture that put a pool of common scouts at the disposal of all member teams. It was a clever money-saving device, but it was a cooperative venture, therefore not a way to compete. Co-op models are the basis of many a successful industry (Ocean Spray, Sunkist, and Farmland are all superb examples), but I cannot think of one where the co-op's members are hypercompetitors.

In baseball, the co-op scouting model guarantees uniformity of thinking. Teams send their own scouts to cross-check the bureau's reports or, as Twins G.M. Terry Ryan told me, use the bureau's conclusions to verify their own scouts' work. But if the player is a diamond, he wouldn't be a diamond *in the rough,* undiscovered by competitors. The only way a team could gain a competitive edge in scouting would be to examine the players the bureau's scouts *weren't* recommending—hardly a high-yield strategy.

While too many HR departments are incompetent, some are quite "good." What they are "good" at is acting like a vanilla HR department, making standardized, mostly uniform decisions, just as the Major League Scouting Bureau, a standards-driven evaluator, does. Smart baseball minds are beginning to grapple with the problem. The current trend is to put more resources into in-house, proprietary scouting analysis. The Boston Red Sox sabermetric consultant Bill James has proposed tinkering with the paradigm for scouting, aiming at vastly more in-depth scouting of significantly fewer potential players. The Sox apparently haven't implemented the James model, but they are open to thinking about it.

But in the hypercompetitive environment, no team can afford to scout just Cuba or scout just college players in the Pac-10 or scout just high schoolers in Florida. Likewise, no organization can afford to give priority to certain degrees or prominent educational institutions. Rigidity increases the chances for failure, something no team can afford to risk.

The danger for nonbaseball organizations with a standards-based, conformity-driven HR department is that they will all pursue the same profiles, missing out on the Roberto Clementes and David Ortizes. As a result, those failures have created a gravitational attraction for letting outside shops (most frequently no better, by the way) do the recruiting and carry the burden of failed hires. That movement has led to many kinds of "sourcing," mostly "outsourcing." Any organization that would outsource its most important function is playing Russian roulette with four bullets.

The approaching economic shock forces all organizations to rapidly internalize the baseball model if they want to survive. How best to do it becomes the key question. One of the best management consultants, Tom Peters, has come up with an idea called "Best Sourcing." Summed up in a single slide, the idea is:

Not "outsourcing"
Not "offshoring"
Not "near-shoring"
Not "in-sourcing"
but . . .
"Best Sourcing"

Peters's argument is simply to use the talent most appropriate for the upcoming task. Don't automatically assume that a specific source is best for everything or that a standard approach will be best for any specific effort. Diversify your talent search to acquire the best available anywhere, because if you don't, a competitor will.

If your HR group is not open to breaking its mold, you're going down the path of a team that uses only the Major League Scouting Bureau. In a noncompetitive arena, that won't necessarily be fatal, it will merely guarantee mediocrity. In a competitive arena, it guarantees high salaries/wages and average performance, a turnpike to performance hell.

The Résumé Is Not the Person: Hiring Doug Glanvilles & Tony Phillipses

Large organizations recruiting for a key position seek stars—people who have powerful charisma and overwhelming skill and accomplishment combined with alpha-dog personality. As in baseball, when you find a Barry Bonds or a Roger Clemens, that's great, because no matter what his personal shortcomings or bumpy stretches, he just elevates your entire organization's prospects. All organizations recognize the value of Barrys and Rogers.

Since they seek Barrys and Rogers with such passion, recruiters and scouts frequently fall into a MBWT (Management by Wishful Thinking) pattern, taking someone who on the surface seems like a Barry or a Roger but who is all hat and no cattle. The swagger, unaccompanied by applied accomplishment, is just ersatz leadership. More often than not, that's worse than nothing—more often than not, the final box score shows a negative result from thrusting an ersatz Roger or Barry into the mix.

Then there are Doug Glanville and Tony Phillips.

While few large organizations know it, all need some easy-to-find Doug Glanvilles. These are people who, even though they don't have close to Bonds-caliber talent, elevate everyone's abilities through broad interests, multidisciplinary involvement, and emotional intelligence. You can't build a team around such individuals, they can't be your "franchise player," but they are terrific catalysts, key parts all successful organizations in competitive fields have on hand. Organizations that ignore the need for Glanvilles or have them but suppress their natural connecting abilities will find it hard to excel.

Glanville was an outfielder in the majors from 1996 to 2004. An intelligent natural extrovert, blessed with highly educated parents and highly educated himself (advanced studies at the University of Pennsylvania), he's verbally adept at a couple of standard deviations above the baseball-player norm. Glanville's path to the elite-talent world of the majors began as a five-year-old when he started playing a baseball simulation (Strat-O-Matic) along with Wiffle Ball. Simulations, especially good ones, are wonderful training tools. He got some programmed knowledge in very basic baseball strategy from a manager's and owner's perspective.

He had baseball skills good enough for the majors, but he reached All-Star–caliber play only one year, 1999, when his combination of .376 on-base percentage, 32 successful steals out of 34 attempts, and best-in-the-league range in center field made him a key asset to the Phillies.

He was a player representative, using his communication and self-described "nerd" skills to educate his fellow staffers about rules and industry trends. He was and is active in the community, bringing his fellow staffers into contact with the organization's customers. He was a talker in the clubhouse, a joker who kept people loose. As a degreed engineer with a background in transportation planning, he went to his team's front office to give them unsolicited counseling in transportation topics around the design and delivery of their new stadium. He was only a backup outfielder, but he was fearless in sharing his knowledge with his "superiors" in an organization in which he knew more than anyone else about a subject. In his retirement announcement, a time that's undiluted sadness for most, he milked it for laughs, arranging after leaving the Cubs to have a one-day contract with his hometown Phillies, and claiming he signed it in invisible ink.

The benefits of a Doug Glanville extend beyond the immediate skills specified in a job description. His average on-field value was significantly expanded by his ability to keep people loose in the clubhouse, to foster communication among various kinds of people who wouldn't have communicated otherwise, to help interpret the details that were hard for some to understand. In short, his rôle was as what author Malcolm Gladwell calls a "connector." His personal productivity never made him a star, but his demeanor and ability to make a team more effective were invaluable though intangible positives. People who work in organizations without Glanvilles miss out on knowledge, connections, and the ability such contributors have to break up stress and the mistakes it can cause.

Tony Phillips is a different but related type. He started his 18-year career as an erratic shortstop for Billy Martin's 1982 Oakland A's. Seven starting positions on the field, seven relocations, and five other teams later, he concluded his productive and versatile career back in the East Bay in 1999 as a utility man.

I met him in April 1986, when he was just starting to be the team's leadoff hitter in the death-pressure assignment of "replacing" the most prolific, productive leadoff hitter of all time, Rickey Henderson. The team had already spent an unpleasant year experimenting with leadoff batters after Henderson left for the Yankees. But already this new season, Phillips had had a pair of games against Seattle where he was a one-person wrecking crew, going 7-for-9 with a walk and scoring five runs.

We talked about the pressure of what he was doing. He explained that in spite of his intensity, he came to understand and hold on to the idea that he couldn't replace Rickey; he just had to do whatever he could, relentlessly seeking education and other ways to make himself more effective. He said he would just have to measure himself every day against his own current potential and look for ways to expand on it.

After that he transformed himself into one of the most versatile players since the deadball era. By year, here is a list of the position he played most, with a few of his accomplishments

Year	Main Position	Noteworthy Accomplishments
1986	2B	Became leadoff hitter and starting second baseman. Increased OBP 31 pts. to .367.
1987	2B	Hit 10 HRs, first double-digit season.
1988	3B	Moved to 3B and OF.
1989	2B	Back to playing primarily 2B.
1990	3B	Signed by Detroit. Back to 3B, 99 BBs.
1991	OF	Moved to OF. New career highs in HRs (17), OBP (.371).
1992	OF	New career highs in 2Bs (32), BBs (114), OBP (.387).
1993	OF	New career highs in BBs (132), OBP (.443).
1994	3B	New career highs in HRs (19) and Slg. (.468).
1995	3B	Traded to Angels. Back to 3B. New high in HRs (27).
1996	LF	Signed by White Sox. Back to OF as primary position.
1997	2B	Traded to Angels, new career highs in 2Bs (34), 5th season with over 100 walks. Moved back to 2B.
1998	LF	Signed with Toronto, traded to Mets. Back to OF.
1999	2B	Finished career back with A's as everyday utility man.

His utility, like Glanville's, extended beyond what he racked up on his Baseball Reference career stats page. When you get a Tony Phillips and deploy that worker in the right ways, you can gain sudden liftoff and win great glory.

According to Bill Bavasi, then the California Angels' GM, Phillips had a galvanizing effect on the 1995 team. The context of the acquisition was important to why it worked, and the glory acquired by the hiring manager, in this case Bavasi, was immense.

"In 1994, we had a young team and we got our butts handed to us," Bavasi said. "In '95, the kids matured. We traded for Tony Phillips and it really turned us around. That really made us a good club. We weren't close yet, our players shouldn't have been quite ready. . . . We shouldn't even have been in that race."

But they were, and it was Phillips, the GM thinks, that put them there after they got him from the Tigers for Chad Curtis. "He is *the* single most influential and best player I've been around. Making that deal was tough. . . . In-house we were divided, 50-50 at best. What put it over the edge for us was that Matt Keough, who'd played with him, said, 'I guarantee he will made Jim Edmonds and J. T. Snow and other guys better players. He will absolutely influence them and drive them hard.' *That* put it over the edge for me. Chad was not going to do that for us."

Notice, it's not just raw talent that guides a GM's decision. It's not résumé, college GPA, pedigree. It's the blending of skills and attitudes that is an essential part of making a successful team.

Bavasi explained the way Phillips worked. "There was a time during that year Tony had something like seven cortisone shots in his hamstring just to stay on the field. And he was driving the young players. . . . You can look at Edmonds's career. That season was his big jump. Tony would go into the training room and flush any player out, get them out on the field, and say, 'What are you doing in here. . . . We're playing today. *You* are playing today.' "

Phillips made Bavasi—then in only his second year in the GM job—

realize how powerful management is. "This guy made me think I could be a GM because of the way we played that year."[15] Both '94 and '95 were shortened seasons, but based on 162-game performance, the Tigers who gave up Phillips declined seven wins, while the Angels flew 21 wins higher with him. Of course, to be a Phillips, you need to be a seriously good player, better than a Glanville, because the teammates have to believe that a Phillips knows more than they do. Phillips was a very good player, although he was never elected to an All-Star team, and few people who aren't sabermetrics geeks would likely vote for him for the Hall of Fame. But he was good enough to carry this peer-leadership mantle, even with occasional times when personal demons or troubles in his real life made him seem undesirable to organizations.

If you're willing to invest energy finding a Glanville and a Phillips for your team, you're at an advantage, especially because the competition tends to overlook them in favor of obvious superstars. When organizations can't find superstar talent, they tend to make the error of taking a chance on someone who really isn't one but who *looks* like he or she just might be. Usually, they're far better off with a Doug or a Tony. His talents at connecting people or galvanizing their performance as a peer transcends the immediate stats he can put up.

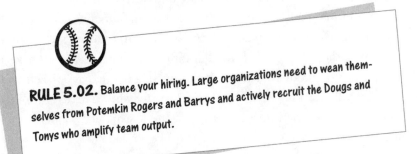

RULE 5.02. Balance your hiring. Large organizations need to wean themselves from Potemkin Rogers and Barrys and actively recruit the Dougs and Tonys who amplify team output.

Shelving Wood, Pumping Hart—
Stealing Second Against the Cult of "At-Will" Employment

Once in a while, there's a lesson in baseball that just turns everything you think you know on its head and makes you wonder why you never noticed reality before. As we slip into the Incongruous Zone, we won't use Rod Serling as our guide, but call upon former Cleveland Indians GM John Hart to point out how much smarter baseball is than business at managing talent.

Take how we hire talent in the late 20th and early 21st centuries. Mainstream U.S. economic wisdom holds that we're exporting unskilled jobs to lower-paying labor markets, and that's great because we're growing skilled jobs here. Those skilled folks will benefit additionally because lower-paying labor will produce goods for Americans at lower cost, so we'll be earning the same and paying less.

Skilled people, by definition, know how to do something valuable. But universally, organizations strive for "at-will" employment, where the employer may discharge the employee at any time without cause, without notice, and generally without a golden (or even tin) parachute. In exchange, the employee may resign at any time without notice. At-will is a rational hiring model for low-value-added commodity businesses with a dynamic labor pool, like seasonal farmwork. Farmers need pickers, but only for a short period, and the skill differences among workers have a small effect on product quality or quantity. In a fair market, pickers and growers will adjust prices to find efficient pay for work. The at-will ability of the picker to pack up her machete in the middle of the day and move to a better-paying spot, or for the grower to give the ax to lower-performing workers if good weather stretches the time for harvest, lubricates the efficiency of a fair market.

With skilled jobs, though, why would we hire people at will, a strategy clearly meant for fungible jobs? Baseball doesn't, even though, synchronistically, at-will was invented by Horace Wood, a creative legal scholar, a year after the founding of the National League in 1876. Baseball signs its talent to contracts with specific durations. Like reliable Java programmers, competent project managers, creative accounting whizzes, smooth salesfolk, or the members of ZZ Top, major leaguers are skilled employees. They are, in management's opinion, the best 1,200 people in the world at what they do.

When an organization spends $35,000 looking for, finding, interviewing, selecting, and making an offer to a person it hopes will be one of the best 1,200 Java programmers, or one of the best critical-care nurses, or one of the best long-haul truck drivers, why does it strive to work out an at-will setup with her? Look at it rationally. You hire someone with special talents. In exchange for the potential benefit of laying her off in a downturn or when stock analysts need to be fed a bit of *ledger de main,* you surrender control over her efforts. The cost of her leaving is not just in recruitment, but in her knowledge walking out the door. That organization can count on training and acclimatizing her replacement, meaning lower initial productivity and schedule slippages. Even the creative accounting geniuses at the U.S. Department of Labor can't tell how much this costs, and perhaps this is why the dysfunctional habit persists.

Baseball knows, though. In 1876, baseball was reeling from five years of labor chaos. Skilled players moved from team to team in response to offers of better pay, or the chance to play alongside better teammates, or in front of more fans. In 1994, American employers were reeling from the effects of skilled employees changing organizations at the drop of a cap to garner better compensation, more interesting work, or better chances to build skills. In both eras, executives were going ballistic about skilled-labor instability.

In baseball, the solution was enforceable contracts. Sign the talent to a relationship of known length. This solution worked for the owners for almost 100 years. In business, the "solution" was . . . at-will employment? At-will, invented in the 1870s, minimizes loyalty while lubricating the ability of skilled labor to move on—that is, it has been a total failure for employers because *even when the shop doesn't intend to chuck the talent overboard,* the threat is implicit every day of the relationship. The more skilled and employable the talent, the more likely they'll jump ship, leaving a higher concentration of roster plaque and passive people. At-will worsened employment instability until Alan Greenspan crashed the skilled-sector economy with his second recession in 2001.

Great managers take advantage of others' counterproductive compulsions. Ex–Cleveland GM John Hart recognized one and revolutionized baseball personnel patterns. Before Hart, free-agency era teams pretty much acted uniformly based on this treadmill.

- ⑩ Bring up a prospect.
- ⑩ Keep his salary as low as possible for three years until he's eligible for salary arbitration. In arbitration, his pay goes way up.
- ⑩ At six years he becomes a free agent. His pay goes way, way up.
- ⑩ Let him go. Sign another free agent or go back to the start of this cycle.

Now, you've lost half the player's highest-skill years to another team, plus you need to pay for another guy, someone you don't know as well and have to invest some resources to learn about.

The Indians' front office, however, invested in a smokin' farm system, generating a lot of fine young players. Then they short-circuited the cycle, signing players to longer-term contracts before arbitration, essentially capturing talented players' best years. Hart eventually moved on to the Texas Rangers, and his front-office cohort Mark Shapiro inherited the general manager job. While a few other franchises have tried to copy the model, Shapiro and the Indians still are the masters of it. Shapiro initiated another round of short-circuiting in 2004–2005, and the team got really competitive in the latter season, finishing 93–69, and presaging an interesting run.

Think about it. How much does turnover cost you in resources you can measure? How much in lost time, lost knowledge, and lower productivity? How many quarters of comparative advantage will you gain over competitors by recapturing that waste and pouring it into productivity? What prevents you starting a Hart pilot right away, and what will you do about it?

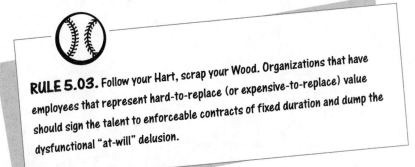

RULE 5.03. Follow your Hart, scrap your Wood. Organizations that have employees that represent hard-to-replace (or expensive-to-replace) value should sign the talent to enforceable contracts of fixed duration and dump the dysfunctional "at-will" delusion.

I'll restate a point I made earlier in this chapter. The managerial activity that will have the highest return for you and your organization is the ability to hire the right talent. That's not the end of the effort. You have to use it well and keep it sharp. We'll cover some of the essentials for that in chapter 6.

6

Charting Hits:
Optimizing Player Performance

See that fellow over there? He's 20 years old.
In 10 years he has a chance to be a star.
Now, that fellow over there, he's 20, too.
In 10 years he has a chance to be 30.
—**Casey Stengel**

Getting the most out of your daily lineup by getting the most out of your individual players is one of baseball's most fertile sources of wisdom for nonbaseball managers.

Baseball's methods for optimizing player performance come from three progenitors and a genius who later synthesized the forefathers' innovations into a system that was more than the sum of the three together. The progenitors were John McGraw (1873–1934), Connie Mack (1862–1956), and Branch Rickey (1881–1965). The synthesizing genius was Paul Rapier Richards (1908–86).

McGraw, known in the press as "Little Napoleon," was a hyperactive control freak who assembled a master plan that dictated every aspect of player behavior both on the field (for example, where a shortstop planted a foot when pivoting on the double play) and off (for example, what food his players ate).[16] McGraw observed what players had done previously, probed every day to learn what they could and couldn't do, and then planned a future for them based on his observations.

Mack, "The Tall Tactician," was a perceptive analyst who looked at a player and knew what to value and what to ignore. That gave him the insight he needed to know to build on the player's distinctive skills. For openers, Mack analyzed tendencies that others didn't, designing manual systems for tracking where opposing players hit the ball so he could optimally move his fielders around.[17] And Mack scouted and signed outfielder Al Simmons in spite of the outfielder's eccentric batting stance and a swing that forced him to "step in the bucket."[18] That was supposed to be poison, but Mack chose to ignore an unbreakable dogma, wisdom that his successful baseball peers considered as unarguable as the rule book itself. Simmons merely worked his way into the Hall of Fame.

Bill James contrasts the two management philosophies. "McGraw's philosophy was, you have to control every element of the player's world and get rid of everything in there that might cause you to lose a game. Mack's philosophy was, you get good people, you treat them well, and you'll win."[19]

Rickey ransacked workplaces beyond baseball for innovations he could apply to the game and came up with some winners from manufacturing and education. From manufacturing, he borrowed the assembly-line model to work out the sequence of lessons for training prospects. He also cloned manufacturers' quality-control processes, creating a system for examining a player's career at predetermined checkpoints to evaluate how well the player was doing. From the discipline of education, he brought systematized methods for both evaluation and training by creating thorough documentation and by enforcing standards throughout the extended team system.

Control (McGraw), analysis (Mack), and systemization (Rickey) each proved to be a powerful ingredient for optimizing player performance, but it took the Baltimore Orioles' organization to bring them all together into a Weapon of Mass Construction—starting a year or so after the sad-sack St. Louis Browns moved to Baltimore and were renamed for the local bird. The prime mover behind their system was Paul Richards, a manager hired away from the White Sox after he'd set in motion a major turn-around of that franchise's fate.

Richards synthesized the Rickey, Mack, and McGraw models for an organization that had operated 38 years without a management model.[20] Never wealthy, the O's had no choice but to rely instead on intelligence, organization, technology, and training to overcome their relative lack of resources.

By bringing these models together, Richards applied the finishing touches to the system that all successful baseball franchises now emulate to a serious degree. Richards's model is highly effective in serious non-baseball organizations, too.

The Four Practice Areas

To win, you have to improve player performance—and do it continually. You do this using four specific practices. The successful manager has to be unyielding in pursuing all four. The underlying challenge is that the choices you make to optimize performance are different for each contributor.

The four practices are:

1. **Experimentation:** Deploying your staff to work in ways that are designed to get the work done, but at the same time to reveal individuals' and group strengths and weaknesses. Baseball shows beautifully how by experimenting with staff skills you can deliver successful results now, at some risk of failure later. But you can minimize that risk by deploying the other three practices.
2. **OMA—Observe, Measure, Analyze**: Monitoring your staff, watching how they handle specific situations, and trying to discern patterns in what they do and don't do well.

3. **Applying:** Taking the lessons you learn from OMA, then organizing work in ways that maximize individual and group effectiveness.
4. **Coaching:** Preparing individuals to become better at what the organization needs them to improve at, as well as delivering individualized motivation and training.

In this chapter, I'll provide you with scouting reports on how to make the most of the first two practices, where you actively gather information. In chapter 7, I'll address the latter two practices, where you apply the knowledge you harvest with the first two.

Experimentation:
Conscious Deployment for Both Testing and Winning

You need to learn what your roster's capable of. That requires experimentation, but most managers are chronically driven from above to improve results *right now.* Most under that pressure prefer to assign all their resources to tried-and-true players, methods, and tactics. Like refusing to set aside time for slack (see chapter 3), tried-and-true stunts the organization's ability to improve, because the manager is finding out almost nothing about what less-used team members can do, how they might be able to help, and which new methods might help the organization respond to the changing environment.

The larger the organization, the more prone it is to this weakness, what I call the Johnny Floggerfaster Approach. The organization ossifies and gets more and more out of touch with the evolving present, until it's so obvious the system is out of whack that the organization feels it has to bring in expensive consultants to lay off people—and make up a new, "improved," static model that will again start ossifying.

One of the hardest acts for managers in and out of baseball to accomplish is to balance what look at first like contradictory needs: staffing tasks for high performance right now, and testing the aptitudes of staff at performing tasks in diverse situations.

Baseball managers have to do this more than most of us because baseball players' ability erodes over a few years, and it's inevitable that they have to be replaced. Staffers outside of baseball are rarely in jobs where age quickly depreciates the aptitudes that got them the job in the first place (some exceptions: construction and farmwork, many factory jobs). But like you, baseball managers still have to figure out a way to win while throwing players into situations that will test and reveal their strengths and weaknesses.

Baseball managers sometimes have clear opportunities to do this, like the late innings of games where the team is ahead 8–1 (or behind 8–1), or late-season games where the team is already out of contention. More often than not, like you, they have to try to test in less forgiving situations.

John McGraw was an early master of experimentation. It was his rabid pursuit of structured control that led him to this mastery. It meant he had a test schedule in mind for every new employee (player), from the moment of recruitment to the end of his career.

The early career of Hall of Famer Frankie Frisch, "The Fordham Flash," is a good example of McGraw's drive to win and concurrently test team members' capabilities. McGraw recruited the cocky infielder for his New York Giants in 1919, fresh out of Fordham. McGraw wanted to initiate Frisch in the minors, but the affluent student-athlete told the manager it had to be the majors or nothing.[21]

The Giants already had a competitive team, and their infield was set. Established stars, Laughing Larry Doyle and Heinie Zimmerman, anchored the two positions Frisch was most likely to play, second and third base. And the Giant shortstop, Art Fletcher, was much better than average at a position Frisch didn't look ideal for.

By June 14, when Frisch debuted, the team was humming along with a 27–13 record. McGraw continued to play to win, but found 29 games in which to play Frisch at second base and 20 games at third. The Giants finished strongly in second place.

The next season, 1920, Zimmerman had been banned from baseball. Doyle was still at second, and the Giants had the services of Dave "Beauty" Bancroft, a Hall of Fame shortstop at the peak of his career. McGraw used Frisch in 109 games at third base and not at all at second. The Giants again finished second, and managed to be very competitive while creating opportunities to test the youngster.

As always, McGraw marinated prospects in his methods while observing them personally. Frisch said McGraw "saw to it that I was given a chance to hit during batting practice. . . . He personally took charge of polishing up my fielding. He would hit grounders for hours. . . . He would even hit to the infield in the pre-game warm-up. If you didn't make the play the way McGraw wanted it, he'd hit you another, five more, ten more, until the play was made the way he wanted it." [22] Managers who delegate *all* the training in your line of work are at a disadvantage—even just a little involvement can work magic.

In 1921, Doyle retired, and Frisch got more playing time at second (61 games), but McGraw took a chance. He made a deal with the Phillies, trading his light-hitting third baseman for the Phils' light-hitting second baseman, giving Frisch more duty at third (93 games). As a full-timer now, though still being tested at different positions, Frisch led the league in stolen bases, and was in the top-10 lists for on-base plus slugging, batting average, slugging average, doubles, and triples. The Giants won the pennant this time, and Frisch's breakout season was a significant catalyst.

By 1922, McGraw had concluded that his emerging star should play second base, so he traded for Heinie Groh, an All-Star–caliber hitter at third base. Because Groh struggled to adapt to the new team and suffered injuries, Frisch logged 53 games at third base while tallying 85 games at second. The Giants won another pennant, as they would with Frisch at second the next two years, for a remarkable four titles in a row.

What Is Past Is Prologue:
The Development of John McGraw

John McGraw started playing in the majors in 1891 at age 18. He was lucky to play as the third baseman for one of the legendary franchises of the 19th century, the Baltimore Orioles of the American Association and then the National League. He was ambitious, too, and that stoked his chances for becoming a manager.

From 1890s baseball, he learned that in a free market, chaos reigns supreme. So the organization willing to push the limits of rules (or simply break them and worry about the consequences later) had a comparative edge. Baseball then was like Afghanistan, pockmarked with here-today-gone-tomorrow franchises, owners who would not pay players, players who would jump contracts, and volatile rules. In that environment, the Orioles set a standard for brawling, high-pressure, Australian Rules baseball, replete with sharpened spikes and a relish for bullying the single umpire appointed to arbitrate a game.

But it wasn't just physical intimidation that set them apart. They were brainy in their criminality, too. Their Hall of Fame left fielder Joe Kelley had good range and a legendary throwing arm and nailed many a base runner at third or home in critical situations. To respect the historical record, though, we should note that he was assisted in this endeavor by keeping a spare ball hidden in the 3½-inch grass that was common in the outfield of the baseball fields during that era (they were called "fields" for a reason). If a ball got past Kelley and was low enough to vanish from the umpire's and runner's vision, he might grab the hidden ball and use his rifle to cut down runners whose judgment had told them the ball was past him. Kelley, according to legend, was finally caught only because his center-field neighbor, Steve Brodie, tore after a ball through the gap, and while Joe grabbed the hidden ball and threw it to the infielder, Brodie didn't see Kelley's trick and chucked the actual game ball back into the infield, too.

The Orioles' strategy was to keep the environment anarchic, changing tactics daily to confound opponents and umpires. McGraw played in this environment during the season, but looking beyond his playing career, he chose to work off-season, and that gave him an alternative perspective. In exchange for free tuition, room, and board, he became the baseball coach at the college known today as St. Bonaventure. He accumulated both credits and knowledge of the complete antithesis of anarchy—the rigor of Catholic education. And even though he was about the same age as the college players he was coaching, he had to be the responsible figure. And he couldn't have his players use his own favorite Oriole tricks in intercollegiate games, techniques such as grabbing the belt of an opposing runner going past him at third base.

McGraw synthesized the creative effervescence of Oriole tactics with the rigorous structure he observed at the college. The result was controlled pressure. "Little Napoleon" learned, too, that adapting to daily circumstances was absolutely vital to survival—he had to, because his on-field and off-season environments were antipodes.

Applied creativity is best served by a foundation of order—not necessarily "control," but a structured system and environment that frees up time and encourages and rewards creativity.

McGraw and the players who toiled for his major-league teams knew this lesson. Sadly, American organizations almost never do. Instead of finding that functional combo, they either become miasmas of sloppiness in the name of creativity or little rules-worshipping dead ends in the cause of control.

The two clear management lessons from McGraw are as useful outside of baseball as they are in it.

1. It's not only possible, but necessary, to find opportunities to test team members, even under the pressure to achieve right now. The higher the pressure to achieve, the longer it may take to find the opportunities to test and confirm the team members (it took from

1919 to the end of 1921 for McGraw's testing of Frisch), but managers must continue to attack both missions simultaneously.

2. For the good of the team, you sometimes have to ask a team member to take on tasks different from those you think she's best at. But just like McGraw in 1922 realizing Frisch was more valuable at second base, you have to work out a way for a star to get back to her highest-achievement potential.

Observe, Measure, Analyze (OMA)

Baseball organizations have always observed and had natural ways to measure, but were very late to come to rigorous analysis. Baseball's accumulation of serious statistics started when Branch Rickey let statistician Allan Roth talk him into letting Roth work for the Brooklyn Dodgers after World War II. Early sabermetricians like Dick Cramer and Pete Palmer commercialized team data collection in the early 1980s. But teams trying to sift through the mass of data to derive new, competitive conclusions based on analysis of historical data seriously started at the turn of the 21st century with a movement made known by the Oakland Athletics' front office, as documented by Michael Lewis in *Moneyball*. Some have tried to create a controversy by pitting statistics *against* traditional arts such as scouting, and while there are a few Talibaptists on each extreme, the statistics are, and have always been, a reference for decisions made through traditional arts. The imaginary enemy of the Moneyball method is John Schuerholz's excellence machine, the Atlanta Braves organization. But the Braves use just as many statistics as Oakland, though with a different focus, while the A's scout just as much as the Braves.

The main reason baseball managers have needed to observe, measure, and analyze every player every day is to understand which components of the game the player is good at, which ones he is shaky at but might improve, and which ones are a black hole that no amount of practice or coaching can fill. The other reason for OMA, and it comes in a *distant* second, is for trying to deliver an overall assessment of a player, for those infrequent occasions when you make a trade or negotiate a contract.

Nonbaseball managers find OMA harder: theorists labor over ways to embody work events into numbers, and outside of manufacturing, it's easier for a rich man to pass through the eye of a camel than it is to get agreement on how to assign meaningful quality and quantity measures to the fruits of work efforts. Look at a few examples of effort and how we measure it.

Manufacturing is easiest to observe and measure. When I worked on the line in a plastics factory, one of my jobs was to fix the soap dishes pulled off the line by a quality-control worker because the pieces had excess material on the edges that needed shaving. I trimmed the excess and put the now to-specification soap dish back on the line. In manufacturing, the quality and quantity of this work was totally measurable; managers could count how many soap dishes an hour I fixed and whether each item in my output met their standard or not. Quality (does it meet spec?) and quantity (how many?) are both measurable through observation.

Agricultural work is more challenging. When I picked citrus as a teenager, the employer knew the quantity of what I picked, and that's what I got paid for. But there was no resource assigned to inspect every grapefruit in the box to make sure it was a good one. After a while, of course, I knew how to recognize excellent from so-so from no-darned-way (to this day, I'm the Greg Maddux of picking out citrus at the produce stand). In agriculture, sorting for quality happened later in the process and wasn't tied to individual pickers. Quantity measurable, quality not.

White-collar work, the highest-paid jobs (and therefore the ones most important to measure) have *no* obvious facets to measure. Yes, for CEOs, computer programmers, secretaries of defense, and university presidents, theorists do sweat to invent meaningful numbers they can assign, but what they report is meaningless. The hallmark of the perversity of American management is that the greater the cost of the human resource, the less accountable her position is—as though accountability sloughing is one of the perks of a privileged job. In services or symbolic analyst work such as human resources or finance, both quality and quantity are nearly impossible to measure.

It's critical to recognize that observation and measurement outside of baseball are almost always done for the lower-return reason, the overarching assessment, the examination of an employee's "performance" at review time or when a possible layoff or promotion comes up. In a healthy organization, this will happen at most twice a year.

But the much-ignored higher-return reason, as in baseball, is the manager's everyday OMA of each team member for strengths and weaknesses at individual tasks and duties. As in baseball, it's to understand what she's good at, what she needs improvement in, and what she will probably not learn to do. The objective is seeking both immediate returns and building a plan for bigger long-term ones.

Employees, like ballplayers, are bundles of strengths and weaknesses. While it's important administrivia to be able to give them an overall rating, when you're in the trenches getting work done, you need to know *what* each excels at, is fine at, sucks at. A single, overarching evaluation isn't very useful there. Consolidating measures into a single number makes the scoring and aftermath of evaluation less effort for the manager—and less useful to both the manager and the organization.

Here's a nonbaseball example. Salespeople tend to have the same distribution of strengths and weaknesses as ballplayers. Just as batters have to face right-handed sinker/slider pitchers one day and fireballing lefties the next, salesfolk meet all kinds of prospective customers. Some calls require adequate technical knowledge, others merely that you dress for success. Some require flirting, some just the facts, some just the lowest price. There are as many kinds of customers as there are pitchers a batter faces, and you'll find a saleswoman who can sell to all of them equally effectively as often as you'll find a Barry Bonds who can hit everything thrown at him.

Why Can't Business Be More Like Baseball?

In baseball, management has to evaluate and deliver feedback to be successful. Managers have to do it in almost all other endeavors, too . . . they just haven't realized it yet.

In baseball, even bad managers evaluate their players constantly, and the good ones practice OMA every moment of every practice and game. In most businesses, employees have to chase around their supervisors with scary-looking dental-surgery implements to induce an annual evaluation. How can anyone in organizational life think he deserves a management job if delivering an evaluation to a colleague a couple times a year is too hard? Because most managers don't do ongoing OMA they don't have confidence in their knowledge, so they feel underqualified to draw up an evaluation. In a majority of big businesses and government agencies, managers also find that employee evaluation holds them accountable, a state that can undermine a career.

It's easy to do evaluations if you do OMA. You have immediate information on which to base directive comments to your team members. I've found that if a manager can set aside time at least every fortnight to meet for a short time with every team member, give feedback, and discuss lessons learned, barriers, and how to focus the next fortnight's efforts, both sides benefit. The manager acquires a deeper awareness of work details; the team member, a clearer perspective on the manager's objectives. Try it for six months, and watch your team's competitiveness go up quicker than ticket prices at a new ballpark.

I've got a simple tool at the *Management by Baseball* Web site, a file you can download that has a basic grid to fill in for regular meetings. It's a respectable foundation for you to turn into something of your own.

Recognize that the probability of success is highly contextual. While it may be relatively easy to come up with a single number that states a sales team member's value (total sales is a commonly used one), in reality, each individual will excel or fall short when matched with a specific kind of customer. Once you embrace this model, you can start deploying sales-folk in a way that increases both their immediate value and morale at the same time. That translates to long-term value.

The trick to having your team excel is to observe, measure, and analyze what all your team members do, even if it seems difficult to assign quantitative or qualitative measures to it. That difficulty can be a barrier, and for some personality types, an impermeable one. I recommend that managers who have not given serious thought to how they can measure work should start reading some of the copious literature on the subject. You'll find some references to tools and readings about metrics at the *Management by Baseball* Web site.

I had an otherwise intelligent boss who shall not remain nameless. He refused to measure output in any meaningful way. After a long discussion about his belief, I can print it for you in close to his exact words. Stewk's Law is "If you can't measure something perfectly, don't try to measure it at all."

A lot of managers channel Stewk. Every one of them is guaranteed to struggle or to fail abysmally. Measuring quality and quantity in nonman-ufacturing jobs is truly a challenge, and you won't be able to come up with a perfect system. Don't be a Stewk; measure and analyze when you can, use technology or don't, do it as well as you can, and know that results are fuzzy, but that measuring them contributes to your group's abilities.

In the early 20th century Connie Mack institutionalized something players and managers had always observed but not recorded. "The Tall Tactician" always carried a large piece of cardstock with him during games, noting where opposing batters hit the ball. He used the information to refine his placement of fielders. It was easy to chart, tedious but not difficult to gather. While it didn't answer a lot of questions or deliver perfectly successful results, it was somewhat useful to apply measurement to an easily measured aspect of the game.

But how much data is enough? You need a serious sample, because a few factoids do not wisdom make. Earl Weaver, a natural measurement and analysis wizard, explained how important finding the significant sample size is.[23] In theory, he believes, a batter needs to face a pitcher 20 times before one can be sure enough to get a decent reading of the matchup's probabilities. If a batter is 3-for-5 against a specific pitcher, that's an interesting early indication, but not meaningful. If a batter is 3-for-13 against a pitcher, it doesn't look good but the jury is still out; if he goes, for example, 0-for-7 in subsequent appearances, he's going to sport a .150 batting average. But if he gets three hits in his next seven at bats, he'll be hitting .300, and just two hits will make for an adequate .250. If those two hits are home runs, the batter will be looking pretty good. The point: at this undeveloped stage, results change quickly.

Televised games, with broadcasters' conviction that baseball is too boring to make the advertisements effective, have a strong compulsion to keep data spewing out of infographics to stimulate the viewers' lizard brains. They'll gladly report that a batter is 0-for-4 against this pitcher, and the color man might reinforce verbally that the pitcher has the batter's number. That's nonsense, just as when they try to make a batter's 2-for-4 against a pitcher a profound judgment of the batter owning the pitcher. The latter just tells you the batter's not helpless against the pitcher.

In your group, as in baseball, when the sample size is not big enough, it doesn't pay to solidify an opinion and shut down data collection; small changes in effectiveness can repaint the entire picture. As Weaver posited, most pitchers and batters learn from their experiences with each other, but individual strengths and weaknesses and the way they match up with the task at hand mean sometimes the mismatch will persist.

Assuming the employee is still alive, there is no point at which a manager's interpretation will prove out with absolute success all the time. You need a reasonable target in your own OMA routine, and if you think about it, you'll likely find it.

Persist in measuring. Even after you have a clear picture of what people can and can't do, continue to observe and measure as much as you can free up resources for. Most people change over time, and you might be insulating someone from a task at which she could be a great contributor.

Index Cards and Apples—to Technify or Not

Should you use technology to record observations and make measurement easier? It's not necessary, but it can be helpful if the work burden of the tools is lower than the benefits harvested. A chosen technology can be an aid or just more overhead. Weaver, for example, used index cards and pencil to track each batter against each pitcher. It was tedious but worth the time. One of my best interviews was a relaxed pregame conversation while he was building his lineup for the day. As he touched each card, he related what he saw on it and what he was thinking. That day, he had his choice of designated hitters and noticed his human hand grenade of a left fielder, Pat Kelly,[24] had career stats of 5-for-8 with a homer against the day's Mariner victim. As Weaver said, he just had to put Kelly in that lineup at DH so Kelly could get another crack at what he looked to be successful at.

Earl's index cards are great. They're portable and easy to manage. For a manager who's comfortable with numbers, the act of entering data and handling the cards reveals much more than the same information generated by an invisible computer process and poured onto a screen or sheet of paper. There's a texture to number knowledge that most people absorb calculating and writing by hand but miss out on if they're just given the result. But while it's better for "knowing" what the source data is, the time it takes to analyze results from data collected this way can limit the number of questions one chooses to answer. And fancier correlations (this batter against that team's right-handed pitchers, at the home stadium) are almost impossibly time-consuming to unearth using a manual system.

That's why as the personal-computer revolution arrived in the early 1980s, Dick Cramer and Pete Palmer, two of the first computer-literate baseball researchers, designed competing systems to track and store in a database every significant event that happened on the field. Cramer's product was a software/hardware combo called Edge 1.000 that required a skilled observer to record pitch-by-pitch events. By the end of 1981's spring training, the company he worked for had a buyer in the Oakland Athletics.

The A's saw an unusual opportunity. The young team had gone from last place in 1979 to a highly improved but distant second place in '80. They wanted a boost that would put them into contention with the Kansas City Royals, the best regular-season team in the league over the previous five years. The A's used Edge 1.000 on a dinky Apple II computer so they could take the equipment on road games.

The A's, incidentally, won the division in 1981. The Chicago White Sox signed on for Edge 1.000 a year later. Team VP Jack Gould wanted business intelligence to judge the true value both of players on his own team (so he could negotiate with them) and of those on competing teams (to assess potential trades). The Sox system operator was Danny Evans, a man beloved by slugger Greg Luzinski, who credited Evans's data with convincing the team to change their left-field fence in a way that made it easier for Luzinski to hit homers. (Evans, incidentally, went on to become the very successful GM of the Dodgers in 2002–2004.) The early-'80s White Sox under Gould became the leading user of computers for measurement and analysis when team executive Rollie Hemond had Cramer refine a system for analyzing scouting reports so Hemond could sift through the thousands of prospective youngsters and come up with, for example, a left-handed-hitting shortstop with a better-than-average glove and sound emotional makeup.

The next year, 1983, the Yankees bought the system. Their motive was to be able to answer the endless micro-statistical questions team owner George Steinbrenner asked. The Yankee data-entry man was Doug Melvin, a washed-out pitcher getting his first big front-office assignment. Melvin has gone on to become the GM of the Baltimore Orioles, Texas Rangers, and Milwaukee Brewers.

I think it's no coincidence that the two grunt workers who had to feed the Edge 1.000 system ended up as accomplished GMs. They were forced to *observe* and *measure,* and they were marinated in the ways you could analyze the information.

GMs can do this by hand. The advantage of a higher-technology approach here is not *better answers,* but the ability to ask and answer *more questions* before the analyst gets fatigued. It won't affect whom you take in the first round, but it will strongly affect what you know about the choices you make in, say, the eighth round. Nonbaseball workplaces are frequently limited by the refusal to apply tech where it's useful, but more commonly they're poisoned by an excess of gadgets and cranky software thrown at unanalyzed problems. Find the right balance as they have in baseball; make sure you're getting the answers you need.

The *PC Magazine* Flub: Throwing to the Wrong Base

It's important not only to measure and analyze, but to do it with the right factors. Just because you can quantify something doesn't mean it's important.

Computer industry monthly *PC Magazine* used to measure the speed of performance of computer programs to hundredths of seconds. Laughably, *PC Mag* used humans with stopwatches to do this work. Humans with stopwatches can't even measure accurately to tenths of seconds, and this was ten times as fine as the tenths they couldn't do accurately.

In baseball, it's almost as easy to find an accurate but meaningless measurement. And widely accepted "facts" about the National Pastime are also pitted with inaccuracies. Since measuring accurately is much easier than figuring out what's important, we'll deal with that first.

Home-run distances are an example of terribly inaccurate measurement. Baseball researcher and architect John Pastier has spent years debunking the ridiculous lengths to which fans and media will go to exaggerate the distance of homers.

In April of 1953, Mickey Mantle hit a homer against the Senators that left Washington, D.C.'s Griffith Stadium. A nice shot. Maybe 490 or 500 feet, the theoretical limit to the distance a batted ball can travel. But apocrypha have crept into the archives. The Yankee publicist, Red Patterson, exited the stadium looking for the ball. Patterson found 10-year-old Don

Dunnaway holding the ball and asked the boy to lead him to where he'd found it, in a backyard across the street from the stadium.

Patterson, being a good publicist, knew a marketable story when he saw one. Without verifying the ballpark's dimensions (ballpark measures are notoriously sloppy), he paced off the distance from the stadium to the place where the boy thought he'd picked it up. Patterson came up with the "565-foot" homer—a piece of mythic legend that has become history.

There were a lot of places Patterson's estimate drifted from reality. First, there was the stadium-dimension factor, compounded by estimating the distance from the fence to the adjacent street, compounded by Patterson's use of pacing as a measuring technique, compounded by the 10-year-old's memory of where the ball was (not where it landed, but where it stopped rolling). And while sometimes a lot of little inaccuracies can cancel one another out, remember it was a publicist doing the measuring—a person who had every incentive to maximize the number to inflate the importance of the story. Bad tools, weak quality control, biased agent: a fatal combo in baseball or in your organization.

So while the 565-foot mark is, absurdly, 13 percent over the theoretical ceiling a batted baseball can travel, this number is widely used and even enshrined in the Hall of Fame.[25]

Tumid estimates of home-run distances seep into folklore and TV broadcasts, and with the American passion for record breaking in a bigger-is-better world, these numbers have to be continually inflated like post–World War I German currency to impress the listener. One Mantle Web site cites a computer simulation of a 1963 homer "The Mick" hit in Yankee Stadium that hit a facade. Had it not, the simulation asserted, the ball would have flown 734 feet, 46 percent above the theoretical limit. Hmm, must have been the Iraqi vote counters, or perhaps the auditors at Arthur Andersen, that came up with *that* measurement.

We can all laugh at Red Patterson and Arthur Andersen for sloppy, self-serving findings. And those errors are easy to avoid, once you make the simple decision to be accurate. The real challenges come when you try to sort out the meaningful from the meaningless.

PC Mag's existential folly didn't end with terminal inaccuracy. Because they had Men with Stopwatches, they *had* to measure in time everything a computer or program did. I can remember a review of database products where the lab techs measured how long it took to sort a big database. The times for the "fastest" and "slowest" were something like 1.12 seconds and 1.29 seconds, one-sixth of a second difference, below the .20 human-error probability. Moreover, white-collar workers can't take advantage of .17 seconds in real life, so the context was as flawed as the numbers.

It was right for *PC Mag* to ask the question and try the measurement, but not to present it to readers as though it held any meaning. Pretend for a minute it's really measurable, that the lab techs at *PC Mag* were minimum-wage members of the Master Race. Even then, it's not the right measure to supply. The vast percentage of time people spend working with software is not spent waiting for it to return an answer. Most of the time they spend (over 90 percent) is in learning how to use it, to make it deliver the information they want, to deal with the program's interface. A program with the best interface design but the worst stopwatch speed is in reality 10 times as "fast" as one with the slowest speed and best interface. *PC Mag* was presenting nonsense merely because it was easy to measure and report.

Roster Tweaking: Acting on What You Learn

As I stated already, during experimentation and OMA you're acting to gather data. When you have enough information, it's time to act on your knowledge even though, like everything else in life with the exception of Cate Blanchett's acting, it's imperfect. It's deep enough into the game at that point to deploy the other two practices, applying and coaching, a doubleheader we'll attend in chapter 7.

7

Drills: Juggling the Lineup

I don't think a manager should be judged by whether he wins the pennant
but by whether he gets the most out of the 25 players he's been given.
—Chuck Tanner, Pirates manager, 1977–85

Experimentation and OMA (observe, measure, analyze) are essential
for gathering knowledge. But unless you convert your knowledge to
action, it's just plaqueing up your cranium. Most managers either refuse
to act (based on that marmot-brained misapprehension that if you do
nothing you can't make an error) or flail at a problem randomly like a
Rock 'em Sock 'em Robot. The sweet spot is in between. It requires crafting considered actions that take advantage of what you've learned about
your contributors, as Ray Miller does.

Miller is unique in post–World War II baseball for the diversity of his
job experience, moving back and forth between being a pitching coach
and a major-league manager. He was a highly honored pitching coach for
some of the great Oriole teams (1978–84). He became a manager in Minnesota (1985–86) and crafted the turnaround in systems and methods
that led to their first-ever World Series–winning team (1987), which he
was not there to share in. Miller chose to go back to being a pitching
coach (Pittsburgh, 1987–96, Baltimore, 1997) and then a manager again
(1998–99). Mike Flanagan, a Cy Young Award–winning Miller student,
is currently the O's GM and brought Ray back as pitching coach. This

span of jobs has given Miller insights into doing both jobs that few people have for even one of the two. Miller has a few guidelines he works from, but the key success factor is applying OMA to his coaching.

"What you do with a player has to be based on what he can do well, not what he can't do," he said. "If this guy has particular trouble with left-handers, then you get him into as many situations against right-handers as you can. You work with him on the side to create new patterns against lefties, but in a game you keep him mostly doing what he does best." Miller, a business owner himself, understands exactly how this relates to nonbaseball management. "If you think about it, if you have a business, that's exactly what you do with your people. If you have an assembly line, and you have the oldest guy doing the most physical work and the youngest guy doing the work that's least physical, common sense says let the young guy push that weight and let the old guy push the button, and all of a sudden your production goes up."

Miller's coaching success comes from this ability: "It's about judging what a person can do and then basing what you have him do based on what he does well. Life is hard enough to start out with." [26]

Letting people loose on what they're good at, and protecting them and your organization from a lot of work they aren't good at, is a hidden but powerful technique for keeping productivity high and keeping the talent motivated.

Applying

Applying team members in your own department to the cornucopia of incoming projects and tasks isn't seriously different from what baseball's managers do with their players. There are two quite different forms of application: the big strategic tendencies (motivating everyone so each knows he has a chance at stardom) and the tactical details (applying each person in situations in which she does best). No contemporary baseball manager is more successful at managing the big tendencies than the Yankees' Joe Torre.

In 1998, Torre's talent-stuffed roster blessed him with regulars at every position in the lineup except left field, DH, and catcher. His starting pitching was anchored by four veteran winners, and he planned to start young Ramiro Mendoza, successful the previous season as a reliever, to complete the rotation. And he applied a system to get the most out of his nonregulars.

At catcher, he used his promising young starter, Jorge Posada, about 60 percent of the team's innings and veteran backup Joe Girardi the rest. Posada was the team's choice for the future, and certainly a better hitter. But Girardi was less likely to allow a passed ball or wild pitch, and was a good bunter (Posada had just one successful sacrifice in his first 581 major-league games), which enhanced his limited offensive value.

In left field, Torre had five contributors. None was a star, but if you rolled together the best attributes of each, that golem would *look* like a star. Chad Curtis was a hustling right-handed journeyman with good baserunning instincts and outfield range that meant a lot in Yankee Stadium's spacious left field. Darryl Strawberry was an aging, left-handed former All-Star—no longer a good outfielder but with monumental home-run power against right-handed pitchers. Switch-hitting Tim Raines at 38 was no longer the greatest high-percentage base stealer of his time, but still a great base runner and sure-handed in the outfield. The rookies were Ricky Ledee, a speedy but erratic 24-year-old lefty, and Shane Spencer, a bulky, slow righty who could hit up a storm, especially against lefties. At designated hitter, Torre could choose from whoever wasn't penciled into the lineup in left field that day.

Mendoza was ready to cement his position as the fifth starting pitcher when Orlando "El Duque" Hernández defected from Cuba and the Yankee organization snapped him up. El Duque had been one of the great big-game pitchers the game had ever known. There were some skeptics, he grabbed his opportunity to start when David Cone was temporarily

Joe Torre's Success Factor

In 1998, Joe Torre put together an extraordinary team accomplishment. Yankee teams are traditionally good at winning just enough during the regular season to get into the playoffs, then crushing their victims in the playoff and championship games. The '98 team excelled all season long, mortal only during an early-September stretch. They went 114–48 for the campaign, winning over 70 percent of their games in a sport where winning over 60 percent is exceptional. They led the AL with most runs scored and fewest runs allowed, and were far above average in defense.[27]

More often than not, teams that lap the rest of the pack by that much don't win the World Series, imploding with all the bad luck and silly mistakes they avoided all season to get to the championship. But these Yanks were different, ripping through opponents like a chainsaw through butter. They routed the Rangers in the first round, massacred the Indians four games to two for the pennant, and excommunicated the Padres in four straight games to win the Series.

Like a lot of dominant organizations in the current global economy, the Yankees generally succeed by using massive resources to corner the market on key commodities to lock competitors out of lucrative markets. They also use sophisticated business intelligence to find competitors' weaknesses and undermine those competitors' aims. They do whatever it takes to reinforce their position of dominance. In this baseball example, that meant scooping up not just all the players who might be useful for the team, but also some that weren't useful to the Yankees but might be useful to a competitor. Dominant outfits that thrive by that model don't usually strive for excellence in all aspects of their business. They don't have to. They know it's a waste of effort in that situation because quality does little to affect outcomes.

But at the same time that Yankee GM Brian Cashman was assembling a squad that looked like an All-Star team, Torre got those Yankees to be different, to strive for maximum quality like a hungry underdog. The challenge of a roster packed with first-string talent is that some first-stringers aren't in the starting lineup or rotation, and highly competitive individuals like major leaguers hate "riding the pine" instead of starting.

The 50th-percentile business or professional-practice manager would pit these competitive people against each other, challenging each to prove he'd earned the right to a starting spot. If that average manager was capable of recognizing which single competitor was "best"—and most managers aren't—he'd get the use of a single talent. Torre, though, went against the norm with a three-step program you should use, too.

First, he worked very hard to gather, Miller style, all the OMA he could about each team member's strengths and weaknesses. Second, he promised all of his non-everyday players that there'd be opportunities for them to play in the spots where they'd have the best chances for success.[28] Third, he delivered on his promise and got most of the best talents of a host of contributors. His model can work for you if you've done the observing and monitoring I described earlier and find out the areas where each of your staff members excels.

---

disabled by his mother's Jack Russell terrier. Hernández delivered, so Mendoza was bumped, idling as a long reliever and fill-in for injured starters. And for the record, I think the story that El Duque slipped the terrier a medium-rare pot roast and two Cohiba cigars is pure apocrypha.

The Torre view, "To get the most from the people you manage, you must put them in the right spot at the right time,"[29] worked a different way at each of the three spots without a regular. In each case, though, he monitored individual performance and tracked variables that were potential contributors to success or failure. In each case, players recognized they were being monitored and placed in their best light—a persistent motivation to be their best at work every day.

At pitcher, it deprived Mendoza of the glory of being a starter, but it increased his value to the team. He was pitching critical middle innings.

This made him more effective. He hurled two to five innings, so hitters saw less of him and couldn't adjust as well. By pitching well and stifling opponents in those innings, he not only gained experience, but also gave his team the chance to come from behind. That added wins to his stat line. Filling in as a spot starter when others were hurt, he had a 10–2 season and got to star in the playoffs and World Series, pitching in innings that counted in games that really mattered.

The strategy paid off the next season, too. In 1999, Mendoza oscillated between starter and reliever several times, thanks to an injury to Roger Clemens and the implosion of Hideki Irabu. Mendoza kept succeeding at both roles, not only because he was the rare kind of player who could do both, but also because Torre prepared him to change gears and recognize how important and special that versatility was. As managers, we can always benefit from recognizing those individuals who may not be the best at one thing, but can be very good at many things. We can apply their skills in ways that benefit not only the group, but the individual as well.

At catcher, Torre was able to choose on a daily basis the player he thought would add most value that day. Like all contemporary managers, he had access to the batter-versus-pitcher stat lines, so he could sometimes nail a decision based on a catcher's success or lack of it in hitting the opponent's starter. And whoever he didn't use as a starter could add value later in the game, Posada as a pinch hitter, Girardi as a defensive replacement. Good managers in nonbaseball organizations learn to keep everyone involved in the work the organization considers important. Engaged staff members pay better attention to detail and individual productivity than those who are left out.

At left field and DH, Torre made sure all five players were getting time in the field, or just at the plate. He based his daily choice on the park, on whether a team member needed a rest or was hot, and on who the opposing pitcher was. He optimized morale by making sure everyone got to play, and that everyone got rest instead of the work at which he was least likely to succeed, which delivered the side benefit of boosting self-confidence.

RULE 7.01. Complement staffers' skill. Finding someone to complement a team member is something managers outside of baseball should do. It delivers much higher performance from their groups and project teams.

It's an easy innovation that requires only applying the OMA knowledge of the team's individuals. Does pulling someone briefly from a less important task to temporarily partner her with the team member on a more critical task who needs a complement seem complicated? Consider how and why they do it in baseball, and how it started.

Platooning for an Edge—
George Stallings's Tactic & The Miracle Braves

Finding a complementary partner in baseball as Torre did is most frequently "platooning": pairing two players who bat from different sides of the plate to share a position. The first noteworthy success with this approach was achieved by manager Gentleman George Stallings of the 1914 Boston Braves, and was one of the factors that led to their nickname "the Miracle Braves."

Stallings signed on to manage the Braves for the 1913 campaign. They finished in fifth place at 69–82. His best-hitting outfielder, the aging and talkative Silent John Titus, retired at the end of the season, undermining an already below-average offense. Going nowhere fast, and without re-sources to acquire stars, it was the perfect environment for an experiment.

Stallings must have been carrying the mass-platooning idea in his breast pocket for a long time, but according to Bill James, he decided in 1914 to platoon at each of his three outfield positions. Most games, this meant resting a man against the pitcher who threw from his side—for ex-ample, resting a lefty hitter against a lefty pitcher, tending to avoid a tougher matchup for his batter. A couple of the early platoon partners (one, a 36-year-old retread apparently brought in just for the experiment) didn't work out well. Instead of giving up on the experiment, Stallings ad-justed his plan and traded for more platoon outfielders.

The 1914 Braves finished first (94–59) as a result of several factors, in-cluding improved offensive contribution from their outfield. They then tore through the Philadelphia A's, *the* dominant franchise of the time, in the World Series, taking four straight games.

According to James, the eccentric experiment and the result of an out-of-the-blue (actually out of the blue and red, the Braves' colors that year) miracle campaign effectively revolutionized roster construction for the next 25 years. The successful results of platooning were shoved into every manager's face. It became almost a given that teams would platoon at one or more positions. But eventually there was push-back from two factors. One most likely won't affect your ability to do this in nonbaseball organi-zations. The other definitely will.

One: the natural law of supply. Stallings had no competition for mar-ginal players with one or two very positive aptitudes; competitors were looking for all-around talent. So Gentleman George was free to browse at his leisure through the remainder pile, looking for players who had spe-cific skills that complemented those the players on his roster already had. But once others noted the utility of platooning, it was more like Filene's basement—a lot of stock, most of it useless, but a number of valuable items and a horde of aggressive people mud-wrestling to get them.

This won't be a problem for nonbaseball organizations.

Two: resentment and personal insecurities, which *will* be a problem. Platooned players want to play all the time. When you start platooning, your staff, especially the ones getting help, will want to go it alone. They won't want to be looked upon as flawed or weak, and most won't want to admit they need help at anything. Most organizations punish people for not being all-arounders like Gary Sheffield, so you'll have to overcome this with some politically sensitive pilot projects and make a big fuss when they're over to show publicly you respect the efforts of both the helper and the helped. One more swing: plan tasks whenever possible so the helped person is the helper next time. It eases ego problems and helps everyone on the team recognize that each member is a contributor.

When you platoon, keep in mind Earl Weaver's approach. You don't remove *all* challenges from a person, denuding him of anything he hasn't had experience with, or previously failed with once. You expose him to work he might learn to do well. Yankee manager Joe McCarthy's use of star catcher Bill Dickey is a good example. Dickey hit left-handed and, like most lefties, hit right-handed pitchers better than left-handed ones. Bill James found that Dickey started 82 percent of the games where the opponent's starter was right-handed, but only 42 percent when the starter was left-handed. Dickey still got to see lefties and build his skills, but his team (and his own stats) benefited from sitting out against many south-paws.

Beyond baseball, the bigger your staff, the easier it is to match them up for a tactical platooning advantage. With two people on your team, it's pretty hard, but having four is almost as good as having forty. Here are a couple of ways I've applied platooning beyond baseball. When I worked at the U.S. Senate and supervised interns, we had Juana, who was a work-horse. She was a messy dresser but could read and digest about a foot of research papers an hour; she could isolate the key points and write them up in a concise though sloppy way. Another intern, Carol, was a clothes-horse, a very well-spoken law student who was very slow to get the full point. Once she'd internalized the point, she had perfect recall. I paired them to work on research projects that would get presented to legislative aides. Juana ripped through the footwork, and Carol did the face-to-face Q & A, where credibility is more important than depth of knowledge. When I comanaged the regional operations of an interstate passenger bus company, I matched driver pairs based on balancing the introverted, safety-first personalities with the extroverted, sociable ones. The passengers got to interact *and* get there in one piece. In endeavors such as advertising and marketing, platooning is an implicit part of most projects. You can play with these as a launching point for your own platoon designs.

Applying the talents of your team players is a powerful competitive advantage. Baseball is quicker than most at grabbing tricks like this, but if you choose to learn from Gentleman George, Weaver, and McCarthy, you'll have an edge. Most competitors won't have the guts and good sense to follow you.

Chicago White Sox Trick:
Not Closer by Committee, Closer by Situation

The White Sox won the 2005 AL flag and World Series with one of the two best bullpens in the league. GM Ken Williams and manager Ozzie Guillen cobbled together what in the 21st century looks like an innovation, what Williams called a "Closer by Situation."

It differs from the standard model. There, the relievers have prescribed rôles of ascending "importance" based on appearing in later innings. That now-standard model was deployed by Tony LaRussa in the late '80s specifically because he had former starter Dennis Eckersley, who threw very nasty stuff but was less effective when he threw much more than two innings. He'd most frequently use The Eck to start the ninth inning of close games the A's were winning, but not exclusively.

It made sense for LaRussa and The Eck because of the specific context of Eckersley's skills and limitations and the other pitchers LaRussa had to work with. Others, as always, imitated success, but in their own context, it was an approach that limited flexibility. Moreover, they started rigidly using their "closer" to start the ninth inning, and rarely other ways. Why should the most effective reliever come in only the ninth and with no one on when the paramount moment might be a bases-loaded jam in the seventh? The closer's skill wasn't consistently applied to the most dangerous situations. But relievers and managers both liked the comfort of prescribed, therefore easy, decisions.

The 2003 Red Sox tried to innovate a more flexible alternative. The field manager, Grady Little, didn't like it, and the personnel weren't quite right and didn't like the uncertainty. When the scheme hit some rough going, the press got all over the team, and they reverted to the start-the-ninth-inning closer. When the 2005 Chicago Cubs' bullpen imploded in late April, manager Dusty Baker decided to move to something he called a "Bullpen by Situation." As opposed to the conventional design, this Dusty model would bring in relievers based on a lot of in-game specific factors and not the predictable parade. Left- or right-handed, ground ball or fly ball or strikeout, rested or tired. Some relievers, Chad Fox especially, said the uncertainty made them uncomfortable. The Cubs changed when failing starter Ryan Dempster, dropped to the bullpen, emerged from the "by situation" pack as the closer.

Chicago GM Ken Williams adopted the crosstown team's "Closer by Situation" model, with a Guillen twist. For Guillen, all relievers are closers. "If I put you there in the seventh, close the seventh," he said. "If it's the eighth, close the eighth. If it's the ninth, close the ninth." This fits the sabermetric model, recognizing that the predictable, ordered parade of rôles with the marquee "closer" in the ninth doesn't leverage the best reliever for the toughest situations. At the same time, there's ego stroking, an ingredient that dampens the reliever resistance Baker received. The uncertainty of "when" is still there; there's certainty, though, in that whenever you appear, you're a critical contributor.

The White Sox started 2005 with a most unusual closer. Shingo "Mr. Zero" Takatsu was an import from Japan who'd addled hitters in his first

MLB season with a glacial 60 mph submarine changeup mixed in with occasional 90 mph heat. In 2005, batters started catching up with Mr. Zero, and by May 11, Guillen had eased him into a role where he still appeared, but mostly in noncritical situations, and slid Dustin "The Springfield Rifle" Hermanson into what most teams would call the closer slot. He was very effective until mid-September, when his back blew out on him. Guillen didn't put his most successful reliever, Cliff Pollitte, in the ninth-inning slot; he left Pollitte in the high-leverage role and inserted young Bobby "Double Wide" Jenks in the ninth-inning slot.

Guillen uses a practice that's a mandatory prerequisite for this nonconformist technique to work: he manages by walking around. He has at least a quick conversation with every player every day, maintaining the "team" connection for everyone who might ever appear in the game. He treats everyone as important, and thereby makes it more likely everyone might do something important that day.

That works outside baseball, too. Your group's productivity can go up if you enable the talent to transcend their job descriptions and instill the idea that everyone might be the star of the day. It won't work unless it's unavoidably obvious to the staff that you know of what you yack. Regular Management by Walking Around is the premier tool for this. And willingness to be flexible in the face of the immediate situation is a requirement.

Bend responsibilities, blend talents. Channel Ozzie and Ken. Win big.

Coaching

Branch "the Mahatma" Rickey is the godfather of baseball coaching—not because he was the greatest coach, but because he set up effective systems for an entire organization to strive for the same outcomes. Unusually, Rickey was able to synthesize a pair of polar opposites and come up with a powerful system.

He adapted his first set of innovations from assembly-line manufacturing, an endeavor aimed at delivering a mass quantity of a product, identically, using identical equipment. A specific batch of parts built in one factory would fit into assemblies from another factory, as would a different batch of that part from yet another factory.

Rickey applied this to developing talent. He and St. Louis Browns owner Robert Hedges had already cooked up the idea of a "farm system," a set of captive minor-league teams that had to surrender all their good players to the major-league club that owned them.

Now he advanced the utility of that pipeline by applying the mass-manufacturing model to the minor leagues. In the farm system, he re-created a decentralized factory for producing execution methods that were interchangeable among individual players. Coaches and trainers weren't ordered willy-nilly to do their best with the teams they were handed. Instead, the organization trained coaches in specific outcomes: how specifically to turn a double play on a ball to the right side, how to sacrifice bunt with runners on first and second, how to slide into second, how to slide into home, and so on.

As a player moved up through the system's levels toward the major-league club, each manager inherited a player with execution preshaped to his own organization's way of doing things. Consistency lowered the overhead of retraining someone to do something *your* way and freed resources for attacking shortcomings or learning new skills. Thanks to the systematic nature of the system, the AA league double-play combination starting the season together would have little problem adjusting to each other's styles even if they had come from different A-league teams.

Many people have tried to use industrial mass-production techniques as a model for managing people. Almost all have failed laughably. What's unusual here is that Rickey succeeded because of his academic experiences. He was a marginal major–league backup catcher, but when it became obvious to him that he would not have even an average baseball career, he went to college. There, as a multitool talent even baseball rarely sees, he was an upperclassman, and taught freshman English, Shakespeare, and Greek drama, and served as a basketball and football coach.[30]

Like John McGraw, Rickey had managed sports in college. Unlike McGraw, an athlete who valued education, Rickey saw himself as a scholar first, an athlete second. He internalized the system of teaching he received and presented in his classroom, and drew on classroom teaching processes in his design for baseball training.

Where McGraw set the tone for most baseball training through thoroughness and repetition, he also saw a single, prescribed path to getting to the goal of executing—the way he himself thought it should be done.

Rickey, however, strongly followed the academic model, understanding that students take many different paths to get to the result, and that all of them are workable as long as the student arrives at the right goal. As the Mahatma said, "Coaching is a matter not of compulsion, but of fertility in suggestion. It may not work for Bill like it would for Steve or John or Dick. . . . It won't work the same for two [different people]." [31]

Rickey's lesson makes sense beyond baseball, where too many managers confuse ends with means, or try to make people work in certain patterns instead of focusing on results. I've had plenty of highly productive employees, for instance, who won't read manuals or walk through tutorials, but who can learn equipment by just banging around in it. Some can benefit from classroom sessions; others learn only by discussing the curriculum with their peers.

Rickey also envisioned having standards for promotion—a checklist of skills a player must master to proceed to the next higher level. If you try this in your organization, and I believe you should, line up several deliverables first.

Start by building a list of accomplishments/achievements/abilities required for promotion, and by making sure the list actually reflects which skills you need. Most organizations have "survivals"—behaviors or standards or beliefs that were functional at one time but no longer serve a purpose. They're like the buttons on the end of men's blazer sleeves; at the turn of the 20th century, these actually buttoned, but now they are present only because designers think blazers look funny without them—

historical but, in the cruelest light, hysterical. It's important to pare the survivals out of the list both to keep players focused on useful goals and to avoid undermining your credibility.

Second, you must publish the list. It must be clear and unambiguous, the kind of checklist an ambitious player could actually consult to track and monitor her progress.

Third, for each promotion standard, create a target, preferably unambiguously measurable, for which the ambitious can aim. It's important that the promotion-standards list be made up of concrete targets, objectives the hardworking can aim for and know when they're getting close. Too many fuzzy, unmeasurable targets open up debate and whining from complainers.

But don't necessarily omit a truly important ability from the standard just because it isn't something you can test for easily. Any job past entry level has performance factors that are too subtle to measure. But make sure any nonmeasured factors are not ones managers will use as excuses for prejudice (race, gender, religious, political affiliation, baseball team rooted for, eye color).

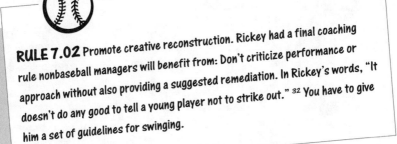

RULE 7.02 Promote creative reconstruction. Rickey had a final coaching rule nonbaseball managers will benefit from: Don't criticize performance or approach without also providing a suggested remediation. In Rickey's words, "It doesn't do any good to tell a young player not to strike out." [32] You have to give him a set of guidelines for swinging.

Rick Peterson's Lesson #1—Coaching Is Learning

There are almost no cases where you can escape coaching or training or mentoring and still get the most out of your team. But here's the secret value; sessions spent coaching contributors are all amazingly fecund opportunities for your own learning. As Angus's Twelfth Law states: "Everyone knows some things you don't. Inevitably, a few of those will be both worth knowing and applicable later."

As the New York Mets' highly successful pitching coach Rick Peterson said, "All great teachers are great students." Peterson infuses knowledge throughout every level of the organization he works with, creating a common set of customized tools to further the craft of the pitching and catching talent, as well as a common set of tools to view and dissect the craft.

When the Mets acquired Pedro Martínez, the premier pitcher of his generation, after the 2004 season, Peterson sought him out and tried to acquire lessons from him right away. That part is pretty obvious: Martínez is not only a monster talent, but appears to have a monster ego, too; humble aw-shucks guys rarely make successful major-league starters.

But no matter how great Peterson's standing as a coach, and his results are deservedly well known, this particular pitcher came into a new organization after feeling bruised by his previous one and taking on a new home city that had shown him a truckload of derision and hostility. The coach coming to the pitcher as a peer and offering to learn and discuss opens up a positive communication channel stripped of most emotional baggage. Sure, any great teacher can be a great student when his student is such a master of the art. When the time comes for the teaching to flow the other way, though, the pipeline is already open, the dialogue engaged.

Too often in management practice beyond baseball, the manager is afraid to put himself in a learning rôle. But if he caves in to his fear, he misses out and probably loses much of his own chance to grow. One of the best ways to learn about a staffer's learning style and the knowledge and skills she brings to the mix is to try to get her to teach you something. You can ask in a straightforward, not submissive but interested way. If the new staffer is capable of healthy behavior, you'll benefit every time. And if the new staffer isn't capable of healthy behavior, why are you still cutting Sparky a paycheck?

When the Mets bring up or acquire a new pitcher and Peterson starts working with him, he strives to integrate the pitcher into the team's "learning environment," a place where everyone gets to learn from the coach, and the coach gets to learn from the students. The knowledge he acquires is something he may use only to help that individual, or to refine the overall organizational plan to everyone's benefit.

Peterson's learning environment will appear to some casual observers as just learning about an individual to manage him better or making the staffer feel like part of the group so as to integrate him better. It certainly leads to those immediate benefits. But every bit of knowledge we acquire, whether from the butt-crack idiot savant who maintains the computer network or the woman who sorts the mail in the mailroom, is something that can add immediate perspective or be something we may draw on later.

If you are open to getting knowledge or insight from the lowliest line worker, you'll be plenty open to getting it from everyone else. It doesn't have to be a Pedro Martínez. With a new hire, just the fact that he or she is an outsider and not yet used to your approach gives that newcomer an outside perspective that benefits you. Finally, the strategic benefit of the Rick Peterson learning environment is that one accumulates individuals' insights, learns the tools and techniques they have been taught previously or just synthesized themselves. No matter how award-winning your own systems are, you can add to or tune your systems.

Please note what the learning environment did for Martínez in 2005—perhaps his second-best season ever, and this after many teams considering his free agency were concerned he might be used up. He was as excellent on the road as he was at the Mets' Shea Stadium, an environment that's difficult on hitters. And look at his month-by-month consistency (BAA is batting average against the pitcher.)

SPLIT	ERA	GS	IP	H	R	HR	BB	SO	BAA
Home	2.76	16	111.0	85	35	11	26	101	.211
Away	2.89	15	106.0	74	34	8	21	107	.195
April	2.75	5	36.0	18	11	1	6	45	.145
May	2.83	5	35.0	21	12	4	6	37	.171
June	2.66	6	44.0	33	13	4	10	40	.208
July	2.83	5	35.0	27	11	2	7	32	.206
August	3.46	6	39.0	35	15	8	10	33	.240
September	2.25	4	28.0	25	7	0	8	20	.255
Total	2.82	31	217.0	159	69	19	47	208	.204

While the organization's biggest overall gains from a learning environment usually come from elevating average performers (how much room does the game of someone like Pedro have to elevate?), it stands to ratchet up everybody's game. What do you have to change in yourself to make a Rick Peterson–style learning environment happen in your group? And what external barriers are you going to start removing or eroding today?

No matter how much motivation and application of OMA you succeed at, eventually you end up with players who can't or won't perform for you. When that happens, you have to act, and I'll give you some baseball methods to deal with those human rainouts in chapter 8.

8

Down to the Minors:
Reprimanding, Demoting, & Firing

Why am I wasting so much dedication on such a mediocre career?
—Ron Swoboda

In chapter 5, I explained that hiring decisions are the most important management decisions you make. If you hire well, reprimanding, demoting, and firing people will happen less often. But they *will* happen.

When you inherit a group from a predecessor who doesn't make hiring a life-and-death priority, or lets a phone call to Miss Cleo's psychic hot line decide who the project manager should be, you're going to end up with roster plaque. When talent that can't contribute to winning a pennant clogs your limited roster, it's critical to move people along. And while it's less obvious, doing a *good* job of executing the cuts is critical for your competitiveness, morale, and the reputation of your organization.

Staffers hired by previous managers are a challenge to the manager starting a new job, especially one who comes from outside. Set aside for a moment the implicit politics, staffers' fear of the new boss, their as-yet-unrevealed hidden agendas, and all the things the new boss needs to know about their skills but doesn't yet. The big hassle is that predecessors can't be trusted to have hired well, because of Angus's First Law (see chapter 5): only 15 percent of people holding a job aren't in need of significant improvement. While your skills at optimizing performance may be good, there'll usually be roster-plaque "low torques" (LTs) you'll need to remove sooner or later.

Managers outside of baseball are lucky. . . . It's a little bit tougher in the National Pastime. Of the players who make it to the minor leagues, 89.4 percent never make it to the majors. Of the remaining 10.6 percent—the 9,881 position players who made it to the majors for at least one game appearance before 1997—fewer than half ever got what I'd consider a minimal "career," that is, played a season's worth of games. Baseball is good at getting rid of players who fail to perform or grow quickly enough in their skills. Baseball managers are better than your average business managers because they have to fire people for performance reasons all the time to stay competitive.

In large organizations beyond and including baseball, turnover is not always the result of a failure to perform. Sometimes a good choice doesn't work out (chemistry, family issues, or managerial style). Sometimes you have to prune your staff because upper management mandates it. Sometimes good talent chooses to move on, especially as an aftershock in work groups that endure staff purges.

Baseball is the world's finest model to follow in the area of demotion and firing. First, there are few embarrassing euphemisms. In baseball, they don't call it a RIF (reduction in force), "leaving to pursue other interests," a downsizing, an outsourcing, a layoff. It's a release or a drop or a cut. Face it, you're *firing* someone. Glazing the verb in a sugar coating doesn't make it any easier on the casualty. You *absolutely should* make it easier on the casualty (and I'll suggest techniques later in this chapter), but pretending you're buying him a skybox at Elysian Fields when you're really taking away his livelihood and his identity is usually a salve only for the manager.[33] When you are talking to fellow managers or your own management, call it what it is: a firing, a cut, a drop (cue a splayed Wile E. Coyote plummeting to the valley floor, ending with puff of dust). You, your organization, and the fired are all better off for direct honesty in these moves.

RULE 8.01. Choose to go in standing up or sliding. Here's a guideline for when you have to choose between the brass and your staff. If the action is important to the organization's survival, and that won't be often, come down hard in favor of the viability of the outfit—it issues your paycheck. If the decision is over dust in the wind, stand up for your staff because they affect your work results every single day and they recognize your stance.

Conundrum

The single most difficult balance to find in managing is between being an "organization loyalist" and being a "player's manager," especially in a normal (that is, unhealthy) organization. Baseball illuminates the challenge of steering between the two, the eternally lurking Scylla and Charybdis of the manager's career. This careful balancing act is required in most of the actions covered in this chapter, from the simplest reprimand to any firing short of catching someone embezzling.

The manager who's an extreme organization loyalist will do whatever is ordered from above, asking questions only to clarify how exactly the top brass wants it done, without regard to the contributors or the content of the work. That's great for a career, especially in an unhealthy organization. It's terminal for staff commitment and productivity.

The extreme player's manager will always speak out on behalf of the staff, defending their interests. That's great for loyalty and commitment but inevitably deflates the manager's career prospects. There is no sweet spot, but if you ever want to be outstanding, I recommend you err a little on the side of being a player's manager in all cases that don't undermine the organization's vitality.

Most managers *hate* these moments. And if you are one of the majority, hate is a better emotion than the one felt by the next-biggest minority—those who *love* it. Layoff-loving managers behave as though they were sociopaths, followers of what I call Theory XYY (chapter 9). XYYs get a frisson, sometimes bordering on the sexual, from knowing they exercise power over individuals. Actually firing someone is perhaps the best (legal) time they ever have in their lives. Finding a serious but cool middle ground, driven neither by your own yuck-fear of the act nor by unhealthy kinks, means accepting it as a fact, being rational, honest, and empathetic with the casualties, survivors, and fellow managers.

Second, baseball staff firings, unlike layoffs in the corporate or non-profit or academic sector, are relentlessly meritocratic and rarely political.[34] Most American managers tend to make both of the two fatal mistakes one can make around firing issues. They let low-torque (LT) roster plaque they should move to another department or demote or fire fester too long, waiting, perhaps, for a fortuitous alien abduction or for the LT to win the Mega Millions. Then, when there *is* a mass cut, nonbaseball managers tend to cut the wrong people, for political or personal reasons, or merely because they lack knowledge of individuals' aptitudes and productivity (see chapter 3). Instead of getting some benefit from the mass cut by dropping those who can't be trained to succeed, the normal result is random, as likely to release the high-production or talented people as the LTs.

The biggest mass purge of talent I was ever involved in was when I was a director at Farallon Computing, a company that no longer exists, in part because of this self-destructive move. Instead of coming up with a plan built around what the executive team wanted the company to be after the purge and then designing staff needs around that new plan, someone just pulled a number out of his cloaca: the number of bodies to be cut. Not total dollars saved through various means, not number of payroll dollars. Just bodies. And then each department was given the casualty count it was to produce.

What wasn't stated in advance but became clear after a few meetings was that the executive team had already picked out the individuals it wanted gone. The choices weren't based on performance or where the company was headed, but for indiscernible reasons. I sat in multiple meetings with the other directors and vice presidents and listened to the "analysis" that was going on. Many participants were afraid. Most were uninformed. I would occasionally ask a Columbo question when a non-managing exec would bring up a name for the dropee's manager to "consider" cutting. I'd ask innocently, "Excuse me, can you tell me what he does in his job?" and I discovered that most frequently, upper management didn't know, nor did they seem interested in finding out.

The cut resulted in a disproportionate firing of talented people. The first wave of disgusted workers who voluntarily ditched the place in the next six months featured a scary ratio of effective contributors. Farallon never regained anything remotely close to its previous results. It sold off superb products to another company, and most of its superb staff was gone. The only thing left intact was the team that had botched the rebuilding and some survivors who acted shell-shocked. In that bloodbath, the executive team made every mistake it was possible to make.

To be realistic, Farallon's mass execution was not atypical, just extreme. Most mass cuts don't prune deadweight and concentrate talent,

RULE 8.02. Call for the double switch. Retrain real contributors for other positions once filled by roster plaque you dumped. Or temporarily demote them with the understanding that you know they'll work hard and you'll jockey to get them back to their level. Keeping skill on your roster is the key to winning.

but if you're going to come out the other side of the carnage at least as capable as you went into it, you need to preserve the players who contribute.

It's vital to release players, and more vital to do it well. Not just because the disgruntled ex-employee can pick up a six-pack of semiautomatics at a gun show as easily as your kids can score cigarettes (and more legally, too), but because the way it's done affects other staff and also the way the departed may present your organization's image in a lot of future messages.

Of course, there's more to know than just how to release a player. Ideally, long before you get to that point, if she has performance or behavior problems, you help correct them (chapter 6). If that fails, reprimand her or demote her to the minors. Demoting to the minors or temporarily benching a slumping contributor is a standard baseball technique that can work for most nonbaseball managers, too.

Reprimanding Bosox & Marlins Style: Loose Cannonades & World Championships

David Wells on Bud Selig:
"I think he's an idiot, to be honest with you.
He's the commissioner, and that's that.
But we don't have to like it."

When the talent *is* the product and you have to recruit high achievers to survive, you end up with more difficult personalities on your roster. If your staff is big enough, you're smart to make room for the acceptable but not outstanding achievers who contribute through emotional intelligence and hold the group together, but they should be a minority. You need all-stars to be a winner. It's not, as Leo Durocher said, that "nice guys finish last," but if you want to finish first, you need the bulk of your staff to be seriously achievement-oriented. On average, high achievers tend to have less bovine, more difficult, personalities. Like Boston Red Sox starter David "Boomer" Wells or Florida Marlin starter A. J. Burnett.

In late August of 2005, in the middle of the Bosox' tight pennant race, Boomer opened his mouth like Vavoom in a Felix the Cat cartoon and created a political tangle. It was perfectly predictable. The Bosox knew something like this would inevitably happen, just not exactly when, or over what, or how many battalions of the Army Corps of Engineers it would take to operate the cleanup effort. There's a great lesson for non-baseball organizations in the Wells brouhaha. The lesson answers the question, "Are you better off hiring people who don't make waves?" The answer is "Sometimes."

The comments that set off the tempest in a teapot (or was that a chihuahua in a teacup?) were an extended response to a reporter questioning Wells about the MLB upholding Wells's suspension. This wasn't an ordinary suspension; this was a suspension that Wells sounded convinced he didn't deserve. Did he deserve it? I suspect not. He was accused of bumping an umpire, and in the abbreviated video—abbreviated allegedly to show the moment of impact—it looked like he didn't get near the ump. Nevertheless, MLB upheld the suspension, and so Wells held forth, and fifth, in an encyclopedic jeremiad designed to irritate the Commissioner of baseball, Bud Selig.

Some selections from the *Boston Globe*'s version of the lumpy lefty's lippiness:

Wells claimed that his regular criticism of commissioner Bud Selig probably led Selig to intervene in the appeals process and tell arbitrator John McHale Jr. to "stick it to him."

Wells went on to criticize Selig's handling of the steroid issue, claiming, "Major League Baseball I don't think has a clue what's going on. They're just hoping that somebody screws up [and fails a test]."

Wells also said MLB waited to announce Rafael Palmeiro's steroid test until Aug. 1, a day after the Hall of Fame induction ceremony, to avoid attention. The Aug. 1, announcement followed a lengthy appeals process; the Baltimore Sun, *for one, reported that Palmeiro failed his test as early as May. Palmeiro, Wells said yesterday, "single-handedly whipped our butts" in early July, when the Baltimore slugger knocked in nine runs in a four-game series vs the Sox, with Boston losing three times.*

The writer noted that Wells had a long history of sniping at Selig, and included a year-old quote from the portly port-sider proclaiming that Selig wasn't qualified to be commissioner and adding: "I think he's an idiot, to be honest with you. He's the commissioner, and that's that. But we don't have to like it." And Wells concluded the most recent rant by suggesting he was not finished and he'd weigh in again soon.[35]

I've managed a lot of voluble employees over the past few decades, but Wells managed to twist his volume knob to 11 on this one. In suggesting to the world that the CEO of an organization that had some power over his employer's results was "an idiot," he was not apple-polishing for his next promotion.

The official MLB public response was predictable. Baseball's labor-relations executive, Rob Manfred, called Wells's description of the Palmeiro events pure fiction. The behind-the-scenes response was just as predictable. The Boston team's management was very vulnerable then to a potentially vengeful MLB HQ. They were in the thick of a pennant race and potentially subject to a wide range of detrimental retaliation, from subtle rules interpretations to the assignment of certain umps to key games. It rarely pays to piss off executives, unless you can depose them in the process, which neither Boomer nor the Red Sox' ownership was about to do here. MLB headquarters didn't have to say anything explicit. Both sides knew all the ramifications.

The Red Sox wished they didn't have to deal with the blowback, but they knew what they were getting into when they signed Boomer—this was not like late-onset Tourette's. This was unreconstructed Wells, the very guy they inked to a contract in December 2004. The Bosox, without a dominant starter in 2005 when the previous year they had two dominant starters, needed Wells to defend their championship. To protect the team and him they needed to apologize *for* him, and to protect the team's chances they needed not to poke a stick at him. It's not as though what he said about steroids would change anything, because basically no one cared what Boomer thought about designer drugs. It's not as though calling the Commissioner an idiot was going to offend any of his teammates; the entire 40-player roster's minutes per day dedicated to thinking about Selig was probably shorter than one of those midshow TV commercial breaks. And those that did think of the Commissioner were at least as likely to agree with Wells as to disagree.

The Bosox measured the magnitude of the tort (loud but harmless), measured Wells's general and current value to the team (number two starter on a team that didn't really have a number three starter, and in the heat of a pennant race), and picked a reprimand. Undoubtedly they scolded him, very likely without treating him like a child or an idiot. Something in the range of, *"We understand you think the Commissioner is a dipstick—sometimes we think he is, too—but you can't say those things about him, and we need you to apologize to make this issue go away for all of us, including your teammates. And don't do it again."*

I don't think it was one of those nudge-nudge-wink-wink moments where the manager tells the contributor "You were right but . . ." The team apologized strenuously, then Wells sorta apologized on his own behalf sorta about the steroids topic alone and left the other topics including Selig's idiocy off the table.

Management executed properly and got what it needed. They measured

- Ⓦ the magnitude of the tort,
- Ⓦ the value of the employee, and
- Ⓦ the current situation

and crafted an appropriate response. They protected their relationship with the contributor to preserve organizational effectiveness. Organizations beyond baseball should replicate those measures as a basis for designing a response. Too often managers borrow a parental model (covered in part 3) and craft a response designed to make the transgressor feel remorse in the hope that remembered shame or remorse will act as a deterrent. That can work, but only rarely. Remember, too, that the CEO Boomer dissed was not inside his own organization. That would be a different tort.

Which brings us to the A. J. "Third Degree" Burnett incident. Burnett torched his very own management in broad daylight a few weeks after the Wells blowout. Apparently talking about manager Jack McKeon and the coaches, he said, "It's depressing around here. There's nothing positive around here. There's nothing positive on the staff now. . . . You give up one home run, and it's a funeral." He concluded, "A positive pat on the back is better than anything. I haven't seen a pat on the back since April." When asked if it was something that happened in the game, his sixth straight losing effort, Burnett replied, "Not today, the season. It's a waste. Kids are out there busting their butts, and there's still nothing but negativity."

Burnett was considered the marquee free-agent pitcher entering the 2006 season. Where Wells was viewed as "workhorse," "gamer," "personal flake," Burnett was viewed as "injury-prone," "very talented," and "very erratic." How erratic? In 2001 at age 24, he tossed a no-hitter against the Padres . . . in which he walked nine, an ignominious most for no-hitters. That was his first full year, and since then he's had but one full season where he excelled, otherwise falling short in either his effectiveness or his ability to stay off the disabled list.

The Marlins' decision was made in an environment different from Boston's, too. With no chance of passing the endlessly excellent Atlanta Braves, the team had fallen out of wild-card contention about ten days before Burnett's rad riff. Further, Burnett had only one start left in the season, and as a free agent, he was going to test his salary value in the open market. Plus, while he had been a valuable starter for the Fish, the team was strong in starting pitching, so he was less indispensable than Wells. And (this is big) he dissed his own management, not an external organization's. These factors tweaked the choice of an appropriate move.

The Marlins did The Right Thing. They exiled Burnett, sent him home for the last week of the season. They didn't fine him or humiliate him publicly or to his teammates. They got him out of the environment.

Burnett's criticism may have been justified, and if so, it should have affected the reprimand. Justified or not, the reprimand was stronger in this case than in the Wells/Selig Brewer-ha-ha; it had to be real, visible, calm, and swift, and it was.

But in an endeavor where you aim to excel, the talent *is* the product, and you're going to end up with loose cannons as a by-product of effective recruiting. Most organizations stay away from them, even decent performers like Burnett and truly talented ones like Wells. Here are the two reasons organizations pass on talented loose cannons, and why doing that over side issues is usually a mistake.

The most common reason is that the hiring manager cares more about her comfort than about her team's performance. Take that attitude to the Fens for a minute: You know David Wells is going to cause a scene or five sooner or later, so instead of Wells, you sign Mr. Cub Scout, Aaron Sele. Sele is the anti-Boomer, the public equivalent of one hand not clapping, a guy who tirelessly helps geriatrics get across busy streets, and looked unrumpled and unflappable even when opponents batted .315 off of him in 2005. The problem was, Sele was having a bad year. For the Bosox, giving Sele the innings they had given Wells would have cost them on the field to the tune of about 5.3 wins.[36] Instead of qualifying for the AL wild card, they would have missed it by three wins, handing it to the Cleveland Indians. In a manager, willingness to sacrifice performance for comfort is not necessarily fatal, but it always surrenders effectiveness.

The Red Sox and Marlins don't do that. (1) They hire loose cannons

Sending to the Minors: Demoting Baseball Style

A keystone of baseball personnel practice that both increases the chances for winning now and expanding talent for later is a minor-league system. It's so successful and logical it's just deranged that nonbaseball organizations don't emulate baseball's practice when they can.

When there's proof that a player can handle the challenges at the current level, the team promotes the player a level. If the player stalls out and can't handle the higher level, the team either sends the player back down or experiments with his talent to test whether there's an emerging possibility of success.

Beyond baseball, the standard practice is binary. Either people are kept on—they succeed and management's content, or they struggle and management decides to live with it—or they are handed a pink slip. In the case of the strugglers or the pink-slip recipients, baseball's model is much more cost-effective and energy-efficient. The cost and effort of seeking out and hiring and training talent is high; once you've made that investment, harvest returns from it.

If you're in a big organization, try sending your struggling players to the minors. That is, put them to work on less pressing or less important tasks. Analyze the specific holes in their game and work on creating skills-building opportunities for them. You'll get some work out of them and find out if it's really worth the expense of recruiting a replacement.

Consider another, equally valuable baseball technique: redefining the washout's job. Baseball reclaims value from disappointment with this approach all the time. The Los Angeles Dodgers perennially rotated disappointments through positions as they advanced through the system. The three-time NL champ Dodgers of the mid-'70s featured a double-play combo of two converted outfielders; their right fielder was a converted shortstop, and their first baseman was a converted third baseman. More recently, the Seattle Mariners took Rafael Soriano, a disappointing minor-league outfielder with a great arm, and redefined his role as a relief pitcher, where he has ranged from better than adequate to totally stunning.

who are talented enough that the benefits outweigh the costs, and (2) they are successful; each has won a World Series in the last five years. They do the math. Clone their winning thinking as part of your methods for both hiring and reprimanding.

Indirect Percussion: Reprimanding Ray Miller Style

As a pitching coach, Ray Miller employs a method I call "indirect percussion." He invites the manager to yell at him publicly when a pitcher deserves a reprimand for sloppy fundamentals or bad concentration. "The manager can jump around and yell at me, and the pitchers can all see that. Then they look to see if I jump the guy when he comes off the field, and I never say anything. Conversely, sometimes the guy is pitching a great game and makes a bad situation pitch, and the manager's screaming, and I'll touch the manager on the arm in front of the pitcher and say, 'I told him to throw that pitch.' The manager will shut up and go sit down."[37]

By doing this, Ray preserves respect for the pitcher, and the pitcher respects his coach for standing up for him. More important, the pitcher gets to hear the manager describe exactly what went wrong without having it directed at him—and all the pitchers on the bench hear it, too. This form of criticism, not colored by the shame of being chewed out publicly, keeps the pitcher from being distracted by emotions such as shame and more able to focus on the functional details he needs to fix the error.

This is a clear case of siding with your contributors (see sidebar, "Conundrum," at page 145) when the momentary crisis is tactical, an ephemeral hiccup in the overall trend. Emulate Miller if you have your superior's respect, your superior knows enough about the craft to criticize meaningfully, and you both have an agreement to play this scene when needed. It buys successfully imparted wisdom and encourages the contributor to internalize his long-term loyalty to you.

RULE 8.03. Fire only as last resort. Firing shouldn't be the first action for someone who's diligent and capable of learning just because he struggles with an aspect of his job you need him to ace. Try sending the disappointment to the minors or redefining his rôle. What is efficient in baseball is efficient in most big organizations.

Releasing the Talent: Before You Cut a Player

Before you pull the trigger on a firing decision, follow the principle of former Chicago White Sox manager Al Lopez. As sabermetrician and baseball historian Bill James describes the Lopez principle: Never give up on a player until you know who you're going to replace him with.[38] This goes for mass purges, too, where the contributor is not going to be replaced but his work will be shifted to a remaining staffer, so I add the words "or who's going to replace the work the casualty did." As James says, this principle seems self-evident, but James thinks, as I do, that an astonishing number of managers don't recognize it.

You have to have a succession plan. What do I need now? Where will I find that ability? Even if the casualty was effective, can I get that work done better in a different way?

More uncommon, but as necessary for your success, you need to keep managing the person to produce in the immediate moment, continue the OMA, and continue the training and optimizing, because the ideal replacement may not drop into your lap like a foul ball into the expensive seats.

Firing first and figuring out the answers later is the normal approach. It regularly fails in baseball, and it's an avoidable failure for you, too.

Releasing the Talent: The Bavasi Way

Most managers have a really tough time demoting or letting people go. Some cower from it and delegate the drop to human resources. I think that's one reason that when they do it themselves, they frequently do it badly.

Baseball has good lessons for managers who fear or just dislike the process, because it's a natural and essential process in the industry. Because off-loading contributors happens so often in the National Pastime, the average ability to do it has got to be better. And there's no way to sluff it off; a manager can't just put a Post-it note on the casualty's chair and write, "Guess what, you're in Lodi next week."

Just because baseball front-office managers are good at firing doesn't mean they enjoy it. But some, like Seattle Mariner GM Bill Bavasi, take it on because they believe that if they do it themselves, it'll be done professionally. Bavasi thought it was so important that he innovated and synthesized an entire process to enforce accountability, to lead with honesty, to keep communication consistent, and therefore to make the cuts a little easier on both sides. This is a process he developed before he had full authority to execute the system the way he wanted.

Bavasi is really good at cuts. "I think I'm good at it for a few reasons," Bavasi told me. "One is I really wanted to play basketball, I loved playing the game. There was only one problem for me. I had absolutely no talent for it . . . none. I ended up playing on a team in college but I watched from the bench. I had a better seat than anyone else in the house. But I loved the game."

When he got into baseball, he was a gofer, the only gofer reporting to California Angel assistant GM Mike Port. Bavasi explained how the first time he cut a player was before he had the authority to do it, and how the act inspired part of his thinking. "I was sitting at a desk working and this kid was sitting a few feet away and he's waiting for Mike at a little table trying to kill time. He's waiting a long time, and he says, 'Where is he? I'm supposed to meet him here.' This kid is a pretty obnoxious kid. And so finally I felt so bad for him and he was driving me nuts, so I said, 'Look, let me do this for you. You're getting released.' That didn't go great, because I didn't have the authority. I was trying to be careful, but at the same time I didn't want him to sit there and have to squirm for another half hour."

Bad form, but Bavasi recognized it instantly. He found Port and explained his foul ball. Port caught up with the kid, and explained to him, "Look, what's wrong is we just don't have a job for you." The kid got to see the person in charge of the decision looking him right in the eye and making it clear. That's accountability. In baseball, as the Mariner GM explains, "You *do* run out of jobs. It's an up-or-out system. And you're dealing with people who do understand that. The minute they start, they know it's up or out. But I did have empathy for these guys and that kid." Bavasi was moved by seeing that kid squirm and have an idea that maybe he was toast, and the thing Bavasi already understood was that timely and straight talk was merciful for both sides.

As in other businesses, a baseball general manager will have other managers between him and the drop. Bavasi knew that layers can erode accountability and consistency. The minor-league prospect's manager usually doesn't want to lose the kid, so it's easier for him to say to the kid, "I really want to keep you but we met last night and we just don't have a job for you, and 'they' are making me release you." By delegating the decision down, the higher-up is making it easy for a fib to get out there, and he will probably have to meet with the (now more upset) cut anyway. In Bavasi's process the player's manager is part of the decision; his communication has to be aligned. There is no "they."

Bavasi explains, "I tell the manager if this kid wants to talk to you, you're going to talk to him. And once I had enough authority in the organization, it became really simple then because I was able to say, 'Look, this kid played for you this spring, and I'm going to release him.' When he comes to see you, if you say anything that's contrary to what we said in that meeting, you're not coming back, you'll go home with him."

As I discussed in part 1, Bavasi started formulating this process, copying some pieces from others, reversing some others, and adding twists of his own. He did that thinking long before he had the authority to apply it, an attribute of successful managers.

If you're firing someone whose only fault is having the bad luck to be caught up in a mass purge, or because even though he tries he doesn't have enough talent, you owe that contributor human decency. Decency benefits the bottom line because the person you cut may be useful to the organization again one day. And even if he isn't, he'll usually recognize that you did the right thing. Empathy is necessary because, as Bavasi understands, "there's a real psychological dynamic here. It's really important to realize. Each of these young guys in their home town, whether it's small like Paducah or a place like New York, he's the baseball player. That's his identity. You just stripped him of his identity and sent him home on an airplane and he's arrived home all in about 12 hours. He's going to walk off that plane and he's *not* a baseball player and he's not going to know what he is."

That's true of much of the talent you'll fire, too. It takes no extra overhead to treat the casualties with a bit of respect, and it usually pays back in multiples.

One of the strengths that Bavasi brings to this process is understanding what it's like to be on the receiving end and applying that understanding without letting past experiences dictate specific behaviors or resistance to required action. That skill set, self-awareness, is the core of the third-base skill set that we'll take up next.

RULE 8.04. Call the outs cleanly. Be bloodless; keep a neutral voice; express sympathy and understanding. When you're letting people go for inadequate performance, remember the upside; you're improving your organization's own performance, the person you're letting go may be moving on to something better for him or her, and you're preserving more resources for the people who remain.

Part Three

Advancing to Third Base— Managing Yourself

There are things I can't force. I must adjust. There are times when the greatest change needed is a change of my viewpoint.
—**Denis "The Langres Lasher" Diderot**

Managers find it difficult to escape the presumptions that bind them to knee-jerk behaviors, cherished concepts, and oft-repeated processes that may have made them successful. Especially in American society, where the title "manager" rarely denotes rigorous training in the discipline, people tend to fall back on previously learned behaviors, both emotional and intellectual.

Further, people have a hard time recognizing that by taking a paycheck to manage, they owe their employer the full range of effective behaviors, not just the ones they use in personal life. But Wait, There's More, because along with displaying a full palette of interpersonal techniques, managers also need to be authentic. Finding the correct level of authenticity needed in each situation is a complicated task few have mastered. To be safe at third base in the *Management by Baseball* model, you must become adequate at all these skills.

As I mentioned earlier, third-base skills are closely related to the second-base skills, except the person you need to be aware of is *yourself*. It's hard enough work to see ourselves as others see us, and triply so to discern ourselves *accurately*.

Baseball's lessons are very clear in this area because the mistakes that happen from the failure to recognize one's own implicit assumptions are so very clear on the field, from Maury Wills's insistence on making sluggers steal to Lou Piniella's Vesuvian excesses to Chuck Tanner's fatal, excessive niceness.

9

There's No "I" in "Team," But There Are an "M" and an "E": Emotional Self-Awareness

⚾

> The only thing my father and I have in common
> is that our similarities were completely different.
> —Dale Berra

When Dick Williams started managing baseball teams, he could look to the managers he'd played for as rôle models. When the job was relatively low stress, he tapped into a few of those former managers' repertoires. But when times got tough—and he was programmed by his upbringing to make them tough—he reverted to the viscerally implanted boss most Americans have: the dominant parent during their upbringing. Sadly for Williams, his father was a bullheaded redneck who had to struggle every day during the Depression to provide for his family. Worse, he'd assimilated his Navy experience as a model for exercising familial authority, and he did not show grace under pressure.

"Today they would call it child abuse," Williams wrote. "Back then it was just another case of a father dragging a son down the basement steps, tying him to a pole, and whipping him." [39] Williams was very self-aware. He later wrote that his sense of order and authority came from his father.

Being self-aware, he didn't physically abuse his "children," his players, but his father was knitted into his behavioral responses. Williams didn't just learn to be an uncompromising hard-ass. He learned positive lessons, too. In a key moment late in the 1984 World Series when he wanted to have Goose Gossage, the Padres' ace reliever, intentionally walk Detroit's Kirk Gibson, he let a determined Gossage pitch to him. The results were fatal, but, as Williams said, "My principle has been: It's his earned run average. . . . It's his butt. If I can help him succeed, fine. But if he fails, he won't be able to live with himself unless he fails his way."[40] He was channeling his dad's belief in accountability and adding his own belief, 180 degrees from anything his dad would have done: delegating to the person who would be held responsible.

We Are Family. But We Shouldn't Be.

Most managers bring to work these family-bred histories that social workers call "family-of-origin issues." If the manager doesn't successfully separate her managerial behavior from her authentic home behavior, those issues invariably undermine performance. Most frequently, as with Williams, managers do things exactly the way their dominant parent would—or exactly the opposite. Some emulate their military experience or the first manager who showed them personal interest.

In the U.S., where being a manager is less a profession than a badge of behavioral conformity and seniority, too many managers bring their personal quirks, or even neuroses, to work. Most don't do it on purpose. They simply haven't been given training in how to apply an alternative model, so they just wing it. Those who intentionally give in to personal quirks may be completely unaware of the effect it has on their organization's trajectory, and most don't care.

Some workplaces amplify this drift of manager-as-parent. Baseball is one, with its fresh-out-of-high-school initiates and temporary societies of farm teams. So are high-tech workplaces that hire bright-eyed college grads, or fast-food and sweatshop work, where a lot of the laborers are actually children. In workplaces that pride themselves on a culture of survival under pressure, the place becomes a surrogate family. Workers might spend more time and emotional energy at work than at home. They "make" the boss a parent and co-workers siblings, or managers shoehorn their supervisory role into a parental pattern.[41]

What do you do about family-of-origin issues? Over the years I've found practical ways to help separate managers' at-home interaction patterns from their management style.

RULE 9.01. Refer to the scoresheet. First, temporarily channel the dominant parent or manager you think is most like your own management persona. When you're confronted with a stressful work situation, before you say anything or cement a decision, bring that person up in your mind. Imagine what he or she would do. Is it the same as your first reaction? Is it the exact opposite?

If it's the same, that doesn't mean it's a bad choice, but think about alternatives. Think about whether it's because you're imprinted or because it is a good choice. The same goes for doing the opposite. It's a terrible fate to struggle against the phantom of a past authority, re-creating its limitations, or delivering a new and different set of limitations as a reaction.

Some managers are constitutionally unable to use this approach. For them, I recommend finding a management peer, outside or inside the organization, whose approach is least like their own. The manager can meet the peer regularly for a quick sit-down and exchange perspectives (knowing the peer is going to see things very differently). The manager may not necessarily buy into the peer's approach, but the act of listening and processing through someone else's filter provides perspective, and perspective is a foundation for refinement.

When you collect a paycheck from an organization, you owe it your best, your full adult intellect, brought to bear with focus. That doesn't mean you leave all your feelings at the door when you enter the workplace, but it does mean you don't let those feelings involuntarily affect your actions.

The Six Deadly Skins

If a manager doesn't recognize certain responses or patterns as part of an involuntary reaction to her environment, she's not really managing. She's just transceiving. What she's transceiving can range from innocuous to toxic. There are dozens of possibilities, but there are six common behaviors usually imprinted from one's upbringing. These are deadly personal skins that managers wear in the work world. I call them the six deadly skins. And all but one have a baseball manager whose id fits inside that skin.

The First Deadly Skin: Uncontrolled Anger (Lou Piniella)

A manager with a parent who was angry all the time, or acted that way to manipulate children, will often slip into anger or intentionally act it out as a major chord in relations with peers and staff. Lou Piniella seems like such a manager. Piniella appears to have real rages during and after games. He directs them at one enemy (umpires) and another (players who fail to perform), but only rarely at a third enemy (his own superiors). Because he generally shows public deference to his employers, or is more passive-aggressive in his relations with them in public, I suspect this is a behavior pattern that was programmed into him from childhood.

At this stage of his life, it's a controlled performance. As a Yankee player, he had Uncontrolled Anger, the kind a parent uses to intimidate his family into compliance. "Sweet Lou"[42] was the only player in the history of the game who actually tried to kill a suited mascot. The Seattle Mariners used to bring the San Diego Chicken in as a special event every year. In July 1979, he was in full feather for a New York Yankee visit. In those days, the Yankees were dominant, the Mariners doormats . . . except when they hosted the Yankees. The M's had already swept an early-season series against the Bombers, and Piniella had been feeble in Seattle coming into this game. The Yanks were trailing again. The Chicken had fans put a fake arm-waving whammy on the ill-tempered Piniella, who got very upset. He instructed The Chicken to desist. The Chicken agreed. Then he immediately started up. The fans loved it, but Piniella went Three Mile Island and chased the Chicken with lethal intent.

Piniella the Elder knows what rage looks like, but his managerial tirades seem more for show. There's usually a three-and-a-half-act farce culminating in an explosion. A Lou Heptathlon usually features dirt kicking or base lifting and throwing, isometric Kabuki scowling, or other *Baseball Tonight* moments.

When I did agricultural work as a teen, a majority of bosses vented rage, either authentically out of control or just trying to scare the talent into working harder. It's a destructive model because some people, like me, will insist on not excelling for such a personality even if they easily could. Others who *do* respond to it burn out quickly, stimulating the boss's anger further.

The Second Deadly Skin: Perfectionism (Dick Williams)

Dick Williams knew parental rage intimately, but by the time he managed in the bigs, it rarely showed, because he really understood it as his abusive father's hallmark tool and resisted it. The father's tool he couldn't overcome was Perfectionism.

Williams had been to the World Series with the Red Sox in 1967 and won back-to-back Series with the Oakland A's in 1972 and 1973. By

1984, managing the ordinary San Diego Padres, he worked all the angles and made the team catch fire. By early August they had a 10½-game lead. As he explained:

> *Until that time it had been a darned near perfect season except for one thing—this imperfect manager. . . . The more we won, the more I expected us to win. The safer we were in first place, the more I demanded and the tougher I grew. The years had taught me how difficult it was to be a contender, let alone a champion. I wanted my players to realize that playing so well didn't just happen. . . . And I was going to get that message through to my players if it killed me.*[43]

Lots of managers who are of the Bob Dole generation use this style, one I call Management by Disappointment (MBD). The MBD features a stern father who believes if he shows any approval, his ward will rest on his laurels and not achieve his full potential. If he becomes an archbishop, the MBD says, "Well, you never got to be pope," and if the ward becomes pope, the MBD says, "You're a failure, you're not God." This deadly skin used to be the most common in workplaces, but it correlates so strongly with the Bob Dole generation that as they retire, it's thinning out their herd.

The Third Deadly Skin: Intimacy (Bobby Bragan)

The third deadly skin, Inappropriate Intimacy, is the most obvious confusion of work life and family life, because a manager with this skin openly takes a family rôle in the life of her staff. I've never had a boss of this type, but Williams did: Bobby Bragan, a successful minor-league coach who mentored Williams and whom Williams respected immensely. But that respect didn't extend everywhere. Bragan sliced one foul when the mentor called Williams into his office to tell the player he'd heard rumors that the young man was dating a woman with an Italian last name (as Bragan called her, "a foreigner,") and that he'd better stop.[44] Williams may have wanted an adult who would interact with him in a fatherly way, but it didn't extend to listening to a bigot try to shape his dating habits.

I've seen a lot of Inappropriate Intimacy folk in the last decade. While the anger types are more often male, the manager who runs a shop with excessive intimacy is, more frequently, a woman, though either gender of parent can slip into this behavior pattern. It happens when people can't unplug from their powerful parental rôle once outside the home, and so bring their parent act to work.

The Fourth Deadly Skin: Denial (Hank Bauer)

Denial is common beyond baseball. Denial is when you once saw the world the way it was, but become lazy and keep seeing it that way even after its time has passed. A classic case was the Jim Fregosi move I discussed in chapter 4, using a pitcher who had no stuff in a World Series—because he'd been great months before. That Denial lasted just a handful of games.

Earl Weaver's predecessor in Baltimore was Hank Bauer, who fell into a multiyear swoon because of his preprogrammed Denial. In 1964, his first year with Baltimore, Bauer managed the team to 97 wins. He tinkered and refined the mix the next year before tuning the system and leading his team to a pennant in 1966. Success like that is perfect for Denial because now you have "the good old days." It's emotionally easier to pretend these are still the good old days than to practice OMA (chapter 6), which is a lot of work.

In 1967, Bauer changed nothing, and the team tumbled into the second division. In 1968, Bauer pretended it was all bad luck, sticking with players who had been successful years before, but had since been neutralized by age or opponents' scouting. In his own mind, this was a winning team. Rather than attack his problem, giving new players a chance to help failing players, he chose to believe that his incumbents would reincarnate. They didn't, and neither did his job. The front office turned the team over to Weaver halfway through 1968, and Weaver made the necessary small tune-up. The O's blasted through the league the next year with a transcendent 109-win season.

I see Denial all the time. Entire organizations are run by wildebeest herds of Denials, fighting with the winning tactics from yesterday's conflicts. For instance, how do mid-2005 auto manufacturers first fight a sales slump of gas-guzzling lard-ass trucks in the face of $2.50-per-gallon fuel? By advertising how much more powerful the lard-ass models are than smaller, less fuel-abusive trucks.

The Fifth Deadly Skin:
Uncontrolled Niceness (Chuck Tanner)

Uncontrolled Niceness is not very common in baseball. But many organizations, baseball among them, will hire a manager who is the opposite of a failed predecessor. Since Uncontrolled Anger and Perfectionism have both been common skins, the GMs will often install followers of Niceness to heal the wounds created by those predecessors.

As with all the other skins, the Uncontrolled Niceness manager is not doomed to failure if he has the exact right staff. Chuck Tanner, the archetype for this skin, led his 1979 Pittsburgh Pirates to a World Series trophy, but it was a great, balanced team with multiple players who were hard-axe clubhouse leaders (to complement Tanner's approach). When the team later fell into a decline exacerbated by hard-drug use, Niceness could not turn it around. In almost every group there are people who equate Niceness with weakness (a false view in most cases), and many of these people are programmed to stomp the weak—a compulsion that leads to workplace hassles. Niceness is pleasant to work around, especially on the right team, but like every one of the deadly skins, when it's not part of a spectrum of responses, it's going to fail.

The Sixth, and Deadliest Skin: Anxiety

The last deadly skin is Anxiety—a managerial skin that is nonexistent in baseball. The anxious manager is the type who defers all decisions when-

ever possible, deluded that (a) simply not making mistakes can be a winning strategy, and (b) a decision avoided isn't actually a decision in itself.
No baseball manager could behave this way, because the manager has to
fill out lineup cards, call plays, delegate, and take action.

The manager who is channeling an overanxious parent (or who is responding to an abusive parent himself) won't delegate and will stall decisions until it's too late because passivity has eliminated all choices but one.
In a small fistful of endeavors this disorder can be useful in moderation:
insurance underwriting, security services, quality control. A person with
this skin could not manage in baseball for more than perhaps two games
before he was chucked overboard. And that's optimistic. But baseball is
wiser than most organizations. In a competitive environment, acting on
anxiety is a 162-game losing streak.

I worked for too many bosses who had Anxiety as their management
"style." On the totally dysfunctional end, I had the title of director while
working for Steve, a high-tech start-up president. I said "title" because
while I had the name, I was allowed no actual authority.

Steve was intellectually brilliant and very capable technically, but
he was not cut out to manage anything but his own efforts. He wouldn't
delegate. He agonized over tiny decisions. He insisted on having make-
or-break authority over decisions he had no qualification to make, then
refused to actually make a decision. He pretty much ignored everyone
who had domain expertise he didn't. Even when he went along with an
expert, he agonized over the possibility that the decision could be a mistake. His company didn't make it, in spite of Steve's energetic efforts—it
couldn't overcome his deadly Anxiety.

All the deadly skins are survivable—especially if, like Dick Williams,
the manager recognizes the pattern. You are what you do, not what you
feel, so feeling anger or excessive niceness is perfectly legitimate. Acting
on them is not.

Theory XYY in the Bronx

There's a cohort of managers who follow a behavior pattern that sometimes works, though it's expensive and wasteful: either they are authentically sociopaths, or they aren't but behave as though they are.

New York Yankee owner George Steinbrenner is as perfect an example of the behave-as-though-he-is-a-sociopath boss as you'll ever witness. In contrast with management's Theory X, which treats staff as machines, or Douglas MacGregor's Theory Y, which uses a humanist approach to maximize staff contentment, motivation, and loyalty to the organization, the functional sociopath pursues what I call Theory XYY—treating staff as organic puppets that serve personal impulses.

Since they won their last World Series in 2000, the Yankees have been a 365¼-day-a-year Roller Derby of the mind, maximum Sturm und Drang. This is a natural consequence of the typically controlling behavior by the headman, behavior that looks to trained observers (and should feel to his front-office staff) exactly like sociopathy. To laymen the indicted felon's boorishness may seem mysterious. It's no mystery.

In big American and Russian organizations, this is a significant style of what's called "leadership." Leadership is rarely worth spending time on. While it can be significant in some large organizations' trajectories, it's overhyped, a small subset of the management tool kit. Leadership is not something that can be taught or trained, and it's generally ephemeral. In a rapidly mutating environment, a specific leadership style tends to be effective only in specific, short-lived conditions, and few effective leaders have, or are able to learn, multiple styles.

But sociopathic-appearing leadership like Steinbrenner's is worth understanding. Some of you may work in organizations run on the sociopathic style. Most of the El Supremos in these organizations—it's usually a male thing—are not actually sociopaths. Most are people who behave that way because they learned it as a style, frequently from the dominant parent, sometimes from an early work or school experience. A code word you'll sometimes hear from the functionally sociopathic is "Machiavellian." That's merely an intellectual's packaging of sociopathy with a classical reference meant to justify it. The Yankees are a play-by-play recap of the style, why it works, why it doesn't, and some of the indicators you can use to recognize it.

Team headman George Steinbrenner has a powerful need to win (good for business) and a powerful need for attention (great for business). He knows that the attention works well as part of a business model, keeping the team in the news during the season-ticket-deposit period. These two drives help keep the team competitive, keep feeding the fuel for success (income) into the Yankee franchise. After five consecutive years without a World Series title, Steinbrenner is priapic for publicity and the trophy.

The Yankees have almost every indicator of an organization run by a functionally sociopathic leader. Perfect example: 2003's intentional public snubbing of beloved longtime Yankee pitcher and good team citizen Andy Pettitte. The Yanks didn't just let him sign with another team, they treated him like dirt in the process.

Pettitte apparently took this piece of organizational manipulation personally. That's always a mistake—when you work for an organization as calculating as a functionally sociopathic one, it's best to buffer the emotional content of your work. The sociopathic leadership style employs Management by Terror (MBT), instilling fear in everyone in the organization. MBT can make some underperformers who are slacking achieve at a higher level or leave, but most just hunker down until the rage period is over, doing less—to attract less attention—and thereby slowing the organization's work processes. And MBT makes some high performers lose some focus or motivation. The net of MBT in almost every organization is significantly negative.

The sociopathic leader will smoke whole populations just to make a point (for example: Joe Stalin or Chainsaw Al Dunlap). Or he can take a more surgical approach, isolating a popular team member, viewed by all staff as a key contributor and a positive influence, and then squash her flat as a bug in a public way, "showing" everyone that no rational force is at work, everyone better get cracking, and you could be next, even if you are excelling. Yankee example? Javier Vásquez, the pitcher who replaced Pettitte in the Yankee rotation, had a decent year, but when he finished the season with below-average performances, he was made a lightning rod for Steinbrenner's XYY impulse, and purged with an exploding-scoreboard display of noisy, flashing public blame.

An XYY manager will also use high-intensity praise and bonuses and apparently heartfelt intimacy to amplify some employees' level of emotional investment in work and the organization. This investment becomes a fulcrum the sociopathic leader can use to lever his manipulation more effectively. So people in these kinds of shops are subject to an emotional roller coaster of highs and lows, terror followed by a dollop of praise or money or other recognition that gives hope things have changed. The person who willingly stays in a functionally sociopathic system is much like a chronically abused spouse, filled with hope for a better future that will almost certainly never come. The exception is either a sociopath himself or someone like a major-league star who makes a life-changing amount of money that can mitigate some of the negative effects.

At about half the presentations where I bring up Theory XYY and the Yanks, someone challenges my assertion and ends up making the argument that XYY behavior is the cause of the Yankees' success and should therefore be a model for nonbaseball managers to emulate. I don't buy it. The most successful franchise from 1991 to 2005 has been the Atlanta Braves. In the 13 years there was a champion in their division, they've been champion all 13 times. The Yankees played beautifully, but won no more division titles. In the 11 seasons since the 1994 work stoppage, the Yanks have had a better record than the Braves five times, the Braves have had a better record than the Yanks five times, and one year they finished with the same record. Sophists can devise arguments as to why one franchise has been "better" than the other, but they're all bogus. If XYY is a necessary ingredient for success, how can Atlanta, without the slightest bit of XYY at all, be the Yanks' equal?

XYY can be competitive only when the organization has a monopoly or a resource advantage so vast that it can afford the overhead of the toxic by-products and the extra money it needs to throw at buffering the wounds. Skeptical? Consider the 1895–1902 New York Giants under the very intelligent but XYY ownership of Andrew Freedman. Freedman, though a clever business innovator, had just average resources. He ran onto the field to harass umps and both teams' players, conspired to undermine other teams' real estate deals, and allegedly physically abused his office staff. During his eight-year tenure, the team made 14 managerial changes, and finished 9th, 7th, 3rd, 7th, 10th, 8th, 7th, and 8th.[45] Theory XYY can work, especially in an organization as packed with roster and front-office talent as the Yanks, but XYY managers require additional resources to reach the same results as equally capable non-XYY managers.

The Curse of the Curse

Luck is the residue of design.
—Branch Rickey

Most people I've worked with believe that there is such a thing as luck—sometimes working in your favor, other times against you. Like Branch Rickey, I believe it's management's job to design the situation so that bad luck has a smaller chance of undermining the result.

An individual's view of luck is an immense gravitational field that colors a manager's view of past work and therefore affects outcomes. Most management work reflects on past experiences to shape current actions, but too much dependence on past good or bad luck may distort and undermine analysis and execution. In baseball, most of the distortions are innocuous—Houston Astro reliever Charlie Kerfeld wore a Jetsons T-shirt during a game, then ripped off six successful outings in a row, so he wore it for the rest of his career. That's harmless next to the teammate's less uplifting refusal to change his socks during a winning streak, which is harmless next to the variety of "curses" that allegedly hung over teams like the Billy Goat of Damocles.

The cute but fictional Curse of the Bambino allegedly haunted the Boston Red Sox from January 1920, when they traded Babe Ruth to the Yankees, through October 2004, when they finally won a World Series. Invented by *New York Times* columnist George Vecsey on October 27, 1986, after the Mets finished off the Bosox in that year's Series,[46] the Curse colored player and manager thinking year after year as Bosox teams struggled to cross the finish line. Each failure was seen as part of this metaphysical pattern. Once uttered and shared, the imaginary Curse took on a gravitational field of its own, a force that dragged human behaviors toward outcomes that "confirmed" it. Players who came to give the Curse credence concatenated small and large errors in execution and judgment, delivering outcomes that reinforced the Curse's presumed power.

There's a putative Cubs curse, too. During a 2004 playoff game, there was an irrelevant hiccup when Cub left fielder Moises Alou failed to catch a foul ball in the stands. Instead of resuming the game, he let that franchise's imagined curse color his response. Rather than telling his teammates to bear down, he had a hissy fit that disrupted the game, the Cubs' momentum, and their attitude. The team's game-losing series of mental errors cascaded into a draining loss. When I asked Cubs GM Jim Hendry, a successful field manager himself once, why no teammate went to Alou to calm him down, Hendry pointed out that on that squad, Alou *was* the senior leader. By allowing himself to be the victim of the imaginary curse, Alou magnified the effects, amplifying its apparent power to his teammates who knew to follow his lead.

We *all* have imagined curses that undermine us for a short period.

When the Houston Astros lost the first two games of the 2005 World Series, both cliffhangers they could easily have won, they felt and acted snakebit. Except for Roy Oswalt, the team's toughest starter, and outfielder Jason Lane, they looked like they expected Enron indictments to drop on their heads, and were just waiting for the inevitable bad news. Worse, you could see it in the manager's face. Phil Garner not only wasn't using his position to reverse the anxiety, he was amplifying it. He was overcome late in the third game and released his frustration with a chair tossing. While he was focused on the first-base skills, he was only a partial manager that game. What surprised me was that after the last game of the sweep, he seemed in a state of grace during the postgame interviews and visiting with Astros fans. He recovered his skill, but not in time to save the third game. The Astros' curse was short-lived but nasty.

You see long-lasting curses in workplaces all the time. Someone asks, "How are you today?" and you hear responses like "Same old same old" or "I'm here, ain't I?" or "As well as can be expected." I call this Droopy-Dogism. People just "know" it's not going to be a productive day, that luck will disfavor them. Their attitude subtly affects outcomes in many ways, and the results seem to reinforce ideas like "We don't get projects done on time," "We can't meet targets," "Things just don't work out." In turn, this reinforces the Droopy-Dogism that inspired the curse in the first place. As we'll see shortly, one can break this cycle with a structured approach, or sometimes on the back of the contributor I call a "rate-buster." At the *Management by Baseball* Web site you'll find a framework for curse-breaking by attacking Droopy-Dogism. The Red Sox crushed their alleged Curse in 2004. When will you break yours?

It's management's job both to recognize that luck exists and to remove as much luck from the equation as it can. As Rickey said, "Luck is a fact, but it should not be a factor." On the field, you don't let an unearned run beat you. . . . You push hard enough to take a five-run lead into the late innings. In the office, you leave some resources in reserve to throw at surprises, and never rely on luck to bail you out.

To paraphrase a Rickey statement, "Worthwhile things generally don't just happen."

Master of Self-Awareness:
Ichiro Suzuki, the Field Marshal Foch of Swat

French field marshal Foch at the Battle of the Marne:
"My center is collapsing, my right flank retreats . . .
situation excellent! I shall attack!"

Occasionally, your organization is blessed with a contributor who not only oozes self-awareness but uses his or her emotional state to smash through constraints imagined and real. Like Ferdinand Foch, a World War I military leader, this dynamo chooses to view what appears to others as adversity as "the current environment to be mined for opportunity." Managers can harness such a contributor's torque not only to improve immediate results, but also to drag teammates into better performance.

Baseball's Field Marshal Foch of Swat is Ichiro Suzuki, a Seattle Mariner outfielder. After being the National Pastime's winningest team of the previous four regular seasons (2000–2003), the 2004 M's melted down like a Moon Pie on a steel sidewalk in the Libyan Desert. The meltdown proffers worthwhile lessons for managers in nonbaseball organizations, since the moments when the fecal matter hits the rotary ventilation device are the times that test strength. All organizations face a disastrous quarter, or project, or product, or program at least once in a while, and this is where the right manager can make the most difference.

Usually, American managers fuel the flames with either of two neurotically inspired behavior patterns: denial (acting as though everything is all right and working politically to cover their behinds) or surrender (not salvaging what there is to salvage, amplifying Droopy-Dogism, ultimately affecting their next effort). These common responses produce a contagion that infects staff both immediately and in the long term, reducing the group's interest, incentive, and intensity.

There are many contributors in all kinds of organizations who are rate-busters—people whose personal currency is doing "better" or "more" than anyone else they measure themselves against. A good manager can turn around a group's prospects with just one rate-buster on board. In a meltdown situation, the manager should tickle a rate-buster's interest. This can change the work environment enough to propel the group toward achieving the next objective. One needs an extraordinary rate-buster to do it when management is actually part of the problem. Ichiro Suzuki is an example of that.

The Mariners' 2004 batting coach in spring training had convinced Suzuki to alter the approach he'd been taking at the plate his whole professional career. Ichiro has unique mechanics and pitch selection—it's rare that he strikes out and rarer that he walks. He makes contact with pitches, good and bad, and runs like hell. The batting coach, the management that caused the problem, pushed Suzuki to take on more normal mechanics and pitch-selection models—another example of the American or Soviet management meltdown created by imposing "standards."

The Mariners started the season with a disastrous April, losing twice as many games as they won against their AL West rivals—highly important games because every win you achieve guarantees a loss to a rival.[47] Suzuki was awful, too, with a .310 on-base percentage and a .305 slugging percentage, rendering him useless as a leadoff hitter. Apparently, he gave the hitting coach's experiment exactly one month. Starting on May 1, he had four consecutive multihit games.

By June 7, he'd increased his OPS by more than 50 percent over April, with .435 on-base and .500 slugging percentages during the five weeks. The M's weren't doing better, having gone 14–21 during that period, still in fourth place, 9½ games out of third place and 11 games behind the leader. The M's playoff hopes were liquidated for the season. Suzuki, however, kept rolling along. He coped with the meltdown by setting his own targets, rate-busting for his own pride or just personal satisfaction. Like any good contributor in or out of baseball, he makes himself totally accountable, embracing achievement as a moral imperative or a self-inspiration tool.

The outfielder is able to go through games where he seems to violate the laws of physics or luck. For his 200th hit in 2004, he orchestrated a home run, a highly unusual event for him. One of his home runs was at the end of an at bat during which the pitcher had thrown one that arrived where his head had been, and he thought it was intentional. Ichiro's 200th hit in 2005 came very late in a season that was lukewarm for him and his team; with three games to go and with 198 hits in his pocket, he blew through the mark with a 4-for-5 game and followed that with a three-hit game, leaving nothing to luck or blown calls.

Suzuki is not only a rate-buster, but an individual who can hyperfocus on a goal and run it down. He's Seven Sigma when he wills it. With the 2004 season in a septic field, he got through by setting himself targets, pushing himself along by chasing measures he could meet or exceed, and by saying hello to Wee Willie Keeler.

By mid-August, Suzuki was maintaining his .400 on-base percentage, most of it through his .360 batting average. The Mariners had gotten a little worse, and had done one of those Stalin-style roster purges that make sense for Dead Teams Walking, bringing up untested minor leaguers worth testing. Ichiro had had two months with over 50 hits each, and was projecting to have a third such month. Three 50-hit months for a player in a single season is a once-a-decade achievement.

At that point, all he had to inspire him at work every day was chasing his own hitting targets. The team encouraged it. There was nothing else to market, no other inspiration to get casual Seattle fans to attend the ballpark and empty their wallets. So Suzuki buckled down and aimed for a few superlatives: one a "real" record, the others what I would call "marks."

The marks: most singles in a season by an American Leaguer (192, held by Suzuki himself, 2001) and most singles in a season by a modern major leaguer (198, Lloyd "Least Valuable Member of the Hall of Fame" Waner, 1927). Wee Willie Keeler, probably the player in history most similar to Suzuki (hit 'em where they ain't and run like hell every time), had 206 singles in 1898 in a 155-game season.[48] Suzuki smoked Keeler's record, passing Wee Willie in his 151st game with a 5-for-5 performance (that pattern again)—all five hits being, you guessed it, singles. Ichiro finished the season with 225 singles and at least one hit in each of his last 13 games, chipping out 26-for-49 over that period, a .441 average.

Singles are overrated, *but* Suzuki's performance is currently being underrated by some sabermetrics people who've forgotten Angus's Eleventh Law (if they ever knew it): "When something overvalued is exposed and set aside, it inevitably becomes undervalued."

The actual record worth breaking was George Sisler's all-time major-league record for most hits in a season, notched in 1920. The following page shows the all-time leader board Suzuki was assaulting, courtesy of Baseball-Reference.com.[49]

Sisler's was a real record, not just a mark. It required hitting well and staying healthy. Playing in all 154 of his team's games, Sisler hit for a .407 average. It also required team circumstances. His St. Louis Browns played in a home park that was friendly to hitting. He had three full-time playing teammates who hit over .300, so the team led the league in plate appearances, giving "Gorgeous George" more opportunities for the lineup to work its way around to him. He was a very good hitter in excellent circumstances.

Suzuki played on a team that tied for last place in getting on base, potentially reducing times the lineup would come around to him. He played in a home park that depresses offense more than any other in the league. Yet he drove himself toward and ran down that record. Ichiro tied and then passed Sisler in game 160 with (Ow-*ooh*-guh . . . pattern alert) a three-hit game, and racked up three more hits in the final two games. He didn't edge Sisler's record; he reduced it to a Fallujah-like rubble, finishing

Rank	Player	Hits	Year	Bats
1.	George Sisler	257	1920	L
2.	Lefty O'Doul	254	1929	L
	Bill Terry	254	1930	L
4.	Al Simmons	253	1925	R
5.	Rogers Hornsby	250	1922	R
	Chuck Klein	250	1930	L
7.	Ty Cobb	248	1911	L
8.	George Sisler	246	1922	L
9.	Ichiro Suzuki	242	2001	L
10.	Babe Herman	241	1930	L
	Heinie Manush	241	1928	L

with 262. He constantly sets a series of objectives for himself and drives himself to meet them, even surrounded by a meltdown.

In nonbaseball organizations, this behavior is just as valuable. Top-performing individuals set themselves high targets. If they fail to meet or exceed them, they reset their objectives to ones they can still attain. Managers can do this for groups by setting ambitious but realistic targets and relentlessly pursuing them. Avoid, however, the common error of over-shooting and demanding something unachievable.

Faced with a failing effort, achieving some objectives is not the same as ultimate total success. It does, however, provide positive feedback, a realistic sense of advance, and a reason for hope. You can't always change the course of history or get a do-over, but you can overcome the torpidity of Droopy-Dogism by recycling your experience of a failure to build for the future. Ride your group back to competitiveness, and if you have a rate-buster like Ichiro Suzuki, slipstream him.

Suzuki is more than just emotionally self-aware. He's equally self-aware intellectually, too. The importance of that ability is the core of chapter 10.

10

Plate Adjustments:
Intellectual Self-Awareness

⚾

The art of being wise is the art of knowing what to overlook.
—William James

Intellectual self-awareness delivers the ability to see with an outsider's perspective one's own unquestioned concepts, ideas, and presumptions. We absorb these throughout our lives, through life experience, family and school training, and work practice, and have them imposed on us as organizational standards. Whereas emotional self-awareness enables us to come to grips with hidden, unexamined emotional issues, intellectual self-awareness gives us the fulcrum and place to stand from whence we pry away unexamined ideas and presumptions about process.

As human beings we are wired to simplify our actions by internalizing lessons and then autonomically repeating them. If you grew up in a home and return to it after being away a few months, it looks very different because you simplified the image and key details of it when you saw it daily. There was no reason to see it with fresh eyes. After a break, you are really seeing it again.

This natural simplifying is "aliasing," keeping an abbreviated symbol that represents the totality of the object or concept, like a notation in a scorebook. The play as recorded in the scorebook isn't "the play," it's a shorthand summary of some of its elements. Sometimes I look at the scoresheet for a game I watched or played in and years later the shorthand is enough to elicit a vivid memory, whereas other times I can't even remember the game.

I asked Dan Wilson, a veteran catcher for the Cincinnati Reds and Seattle Mariners, about plays at the plate where he took imperfect throws from the right fielder and put the runner out.[50] Such memorable plays at the plate are a zenith of catcher defensive performance, and something Wilson was exceptionally good at. He remembers some vividly, but says that most blur together. It's not the most recent or important that remain; his facility for remembering them, like most of ours, is random.

After we talked, I flipped through my scorebook and found some of those plays. For me, too, some are vivid, some just graphite glyphs on a paper form that generate no memory. I selectively remember the ones where *he* made the play and no other catcher could have made it a putout. We alias based on our own preprogrammed priorities and biases, leaving out the details we don't need to remember or prefer to forget.

To achieve third base in the *Management by Baseball* model, you need to overcome this aliasing process. If you don't, you are stuck with the implicit assumptions—your own and other people's—that become invisible to you. You need to become like relief pitcher Al "The Mad Hungarian" Hrabosky. Many remember the 1970s reliever for stalking halfway to second base between every batter, closing his eyes and standing still, then turning around, stalking to the mound, and firing the pitch, all so fast you'd have thought he was holding a hot coal instead of a ball. His routine covered for the fact that he was crawling through his mental file, remembering every pitch he had ever thrown to the opposing hitter and what the batter had done with it. No aliasing here, just staying aware of the details of his experiences.

Stealing Third: Ichiro Suzuki's Mastery of Tools, Synthesis & Self-Awareness

I mentioned in chapter 9 that Ichiro Suzuki is a superb example of emotional self-awareness. He's a champ in intellectual self-awareness, too. He takes close to nothing for granted and never approaches the game by pretending that what was successful in the past can go unexamined today.

That's clear from the book he released in 2004: *Ichiro on Ichiro: Conversations with Narumi Komatsu.*[51] It's not a great book (few baseball bios as-told-to are), but it has some great insights of use to managers in their everyday work because Suzuki is totally rigorous in his mental approach to the game. You'll never hear him utter the two cop-outs less-introspective players do: "The Lord did this through me" or "See the ball, hit the ball." He knows what his own strengths and limitations are.

It's one of the reasons that while Suzuki is not really a Most Valuable Player (MVP), he's clearly at the top of the MWP (Most Watchable Player) list for me and for many other serious observers of the game. An important aspect of that watchability is his relentlessly analytical approach to making himself effective.

One of his self-awareness advantages is his ability to work with what the environment gives him. Most managers fail at this skill. They succeed with a certain set of techniques in a specific situation, but when a similar situation comes up later, they autonomically apply the same package of techniques.

That's rarely the best policy. It's true that what's past is prologue, and it never pays to ignore past success or failure. Doing what you did before is much easier than standing back and rebuilding an overall plan from scratch. It's much cheaper in time and energy. But environments and conditions change. Not only that, but the very definition of what constitutes success can change.

Johnny Neun was a part-time player for a handful of years in the

1920s. Neun's repertoire: he played first base reasonably well, had decent speed, and was a contact hitter who could walk a little. He hit home runs about as often as Noam Chomsky appears on *Jerry Springer*. A very educated man, he spent 10 years managing in the minors. In 1947, he got his chance to manage a full year in the majors, with the Cincinnati Reds.

The Reds' special strength was a pair of infielders who could hit (a rarity). That's a great advantage because first basemen and outfielders who can hit are so easy to acquire. However, those Redlegs suffered from the absence of any outfielder who could contribute hitting to complement the infielders. On the Reds' AAA team, Neun had one of the purest power hitters in pro ball, Hank "The Honker" Sauer, an awful fielder who struck out a lot (like the Reds' current star Adam Dunn). On some teams, The Honker wouldn't have been of exceptional value. But in the hitting-of-any-kind-starved Reds outfield, he would have been incomparably useful.

We all believe the things we ourselves do well have value. Looking through the filter of his own aptitudes (contact hitting, some wheels, some glove), Neun couldn't see value in Sauer. He left Sauer in Syracuse to incinerate AAA pitching (50 home runs). By the time Neun got it together to promote The Honker, his own job was about to tumble off the upper deck. Sauer went on to have the best slugging career after age 31 (when he finally made it to the majors and stuck) of anyone whose first name was not Barry. He was picked for a couple of All-Star teams and won the NL MVP award in 1952.

Neun wasn't wrong in thinking his own skill set was useful; he was wrong to think of "success" as a static goal unaffected by the environment. A player like Neun wouldn't have helped that Reds team very much; a player like Sauer would have balanced the recipe and led to explosive results. Context in baseball changes which aptitudes have the most value. Time changes presumed benefits and can trash them for non-self-aware organizations.

Airlines skated for years on cheap fuel. They had every reason to know energy prices would shoot up when fuel demand started climbing after the start of the wars in the Middle East. Their fare-pricing behavior didn't change until the hikes were actually showing up at their pumps, and when it did change, too often it was secreted away as hidden surcharges that didn't show up in advertised prices and angered the kinds of people who are their most frequent customers. Most botched the planning, and then let the implementation, an easy grounder, dribble through their legs. Starbucks assumed people in Chicago would uniformly like the same ultra-dark incinerator roast that people in Seattle uniformly liked, so when they rolled out their stores there, they started brewing only those hometown flavors, and had a time of trying to come to grips with the fact that Chicago didn't prefer the exact flavors that led to Starbucks' success in Seattle.

Suzuki, on the other hand, presumed environmental change would change the way he needed to approach his craft. He never assumed that the title-winning batting methods that put him at the top of statistical measures in Japan would work when facing major-league pitchers in major-league parks with major-league umps.

He elaborates in his book. When playing for the Orix team, he'd had seven full seasons and, remarkably, led Japan's Pacific League in batting average in all seven years. The interviewer mentions to Suzuki that when he started practicing with his American team, the media and his own manager, Lou Piniella, were concerned about his hitting everything to the opposite field (he's a left-handed hitter, so to left field), which wasn't the normal pattern of how he'd hit in Japan. Finally, Ichiro diversified his approach and started hitting to right field as well, pulling the ball. He explains his reasoning:

This is a little complicated, but first of all it has to do with the strike zone. The major-league strike zone, compared to Japan's, is much wider on the outside. I had to get used to this. Inside pitches, if they're over the plate, are strikes in MLB, but different from Japan, if they miss one balls' width on the inside, they're seldom called a strike. I'm not saying they never are, but compared to pitches on the outside of the plate, they're much less often called strikes.

I have to be much more aware of outside pitches than when I was playing in Japan. As I stand in the batter's box, I have to somehow handle inside pitches while also paying attention to the ones on the outside part of the plate. But it's really hard to pay attention to inside pitches and pick up pitches that are one or two balls' width outside. Which means I have to focus my concentration on the outside of the plate where it's easy to get called on strikes. . . If you hit those pitches on the outside, they're naturally going to go to left.[52]

So Suzuki, attentive to differences in his environment, worked with what he got (a lot of outside pitches he had to swing at), paid attention to what was different (the relatively far-outside pitches), and took the best path he could with them (hit them the opposite way). This cost him some hits he might have had on inside pitches because he had to make the adjustment.

Overall, it worked for him. It sucked away a lot of what power he had in Japan, but it made him the most successful singles hitter of a generation, and while singles are not the greatest asset ever, if you can generate them at the rate Ichiro does and roll in his basepath speed you are going to help your team. While his manager wanted to move Suzuki to batting third in the lineup, Suzuki had analyzed the situation better than Piniella had. He'd seen that to be successful, he had to adapt to what his skill set and the environment would give him. He couldn't be the mean-average-power-plus-top-average batter he had been in Japan, nor the power-hitting Edgar Martínez-with-speed Piniella wet-dreamed he could be. If the major-league umps had had a strike zone that was sculpted on the Pacific League zone, perhaps he could have been, but instead of fighting the American strike zone, he worked with it. Ichiro didn't allow his past success to fog his thinking about success in his new environment.

Suzuki describes, too, how major-league pitchers' deliveries differ from those he'd devastated in the highest level of Japan's competition. Japanese pitchers generally have a hesitation or other excess motion (if you've seen Hideo Nomo's tornado motion, that's one type; San Diego reliever Akinori Otsuka's octogenarian tai chi master with a sore hamstring is another). In moving from college ball to the Pacific League, Ichiro had to add a hesitation of his own, a leg lift that kept his weight back. When he moved to the AL, he had to resurrect his old, pre-leg lift batting form to cope with quicker deliveries. Self-awareness on two counts: what was working must change, and what has been discarded isn't "bad" or "useless" but a tool you can pick up again if circumstances change. American culture gives us an explicit faith in "new, improved" products, and gives us an implicit loss of faith in what they replaced. Because Americans (and Japanese, too) throw away old products, it becomes a habit to throw away old, useful ideas along with the old, outmoded ones.

A final secret about Suzuki: the home runs he hits he hits "intentionally." A common hitting model is to make solid contact and swing through the ball, with the intent of hitting it hard and sometimes getting a home run. Suzuki does it differently. His homers come off swings that he designs specifically with a homer in mind. In 2005, after averaging nine homers in his first four seasons in the majors, he hit 15, the same as his Pacific League average of 16. Self-awareness: he knows he can hit a homer only with different mechanics, and he reserves these for situations when his team really needs only that event or he needs to make a statement.

There are far more Neuns in big-organization management positions than Suzukis. Entire giant businesses are built on investing up front in creating or copying a stable model and cookie-cutting solutions against it, limiting development costs and research expenses. Wall Street loves the for-profits that do this. As I said in Chapter 2, big-time management consulting itself is based, more than any other technique, on this concept: create a solid solution and sell it over and over to many customers, regardless of contextual differences. Governments are sucked into this one-size-fits-all solution by gravitational forces, and the bigger the governmental unit, the more attractive the approach seems and the stronger the gravitational field that amplifies this diseconomy of scale.

As big organizations, larded with this overhead, struggle to achieve organizational self-awareness, inertia reifies one-size-fits-all into management behavior. They tend to either hold on to their old tools necrotically with their cold dead hands or jump on a fad and throw the previous tools out, even the still-useful ones. In the standard rhythm of their daily efforts, they forget that they can take advantage of another set of behaviors to achieve a less usual objective, as Ichiro's home run swing does.

Stealing third base, even for a skilled sack pilferer, is a challenging accomplishment that doesn't happen often. Managers will struggle to get to third base in the *Management by Baseball* model, but it can be done by paying attention to what "success" is in different situations and in different contexts and acting on the differences. Simply put, it's being like Ichiro Suzuki.

In chapter 7, I discussed "survivals," behaviors or standards or beliefs that were functional at one time but no longer serve a purpose, like the batting mechanics you used in a different league or saying "God bless you" when someone sneezes even though you don't believe evil spirits are going to possess him if you don't. Those who lack self-awareness repeat hundreds of survivals at work every day without ever noticing them. When survivals are innocuous, like the unnecessary buttons on sports coat sleeves, they're an avoidable but acceptable cost. When survivals are mass delusions no one reexamines ("More with Less" and such), they are expensive and can be fatal. A mail-order operation that used to serve business customers only (average purchase, $550) always required buyers to give them a PO number and always printed a duplicate invoice that shipped with the order along with an itemized list of contents used by the packer. When their business shifted to individual consumers (average purchase, $35), no one questioned asking every buyer for a PO number or shipping all buyers three pieces of paper, average cost of time and materials around $4 per shipment. Be attentive to survivals; just being aware of an unquestioned assumption is a big step toward intellectual self-awareness.

Unquestioned Assumptions: Return on Equity Is the RBI of Business

Some business executives manage their operation for return on equity (ROE). The experience of these folks offers an excellent example of missing the point even when they have accurate data (chapter 6), because they can achieve a target that doesn't advance their operation. They have an analog in baseball: teams that value players based on runs batted in (RBI). ROE is a perfectly logical-sounding statistic that encourages its devotees to distort their investments in ways that undermine the business' vitality and long-term survival. RBI is a perfectly logical-sounding stat that encourages many general managers to pay extra millions for ordinary players based on those GMs' inability to step back and examine their implicit faith in "the way it's always been."

ROE is one small measure among many, it's highly contextual, and it may mask more important factors. An exec can increase a company's ROE in a dozen ways that will undermine a company. If I cloned myself and managed two companies with everything identical except that Company A had less equity as a result of some poorly chosen spending and Company B was storing cash for some prudent investments, the clone who managed A would have better ROE than the B clone. Not because of skill or ability to advance the company, but simply because of the "benefit" of having less equity.

The RBI is parallel, a highly contextual measure, and it may mask more important factors. The most prolific homer hitter in the majors the last five years (2001–2005), Alex Rodríguez is a great RBI man. The Yankee cleanup hitter has had 100 or more RBIs in eight consecutive seasons

(1998–2005). Awesome. But he's a cleanup hitter, so he usually has the three other Yankees best at getting on base batting in front of him. When he comes up, there's a better chance of him hitting with men on base, runners who represent RBI chances.

Let's test opportunity. Bat Alex cleanup and clone him thrice. Bat his clones leadoff, fifth, and eighth. In the first inning of every game, Leadoff A-Rod is the first one to the plate, so once each game he's guaranteed an at bat with no one on base to knock in. His next time up he's likely to bat behind the number nine batter (usually the least-skilled in the lineup), incrementally reducing the probability of runners to bat in.

Batting-Fifth A-Rod isn't quite as hosed. But the guy who bats in front of him (the Original A-Rod) is the most productive home run hitter in the majors over the last four years, and when he's whacked one over the fence, the fifth hitter is coming up with the bases empty. In fact, Batting-Fifth A-Rod, by being a very scary dude to pitch to, is going to see fewer base runners during the season because pitchers aren't likely to intentionally walk the cleanup hitter to face Batting-Fifth A-Rod.

Batting-Eighth A-Rod is dinged, too. The batters in front of him, hitting sixth and seventh, are among the weakest in the lineup, and their strength is likely power hitting, not high on-base average, so they may not be on base when our last A-Rod gets up. To undermine our clone further, he's going to have the number nine batter, the least-skilled on the lineup card, next up. Of course, this increases somewhat his chance of being walked intentionally, and with men on base, increases greatly his not getting good pitches to swing at, because an opponent is more afraid of being hurt by a scary hitter like Batting-Eighth A-Rod than by walking him and facing number nine's dubious batting skill.

Like a sales team that has regions or account portfolios with highly variable potential, RBI opportunities are not evenly distributed throughout the lineup. Therefore, it's not a solid measure of helping the team, or "how good" a player is. A batter can do a great job but have fewer opportunities, while another has more opportunities and delivers less, and the

RBI will reward the less-effective one. Sales managers too often use "gross sales" as a metric the way team executives generally use the RBI: a survival that's become an article of faith.

You can make useful measures for employees, sales or otherwise, the same way you can make RBIs a useful stat. Adjust it for opportunity as researcher Tom Ruane did. One, take the league average probability of delivering an RBI in every combination of base runners on and number of outs for a batter at the plate. Two, find out how many times that batter has been up in each situation. Three, project how many RBIs the league average should be, and compare his actual RBI count to what the average would achieve in that composite set of situations.

Look at Ruane's table of the best and worst performers in opportunity-adjusted RBIs since 1960. RBI is what you think it is, and ERBI is the number of RBIs a league-average batter would get in the runs-on-base and outs situations the player faced. Over is the number of extra (or when negative, fewer) RBIs the batter had than that league average. RPRW is the ultimate value, RBI adjusted to the context of the batter's home park and then converted into the number of extra wins a batter's actual RBI production would add for his team. So Barry Bonds in 2001 added about nine wins to the Giants' season over the league average with his RBI production, and Neifi Perez in 2000 cost the Rockies between four and five wins.

BEST	Year	Team	RBI	ERBI	Over	RPRW
Barry Bonds	2001	SF N	137	52.3	84.7	9.4
Mark McGwire	1998	STL N	147	65.6	81.4	8.9
Harmon Killebrew	1969	MIN A	140	67.7	72.3	8.5
Dick Allen	1972	CHI A	113	52.0	61.0	8.5
Roger Maris	1961	NY A	141	67.2	73.8	8.4
Sammy Sosa	1998	CHI N	158	78.1	79.9	8.4
Willie Stargell	1971	PIT N	125	59.0	66.0	8.3

WORST	Year	Team	RBI	ERBI	Over	RPRW
Neifi Perez	2000	COL N	71	90.6	−19.6	−4.6
Neifi Perez	1998	COL N	59	79.6	−20.6	−4.4
Walt Weiss	1995	COL N	25	48.5	−23.5	−4.3
Ivan DeJesus	1978	CHI N	35	61.5	−26.5	−4.3
Walt Weiss	1996	COL N	48	66.2	−18.2	−4.0
Larry Bowa	1974	PHI N	36	65.8	−29.8	−4.0
Felix Fermin	1989	CLE A	21	53.7	−32.7	−3.9

The uncloned, real-life Alex Rodríguez is in between these legendary successes and failures as an RBI man. Here are his numbers adjusted for opportunity during the period 2001–2004 (Ruane hasn't yet published 2005 data).

Name	Year	Team	RBI	ERBI	Over	RPRW
Alex Rodriguez	2001	TEX A	135	84.4	50.6	4.9
Alex Rodriguez	2002	TEX A	142	80.3	61.7	5.6
Alex Rodriguez	2003	TEX A	118	73.9	44.1	3.7
Alex Rodriguez	2004	NY A	106	85.0	21.0	2.2

In A-Rod's best year, 2002, he led his league in adjusted RBI. He's been a good performer, adding to his team's ability to win by knocking in runs.

In baseball, the momentum of the implicit has been hard to overcome. Branch Rickey pointed out ages ago three reasons to ignore unadjusted RBI, but even a recognized genius struggles to overcome the faith of the lazy-minded. In your organization, there are a breathtaking number of implicit, unquestioned assumptions. A key element of intellectual self-awareness is to question one's own and one's employer's implicit assumptions. Otherwise, one invests in illusions like ROE or whatever distortions hold sway in a shop.

Only when you overcome the limitations of your own and others' implicit assumptions can you consistently meet and manage change, our inevitable battery-mate.

Part Four

Crossing Home Plate—
Managing Change

You can never step on the same home plate twice.
—Heraclitus

Managing change is hard. That's why it's the last stage of the *Management by Baseball* model. The skills that get you to third base successfully may actually undermine you when you try to get to home plate safely by managing change. Since you don't know when most changes are going to happen or exactly how, data collection and most of the specifics of people management and self-awareness are less useful. Because the skills of otherwise good managers are not usually attuned to change, few managers excel at managing it. That's why there's an entire specialized career called "change management," an endeavor as difficult as stealing home when the opposition knows you're going for it.

Change is the toughest base to coach. The most direct form of coaching is teaching rules . . . *if* this occurs, do *this* or *that* unless *the other*. But in times of change, the rules are usually the first things to fail. That's what can make change devastating. If a manager is repeating the normal winning responses and not paying really close attention, allowing aliasing (chapter 10) to gauze over reality, it's possible for even a quick-minded superstar to "get Vinced," that is, run over by a minor trend without realizing it was ever a threat.

I call it that to commemorate the fastest man in the league getting knocked out of the World Series by the slowest piece of equipment in St. Louis. Vince Coleman was a rookie outfielder for the Cardinals in 1985, harvesting 110 steals and regarded as the fastest player in the league. While standing on the damp field before a playoff game, he failed to notice the ultraslow electronically operated tarp. It rolled over him, squashing his leg and knocking him out for the year. A blind adherence to established rules is the last thing a manager should count on in times of change; she can get Vinced even by the banal.

There's another surprise about change that's slipperier than Astro-Turf in a muggy stadium. Seemingly small changes can remake an endeavor in ways the participants never imagined. But giant, earthshaking changes *don't* always require a change in methods or management practice.

To get to home plate successfully, you first have to recognize that a change you need to work with is happening or about to happen. Then you need the tools to separate the kinds of change that actually matter from those that don't. You then develop a stochastic response (chapter 4)—not a rigid automatic approach, but a flexible one based on flexible responses focusing on shifts and a willingness to test and fine-tune until you get it right enough. Finally, you have to exercise judgment, because most changes that are part of human systems change even as you're trying to adapt to them. That can work to your advantage if you're driving the change—or to your disadvantage if you're not. Let's see how.

11

Lowering the Pitcher's Mound: What Is Change?

People who live in the past generally are
afraid to compete in the present.
—**Sparky Anderson**

Runner on first with nobody out. If the team in the field considers the runner even a remote threat to steal, the first baseman will stand between the runner and the bag, threatening a pickoff throw. Which means there's a bigger gap between the first and second basemen, a gap easier for the batter to hit through.

The defense may try to fill some of that gap by moving the second baseman toward first by two steps. If the batter is a right-handed pull hitter unlikely to poke a ball into that gap, the second baseman might not move, challenging the batter to try to do what he usually doesn't. And if the pitcher thinks the batter will take the challenge, he might pitch inside, making it harder to hit one through that gap. It's rococo choreography, the pitcher and fielders on one side, the batter and runner on another, making lots of incremental, conscious decisions, intentionally changing the environment every second.

Human activities are not a passive vessel for change, but a definition of change itself. Inside and outside an organization, nothing will stay still long enough for an observer to nail it down. Because of that, it's terribly difficult to coach people in managing change. The lesson you give today will sit astride a set of circumstances that may never assemble themselves that way again. The best lessons are not about "facts," but about "patterns." The best solutions aren't built out of "results," but "probabilities." The future brings changed circumstances as constantly as the sequence of each daily sports section's stats tables. In dealing with change, success is beautiful but ephemeral.

The Extinction of the .400 Hitter: How Changes Change Assumptions

Managers' strategies must constantly be tuned, improved, refined, and, ultimately, trashed and replaced. Gains one harvests by adapting to change are always temporary.

To understand the essence of change, take a look at early baseball, where everyone had to get a handle on trends before the trends manhandled them. The essential rule of thumb was described by paleontologist Stephen Jay Gould in his essay "The Extinction of the .400 Hitter." [53] The last full-time major leaguer to hit .400 was Ted Williams in 1941. What's happened since? Gould's theory is that the talent is better now on average, but that as systems like "The Book" got refined through managers' and contributors' efforts, the worst tactics and the worst players got winnowed out.

In early baseball, there was no Book on where to place fielders in general. Fielders' gloves were as useful as pieces of burnt toast. When players, even pros, stepped onto the field, every game was a rough-draft experiment in strategy, tactics, and execution. And it was even harder to nail down "the way we do it," because the rules kept changing.

Before 1879, there was no standard ball. In 1880, the batter had to take seven balls to walk. In 1883, a foul ball caught on one hop stopped being an out. In 1884, a walk required six balls, and in 1886 it went back to seven. The league tinkered with the ball's resiliency, juicing it some years, deadening it others. In 1887, outfielder Tip O'Neill of the American Association St. Louis Browns hit .435 by the rules of his time—four strikes, you're out—yet under those same generous rules, his team's regular catcher, Jack Boyle, managed only .189.

Despite all those rapid-fire changes and many more, by 1890, the 15th year of the National League's existence, there was a Book on how to play. As in all young endeavors, there was still room for plenty of experimentation, but baseball had worked out the basics. If a grounder was hit to the first baseman away from the bag, someone would cover the bag for him. The catcher moved close behind the hitter because someone had discovered that if you caught the ball before it bounced, you were less likely to lose it. By 1898, the best batting average was Baltimore outfielder Wee Willie Keeler's .385; the worst, Pittsburgh Pirates shortstop Bones Ely's .212.

Already, you'll notice, the best is not quite as high, the worst not quite as low. Overall, batting averages have remained around .260 most of the time throughout baseball's existence, but high and low marks have gradually gotten closer to the league average. Variation has narrowed. Some observers, especially those who romanticize the past (a cognitive disease that affects most endeavors and family members over the age of 50), think that "back in the good old days" everything was better. I call people who suffer from this romanticism "Bitgods," the acronym for their belief. They believe that batters were better because they could hit .400.

In reality, all the industry's systems are more sophisticated now. Complete failures are less likely to stay in uniform now than in 1895, when Dewey McDougal got to pitch 114 innings for St. Louis and surrendered 233 base runners for an opponent batting average of .360 and an ERA of 8.32. Dewey's 2005 equivalent (worst National League pitcher) was Cincinnati's Eric Milton, with an opponent batting average of .302 and a 6.47 ERA—very ugly, but 23 percent better than Dewey's. If you were a batter, who would be easier to hit .400 off of?

Immutable Law of Organizational Change #1: Punctuated Equilibrium Is Why Bob Gibson and Luis Tiant Get to Stomp You Silly

Punctuated equilibrium (PE) is an explanation of how evolution tends to happen. Here, I give you only the essence of what you need to know about PE as a manager. In thinking about trends, substitute "ideas" or "practices" for "organisms" and "species."[54]

In contrast to the little-at-a-time view of "progress," usually presented as small changes from one simple organism to a more complex one generation by generation, one step at a time, PE supports a model where populations are relatively stable for a long time. Mutations happen, but mostly they are not advantageous, so they don't spread. Then a big change (environmental cataclysm, climate shift, Dusty Baker gives up chewing his toothpick) guns down the dominant species. With no dominant species tapping into available resources, wacky experiments are more likely to find a temporary foothold, so there's a flowering of new species and variation within species. In nature, as in most endeavors, most experiments fail. Successful models start to dominate resources. Overall, there's less variation, more uniformity—until the next big change. Stability over a long period of minor variation gives way to sudden lurching collapse, creativity, appearance of new dominant models, stability over a period of minor variation, repeat. Change is rarely gradual.

On charts, nonbaseball managers usually make projections that are straight lines. Most functions over time do not reflect a straight line. Aging baseball teams don't usually fade over a few years; they tend to collapse suddenly. Levees don't break slowly but surely as water pressure builds up; they hold completely, spring a small leak or three, then suddenly collapse. Pop music tunes don't climb the charts steadily for months until they get to the *Billboard* charts; they build up steam and then rocket up to the top out of "nowhere." The adoption of popular management methods doesn't happen on the smooth straight line; it also spikes and plummets faddishly.

In 1963, the baseball rule book enlarged the strike zone, raising the ceiling from the batter's armpits to the shoulder tops. Batting averages dropped about 12 points, and on-base plus slugging (OPS) fell sharply from about .718 to .679.[55] In 1964, hitting picked up a little, probably because hitters adjusted a little. In 1965 it was a little down (probably because pitchers had learned a little more about hitters' adjustments), in 1966 it went sideways, and 1967 showed a small shift toward the pitchers.

Then 1968 happened. There was no rule change, but the relative equilibrium was punctuated. What arrived was a blossoming of pitching as significant as any in baseball since 1901. Both leagues' earned run averages were 2.98. The Cardinals *team* ERA was 2.49. Their stopper, Bob Gibson, a gifted pitcher who was especially gifted at the high unhittable strike, led the NL in ERA with a 1.12 mark. Five AL starters posted an ERA under 2.00, led by Luis Tiant at 1.60.

At the end of the season, the owners lowered the pitcher's mound height from 15 to 10 inches and went back to the pre-1963 strike zone. Along with expansion as a possible contributor, league ERA went to 4.07, followed by a long period of stability with minor variation.

Beyond baseball, this is a common pattern. The auto industry, as Gould noted, went through the same PE cycle. Many competing 19th-century engine types and dozens of creative manufacturers with their own designs, techniques, and distribution models narrowed to a couple of engine types and a handful of dominant manufacturers building vehicles based mostly on identical principles. Auto companies that survive the next 20 years will find many of today's presumptions made extinct, from supplier relations to engine types to buyers' emotional relationship with their vehicles. The stock market does this PE routine every few years, where all the presumptions implode, leaving retail investors and younger brokers bewildered as though it had never happened before.

There are plenty of trends that can be managed with incremental actions. But it's essential to realize that most big trends managers need to respond to will parallel the PE model. Surviving, more often than not, requires a nonincremental response, usually executed in double time.

While the lines aren't perfectly smooth, the trend is unarguable. Over time, the best and worst players tend to produce results closer to the average. It's the same in the workplace as on the field. As competitors gain experience and rules are standardized, as professionals work out the details of their work, practices become more universal. "Normal" choices have ever-fewer variants. Experiments happen less often, as players allocate more resources to squeezing out microbenefits by fine-tuning accepted strategies, and less to revolutionizing The Book. Newcomers optimize on predecessors who had success. The worst strategies tend to appear less often, while the most successful are emulated more and more—and yield less to those pursuing them.

The first stock pickers who realized the odds of making money on an initial public offering—by buying it at the offer price and selling it quickly after it went public—made good, almost assured, profits. But then people wrote about it, so others imitated. Then it became harder to actually buy the offering before it went public. Further, it was such an effective way to manufacture one's own money that executives taking their companies public would force their market makers to let them buy into the other IPOs the makers were working on. The pool of stock available to "the market" of people hoping to cash in shriveled quicker than Tommy Lasorda on Slim-Fast, because the executives of IPO companies got to reap one another's easy pickings, leaving less for everyone else. Just as in baseball, success creates the gravitational field that undermines it.

In the middle of 2005, an ad agency discovered that the infrequently used tint bright yellow worked as a background for ads, and snared a lot of attention for its client. Other ad agencies' design staffs saw this and got on the bus, and the media, television especially, were a veritable Yellow River of citron backdrops, meant to support the sale of everything from mobile-phone carriers to burgers to mediocre cable-television providers. Everybody "knew" yellow was *the* color. Each follower undermined the surprise factor, strip-mining the effect for himself and the innovator, too. Eventually the shade of the moment becomes passé and people go back to a range of choices until the next surprise color comes along, when the explosion starts again. That process is called punctuated equilibrium (PE) (see sidebar).

1968 Meets 1909: Environmental Collapse

The Orioles were just getting their dynasty going when they ran into a sudden change. For a decade, they'd developed players and managers in the minors on a system that required successfully identifying tendencies and rules for winning. They became devout adherents of pursuing the big-inning offense, or as Earl Weaver sometimes called it, "a walk, a single, and a three-run homer." They diminished use of one-run strategies like sacrifice bunts and steals.[56]

There was only one flaw in Baltimore's flawless design: 1968, a highly anomalous Year of the Pitcher when one-run strategies became relatively valuable and big innings rarer than a Dixie Chicks tribute album of Ted Nugent and the Amboy Dukes tunes.

The stinging line drive that knocked their manager, Hank Bauer, out of the box was a change he didn't adapt to quickly enough. Like his peers Cal Ermer in Minnesota and Eddie Stanky in Chicago, Bauer didn't tweak his decisions to adapt to 1968's run-stingy environment. The O's started losing a lot of low-scoring games. Everything Bauer had mastered, refined, and learned to act on had changed. Bauer was made torpid by his inner Bitgod nostalgia, and was replaced midseason by Earl Weaver, who snapped passivity, as I'll explain in chapter 12. Bitgod mentality can develop quickly, even in just a couple of years, if the positive feedback is strong enough.

Beyond baseball, intelligent people are more likely to let the comfort of success drive them into the ground like a swinging bunt whenever a change comes along that requires them to discard their successful patterns. One of the three most brilliant software designers in the world, Paul

Mace, struck it big in the mid-'80s with a packaged set of PC utilities that did unbelievable things. The product sold decently until a leading columnist wrote adoringly of it. Paul went from modest success to immodest success, and ultimately sold the product to a bigger company.

He still had the same skills, but now he had better capital and connections. He released another innovative product. And waited for a columnist to notice it. Then he waited some more. Working for Mace, I tried to convince him to run some proven marketing programs, boring stuff that works. He had become a Bitgod and wouldn't change his playbook.

In the early PC days Mace had been a hero among computer users, when users meant "hobbyists." In the early '90s, the market had changed to mass-market consumers who didn't know or care who he was. By then, oligopoly distributors, making money by pocketing vendors' marketing funds and not by selling products, didn't want anything to do with entrepreneurs. They wanted big pelf, and Mace wouldn't and couldn't ante up the kind of mordida they were looking for. The product never took off. It couldn't, because change had messed with proven success.

Success is the enemy of adaptability. The more success a manager has experienced, the more likely she is to miss seeing a change and its consequences. Even if she sees it, the more likely she is to be a Bitgod, comfortable with the easy status quo, and the harder it is for her to overcome her inertia and act.

Errors on Easy Grounders: Small-Looking Changes

Many of the changes a manager has to handle are easily foreseen in advance—like shifts to regulations such as the North American Free Trade Agreement, or rising demand for fuel that in turn affects prices. Some are outside the domain of planning, but still predictable, such as colder weather patterns in winter, or the inevitable decline of growth in a high-growth market. Predictable, yes, but some people aren't moved to insulate their homes until the first whopping gas bill arrives, and some manufacturers get shut out because they design their "plan" around a market that will keep growing at 60 percent a year forever.

Sometimes changes are not only predictable, but initially seem small. In the off-season between 1972 and 1973, the American League insti-

Immutable Law of Organizational Change #2: The Law of Comparative Advantage

As we see with teams' responses to the DH rule, organizations that are comfortable with the status quo have to fight gravitational fields that keep them from making the moves necessary to meet the future. Less comfortable, less secure organizations don't have these fields to fight.

Anthropologist Leslie White documented this gravitational field; he called it the law of comparative advantage. Writing soon after World War II, he described how going into the war, the industrial plants of Great Britain, Japan, and Germany averaged roughly the same vintage. But Britain was successful in preventing consistent, targeted bombing of its plants, while Allied bombing flattened a serious portion of the German and Japanese plants. By the end of the war, most of Britain's prewar plants were still standing, but postwar reconstruction replaced the portion of Germany's and Japan's older plants with newer designs and newer technology. By starting from scratch, the losers got better siting and integration with contemporary demographic and transportation needs. Comparative advantage shifted to the defeated, while Britain was stuck with what it had defended—relatively aged capacity. Successful action led to conditions that bred comparative disadvantage.

In baseball, a new manager of a team that's obviously failing can have an easier path shaking up everything than one who inherits a roster that's been winning. Beyond baseball, managers who need to alter process or staffing or assignments or strategy face the same pattern.

tuted the designated-hitter rule, allowing a team to appoint a batter to hit for the pitcher in all at-bats. It appeared to be a minor change. All the teams knew in advance, so they could adapt.

Nope. Not all teams had luck adapting. The previous season's teams with the best offenses, New York and Kansas City, had below-average offenses in the first DH season. The previous season's teams with the worst offenses, Texas and Cleveland, showed the most improvement (still below average, though, proving you can *always* mess with Texas). How come? Teams that already had a successful offense did less to take advantage of the added offensive oomph the DH allowed. Teams that were struggling the most before the DH rule perceived the urgent need to use it to boost offense—and acted on it.

Success is more likely for those who embrace every change as an opportunity, as I'll explain in chapter 12, which is about adapting to changes.

What is change? The way I use the term, "change" encompasses the recognition of shifts in human-made trends, such as regulations or diktats from the finance department, as well as in more unforeseeable or random-appearing trends, such as economic earthquakes or suddenly appearing inventions or innovations that shatter the status quo of entire industries. It includes overcoming your inner Bitgod, knowing how to recognize what needs action and what is just cosmetic. Change includes knowing how to tweak all your systems and how you look at them and at yourself to stay adapted to the present circumstances.

12

When They Rewrite the Rule Book: Responding to Changes

An error shall be given to the pitcher when the
batsman is given first base on "called balls" (a walk).
—The 1883 Rule Book

Unlike the organisms Stephen Jay Gould talked about, human systems like baseball and your work can "prevolve." Prehistoric trilobites didn't think, "Jeez, wouldn't it be useful to produce offspring with an extra row of eye lenses?" Mutations happened. They either stayed in the breeding pool long enough to take hold for a while or they didn't.

People at work are different: we can say, "There's a runner on second and she might relay my signs; I'd better hide them," or "A lot of the other spot welders have been going to the hospital with eye injuries—I'd better get and wear protective goggles," or "We have too many sales folk on the floor Saturday mornings—I'd better delay some start times." That's prevolution.

You Say You Want a Prevolution

Prevolution is premeditated change. As a species, we managers can plan and execute incrementally and respond on the fly, so we can adapt to environments in ways that trilobites couldn't. We can keep our old patterns while testing different new ones in our attempts to find a way to avoid extinction.

There are two kinds of change: foreseeable changes such as altered regulations or a jump in the price of energy, and unforeseeable or apparently random shifts. In all cases, the best approach is to:

- ⚾ observe systemically,
- ⚾ attack stochastically,
- ⚾ optimize the resources you have at hand, and
- ⚾ respond to feedback from your organization and from others.

The observation step is like OMA (chapter 6), but instead of observing, measuring, and analyzing your *staff*, you're applying OMA to *current events* in and out of your line of work. If it's natural for you to think inductively, start playing out imaginary future histories and potential chains of events using daily news stories and trend pieces as fodder. If inductive thinking isn't part of your nature, imagining the future is likely a poor investment of your time. While there's a lucrative industry in "teaching" creative thinking, I've never seen any program that can teach someone who's not already good at inductive thinking how to become accomplished.

All managers, though, can reverse-engineer big changes that have already occurred in their line of work, laying out the chain of events that led up to the shocks or smaller changes they had to adapt to. What's past is prologue, and that approach guarantees little, but the changes you'll be looking out for with this technique are at the very least ones that *can* happen, so it's a great place to start.

After observation comes testing, stochastic experimentation. The essence of testing is to practice coming to grips with the change by applying a variety of approaches to see which work in which situations, as opposed to picking up an unproven approach and applying it whole hog. It

Charting Pitchers & Guessing Pitches: Stochastic Responses

Stochastic problem solving is the approach that works best most of the time. The root of the word "stochastic" is the Greek verb that describes shooting an arrow at a target. Stochastic problem solving deviates from the standard practice of trying to repeat what's perfect today over and over, aiming single-solution arrows directly at the bull's-eye of current reality. Understanding that the real-world bull's-eye is likely to move between each shot, stochastic solutions aim toward it, but cluster a lot of possibility arrows near the center, and progressively fewer the farther away from the center the possibility is.

Committing all your resources to one solution presumes you know exactly where the bull's-eye is going to be. A stochastic pattern directs several investments at the most likely possibilities, but hedges gradually fewer resources on less and less likely outcomes. The pattern gives you more chances to hit a bull's-eye or get very close. Resources are not just dollars; human effort is limited, too. It doesn't make sense to spend as much time developing a contingency plan for the U.S. converting to the metric system or the National League expanding to Havana as it does to prepare for the price of oil going up $5 or $25 a barrel.

Stochastic strategies are why baseball teams don't have an entire lineup of right-handed sluggers or a staff of only finesse pitchers. Sooner, not later, a team will run into a pitcher that strikes out all the right-handed power hitters or a lineup that chews up finesse pitchers. Teams need to have something in reserve to counter the opponent's strength. Stochastic strategies are why companies in most industries have more than one distribution channel, but don't put the same focus on each, and why governments investing in research put money into a range of competing technologies.

means applying the most investment in the more likely new approaches and less in the less likely ones, then gradually shifting the balance in response to what's bringing you success. And you don't entirely dump your old tools while experimenting.

More than anything else, effective responses require not overoptimizing—creating a Soviet Five-Year Plan and expecting the fifth-year targets to be as accurate as the first or second year's. Allow slack for inaccuracies and execute midcourse corrections.

Successful American family farmers, at least the ones whose choices are not tugged at by crop subsidies, know this principle intimately. They may specialize in a crop or two, but tend to hedge their bets with others most years in case there's a crop-specific blight or weather that disfavors their main crop. Family farmers don't "put all their eggs in one basket." Nor do they on the other hand refuse to plant anything at all because the weather might be terrible. They are, as a category, highly experimental, and understand and implement pilot testing better than any industry except baseball.

Slow-Draw McGraw, Stochastic Adapter

Having played during the 1890s, when the owners alternately juiced and deadened the ball and tweaked the rules, John McGraw never presumed baseball was a stable system you could thrive in without change. Even though he managed through almost 20 years of the Deadball Era, McGraw was prepared when Ed Barrow unleashed Babe Ruth on the pitchers of 1920 and the entire American League chased the home run trend. The National League trailed a year or two in the run-happy shift, which afforded McGraw another advantage: time. The changes included a livelier baseball, the banning of the very tough-to-hit spitball,[57] and a procedure where dirty or roughed-up balls were taken out of play and replaced with whiter, easier-to-see ones.

The Giants already had a good team, and played in the funky Polo Grounds, very punishing to homer hitters unless the batter pulled the ball directly down one of the minuscule foul lines.[58] Little Napoleon couldn't throw away his team and the park to start from scratch. He didn't switch his team over, or "cut over" as they say in business process design, to new offensive patterns either.

He started with the other side of the equation; he innovated new pitching schemes. He pioneered deploying a larger, more diverse pitching staff to keep big hitters off balance. He used more relievers. He gave starters more rest so they could be sharper, which they needed to be after the ball became more lively.

Year by year he smoothly dampened the Giants' use of deadball-era tactics such as steals and sacrifices, while retaining use of the hit-and-run.[59] After Frank Frisch (chapter 6), he recruited fewer slashing speed players and kept hunting for very young dead-pull power hitters until he found 17-year-old Mel Ott. Ott's swing was perfect for the Polo Grounds, a very precise talent that got Ott 511 career taters and earned him a spot in the Hall of Fame. He wasn't a superb home run hitter; he was a good home run hitter who mastered his home stadium. Of his 511 homers, he launched 323 (63 percent) at the Polo Grounds, an aberration unprecedented among players who hit 500+ homers. Melvin was what I call a "flamingo"—a term I'll explain in chapter 13—but a very successful one, and a flamingo whom McGraw was able to apply to respond to change.

By changing the pitching approach and recognizing his park would only support the new offensive style for very specific kinds of batters, he worked with the resources he had and prevolved the team by innovating systems in areas his competitors ignored.

Heraclitus,
The 2002 World Champion Angels & Peter Drucker

It is not necessary to change. Survival is not mandatory.
—W. Edwards Deming

Managers can win, briefly, without embracing change only because (a) they are lucky, (b) they master some small details that the environment is rewarding at the moment, or (c) they rapidly act on good observation before the system can change out from under them.

The Anaheim Angels went to the World Series in 2002 and beat the San Francisco Giants for their first-ever championship. The following year they struggled, finishing in third place, four games under .500.

ESPN's Rob Neyer observed before the 2003 season that the Angels' success was built on batting average alone. A team with little power and almost no walks is an intrinsically fragile model. Sure enough, in 2003 five everyday players had markedly lower batting averages than in 2002. Pitching was good enough, but the team was 11th of 14 in scoring runs. On most teams, this might not have been a problem, but Angels GM Bill Stoneman had made a decision after the team won in 2002 that may have been a first in modern baseball: of the starting lineup—the starting rotation and the five top relievers—he changed not a single player, not one of 19.

As a Neyer's Law of Baseball states, "You should never think you're good enough." As Neyer said of his conversation with Stoneman, "When I talked to him last March [2003] Stoneman expressed regret that he didn't have exactly the same 25 players that won the World Series last October. His exact words? 'I wish we were more the same.' "[60]

Because of individuals' variability and an ever-changing rate and direction of change, stasis guarantees slow death. It's true in baseball, and it's true in any organization that operates in a dynamic environment. I'm not an advocate of the grow-or-die cult; there are as many environments that reward focused smallness as ones that reward lumbering behemoths. To optimize productivity, organizations must change size and departmental ratios in response to changing requirements. But if an organization is perfectly, absolutely tuned only to the immediate environment (like insurance companies that optimized on the Clinton years' high stock-market returns to subsidize policies and undersell the competition), it will struggle to survive, even with billions of dollars of cash flow and book value.

The executives of a tool company that hired Peter Drucker to consult told him that the firm's drill bits were improving in quality and declining in price, yet their sales were going down consistently. After exploring the drill bit marketplace, Drucker says, he came back to the company and told them, "Customers don't buy ¼-inch drill bits, they buy ¼-inch holes." His zen saying meant that the company was so focused on the repetitive mechanics and tactics of what it was doing so well, it forgot what business it was in. As times change, the environment changes; if you define your business as subcomponents, even great subcomponents, customers will slowly move away from your business.

Stoneman fell in love with his great players (components) who brought the Angels their first-ever World Series victory, and forgot that his business was fraught with change. Stoneman's quote is the perfect mantra for dissolution.

Most of the insurance companies that used investment income to subsidize policy prices in the Clinton era either didn't have a contingency plan in place, or had one but didn't have the organizational courage to keep from belly flopping into the sulfurous pits of financial torment.

If trying to re-create past success by ignoring the present guarantees challenges, how *do* you change a successful organization without undermining the factors that brought it the success you're trying to perpetuate?

Jocketty Knows:
Whatever Doesn't Make You Stronger Kills You

In baseball, as in most endeavors, the definition of "winning" is different for different competitors. Let's look at some individual teams' specific definitions for the 2005 season.

For the Milwaukee Brewers, starting a sustainable upward trajectory and examining their young players was the "win" goal. For the Tampa Bay Devil Rays or Pittsburgh Pirates, just playing .500 ball early in their development cycle was a moral victory, and ownership and fans would view it that way. For the Baltimore Orioles and Houston Astros, anything less than divisional contention was going to be viewed as a loss. For the Philadelphia Phillies and Minnesota Twins, making the playoffs was the "win."

For the 2004 Cardinals, it was getting to the World Series and possibly even winning it. For the 2005 Cards, having made it in 2004 to the Series and getting swept by Boston, I suspect winning the 2005 Series was the "win" and that falling short was just another form of loss. Very binary for both 2004 and 2005.

That binary win/loss setup, where an organization can win only by being first and in no other case, isn't all that common outside sports. If you open a new retail or manufacturing or service business, say a tavern or a metal-fabrication shop or a dental practice, and in your market area you have the same number of competitors as a baseball team, 29, you don't have to be the largest in after-tax margin or customer satisfaction or gross volume or anything else to "win." Sure, there are entrepreneurs who, like George Steinbrenner, have the personality that drives them to always be number one. And there are some others who believe that striving for number one status in a chosen metric is a necessary component for continued success. In most cases, I tend to agree with them, though not with their usual chosen measure of success, which too frequently is *gross sales* or *market share* . . . both very Soviet-style metrics focused on *Bolshoi-bigness* as opposed to quality.[61]

When the conditions for winning are binary, where winning is *the only* measure of success, focusing on change every day becomes the difference between the possibility of success and the likelihood of failure. In 2004, the Cardinals had an extraordinarily good season. I suspect it even exceeded the front office's optimistic projection. At the two-thirds point of the season they had established a dominant position. If ever a team could "afford" to ease off, it was those Redbirds. Take a look. RS is team runs scored, and RA is runs allowed.

2004 NATIONAL LEAGUE STANDINGS—AUGUST 8

EAST	W	L	PCT	GB	RS	RA
Atlanta	63	47	.573	–	530	444
Philadelphia	58	54	.518	6	550	544
Florida	55	55	.500	8	483	488
NY Mets	52	58	.473	11	492	487
Montreal	44	66	.400	19	405	508

CENTRAL	W	L	PCT	GB	RS	RA
St. Louis	72	38	.655	–	589	449
Chicago	61	50	.550	11½	523	433
Houston	55	56	.495	17½	512	472
Cincinnati	54	57	.486	18½	529	619
Milwaukee	52	58	.473	20	444	500
Pittsburgh	51	58	.468	20½	475	487

WEST	W	L	PCT	GB	RS	RA
L.A.	65	45	.591	–	506	442
San Diego	59	52	.532	6½	493	460
San Fran.	60	53	.531	6½	567	564
Colorado	50	62	.446	16	610	655
Arizona	35	78	.310	31½	456	653

At that point, the Cards were not just in a controlling position over their Central Division, they were the best team in the entire league by seven games. Their team statistics were at or near the top of every good category: third in on-base percentage, second in slugging percentage, fourth in net stolen bases, fourth-fewest double plays hit into. In the ultimate measures, runs, they were second in scoring and third in preventing opponents' runs. Statistically, they were the best overall team in either league, with no clear weakness.

They got to this point without any major deals during the season, and that's understandable to those who buy into the conventional Confucian dogma of "If it ain't broke, don't fix it." But in the situation where being number one is the only alternative to being a total loser, an Anaheim 2003–like Confucian stillness is fatal. Teams playing that well during a season can be too relaxed and get smoked before they reach the Series, like the 2001 Mariners, or so smug down the stretch they don't even get to the playoffs, like the 1995 Angels. Whether it's chemistry or the individual consciousness of key individuals or physical wear and tear, few teams embody the start-to-end excellence of the 1998 Yankees, who had the best season record and rolled through the playoffs and World Series.

Knowing this, the GM of the Cards, Walt Jocketty, decided to fix what wasn't broken. Given that he had a team that already had two of the most all-out, pedal-to-the-metal demonic competitors (what I call "hockey players") with both talent and baseball savvy in Scott Rolen and Jim Edmonds, he went out and got the aging poster boy for that model: Larry Walker and some cash from the Colorado Rockies for a promising young outfielder and minor leaguers.

It gave the Cards another hockey player but one with a lot of hunger for winning. Walker had played on some good teams, but only once a long time before had he been to a playoff series. I'm a little biased because Walker's one of my absolute favorite players to watch. But I think Jocketty got the single best nonpitcher he could have in his situation, namely trying to alter the recipe of an already successful team while making it more competitive for the next few months. Moreover, because the Cards were already a healthy organization, the teams were able to convince Walker to waive his no-trade clause, required to make this deal and something Walker had allegedly invoked previously when the Rockies had tried to trade him.

By changing the recipe, the front office's move achieved a few things:

- ⑩ It added offensive quality to the lineup.
- ⑩ It put one of the savviest and most accurate-armed outfielders in the Cardinals right-field position (where arm is very valuable), moving a slightly-better-than-average Reggie Sanders over to left.
- ⑩ It juggled the batting lineup, forcing the hitters and fielders to refocus on new situations. How fast is the guy in front of me on the base paths? Where should I stand in the cutoff for that guy given his pattern and arm?
- ⑩ It provided the team as a whole with a new social/communal task of integrating a new contributor.

Jocketty made measurable skill improvements, but he also gave this winning machine other reasons to pay attention, stay sharp, and be a team. A GM couldn't have done any more, and the Cards flew home with a strong finish to the season. They stayed focused through the playoffs until they met the buzzsaw of destiny in Boston.

Managers beyond baseball should take two basic lessons from Jocketty and his acquisition of Walker. First, even very successful teams need improvements and tuning. In a competitive situation, whatever doesn't make you stronger can be the source of your demise. Whether to counter smugness, a lack of a day-to-day need to excel, or simply a loss of sharply focused attention, competitive organizations need to shuffle the deck a little to stay fresh.

Good work groups can go sour. It happens way too often. In shops that have a history of struggling with quality or meeting deadlines, managers executing properly can be so surprising to the staff that they lose focus. An associate of mine reorganized warehouse operations at a chronically chaotic assembly house that as a result very quickly approached perfection—until staff came to believe that they could ease back and still achieve. A chronically successful professional practice in San Francisco I worked with found its partners making an increasing number of little, but easily avoidable, mistakes. None of the partners I interviewed believed they had any additional goals worth meeting. In their case, we worked out a mentoring program for graduate students that forced them to get out of the stale rhythm of their mastery and helped them get new insights from current academia that delivered potential for them to learn, too.

A work group doesn't need to be demolished as though in a Godzilla attack from the original Sim City. The workers just need to stay challenged. One way is to add a new senior talent ("veteran leadership," as the Cards did) who can bring additional perspective and expertise into the group's toolbox. Another way, but one that will require a bit more time, is to add a junior person with a yen to learn how to be successful or to acquire domain expertise.

You can expand the team's span of control, giving it new, related tasks to handle. In an organization with struggling teams, you can (I love this one) lend a successful team out as internal or external consultants to the strugglers so that the two can collaborate on improvements. Just remember to create some slack for this, and make sure to let the successful team get public credit before you try to use them as consultants.

How Did Earl Weaver Adapt When Hank Bauer & Kansas City Couldn't?

Back in chapter 11, I explained how Earl's predecessor, Hank Bauer, refused to change his roster or tactics after his outstanding 1966 success. One of the biggest contributing factors in his team's 1967 decline was losing low-scoring games, contests where the winner scored three or fewer runs. In 1966, the O's were 19–19 in low-scoring games. In 1967, Bauer's big shear-off, the small base-stealing and hit-and-run components of their game sagged because they rested heavily on a single individual, the wonderful but aging shortstop Luis Aparicio. The years had cut into Aparicio's ability, but Bauer wouldn't tweak the lineup to get new legs into it. In 1967, the Orioles went 15–23 in low-scoring games as the major-league average of runs scored per game slipped from 3.9 to 3.7. In 1968, team scoring per game imploded, free-falling to 3.4, the lowest it had been in the AL since 1909, when the ball had the consistency of overcooked Pablum and required an INS visa to travel beyond the infield. Bauer couldn't adjust.

Weaver didn't hesitate when he got the job in mid-1968 with the team 43–37, respectable but not driving. He knew he couldn't be Krazy Glued to the big-inning approach, his fave, because the environment had changed. He pushed the team to scramble for hits and bunt for singles. He amped up the stealing by tripling the number of appearances of Don Buford, his fastest base-stealing outfielder. Over the rest of the season, he improved the team about four wins, to 48–34, and more important, gave young players experience that would pay off in the 109-win season that followed.

Faced with a changed environment, Weaver adapted by using the four-step strategy detailed in this chapter. Observe and think systematically. Experiment stochastically. Optimize using resources at hand. Respond to what you have learned. He also used the end of the season to test hypotheses to set the table for the next campaign while still performing better than adequately in his present one.

As I explained in chapter 11, the Kansas City Royals and New York Yankees failed to get competitive value out of the designated-hitter rule instituted in 1973. Weaver mined it for value. Here's how. Most managers felt the DH was, in effect, a pinch hitter who was *already* in the lineup. Since that pinch hitter was in the lineup all the time, their response was to carry one fewer pinch hitter in favor of an extra roster spot for a pitcher. What they didn't think about was exactly how useful that extra pitcher might be compared with the missing pinch hitter.

Earl Weaver did. He saw the DH as a way to overhaul his roster plan. He used the spot for an extra batter. It provided him with flexible choices. To help his pitchers, he could start a nonslugging great defender in the field because the DH was adding incremental offense to balance the defensive artist's lack of hitting. Later in the game, his extra batter gave him extra pinch-hitting choices for the low-offense defender, and he'd still have a defensive specialist as a replacement.

As Weaver correctly saw it, there was more value in cobbling together complementary lineup and defensive rôles he could apply in every single game than in keeping an extra pitcher. The extra pitcher was by definition the least good on the team (if he had been better than someone else already there, Extra Dude would already be penciled in) and would appear rarely, merely to soak up innings in a blowout or an extra-inning game. The extra hitter could be a factor almost every day.

Government agencies, especially smaller ones, tend to be sharp about this. A position gets funded with earmarked dollars even though the operation already has as many people for that function as it needs. The manager will shift that new income to pay the person already doing the job and shift those freed-up funds into a needed position or the savings to meet payroll cuts.

Most managers see only the costs of change, but if you recognize change as proffering as much opportunity as risk, you can frequently ride that opportunity to advantage. Fine-tune the way you invest staff time and tweak processes affected by change. Remember, most competitors will view the change as "a problem," not as something that can give them an advantage. Most won't act at all before they have to. And by being defensive, the best they are hoping for is no setbacks. They aren't looking to derive improvements the way you can if you're looking for that opportunity.

In all cases, keep an eye open for that pitch you know you can drive—the opportunity to trigger change instead of just reacting to it.

13

The Man Who Invented Babe Ruth: Getting a Step Ahead by Initiating Changes

The art of progress is to preserve order amid change
and to preserve change amid order.
—A. N. "Mad Dog" Whitehead

If you're the kind of manager who's good at responding to changes, you're a pearl, an autographed baseball from the 1906 Chicago Cubs, a thing of value and something to treasure. But another set of skills, innovating changes others have to react to, is even more precious. Changes that put the competition off balance include strategic (such as applying a business model that's not being used in your field), product (such as inventing one or moving into a new category), personnel (applying the talent in new ways or devising new employment models), marketing (creating a new segment), and tactical (such as the application or discarding of technology, new pricing models, and defining new processes). When you're driving changes instead of just reacting, you are putting your competitors into a hole that few will be able to dig out of.

Some people innovate just for the heck of it. Others set aside the time and effort only when continuing with the status quo is not an option. Branch Rickey's first general manager-like job was with the St. Louis Cardinals in 1919, poor both in wins (last place in '18) and in investment from its millionaire owner. Rickey, who was responsible for three of the most revolutionary changes in baseball, argued that his first change—the farm system—was a "case of necessity being the mother of invention."

Historically, competitive balance in the majors was worse than it is today. It was especially out of balance before Rickey's first revolution. It was skewed in part because the minor leagues consisted of independent, competitive, entrepreneurial teams interested in making money and winning games. A major-league team wanting to buy a minor-league player would compensate the seller for the loss of a player's services. But that affected the minor-league team's ability to win, which affected attendance, so buying good minor leaguers was expensive. Major-league teams that spent more bought the most and best players, and that perpetuated imbalance. Low-payroll teams like the Cards and A's and Senators tended to struggle year after year, bidding on young talent and losing to competitors with higher budgets.

Bob Hedges, the owner of the St. Louis Browns when Rickey had played for them, had talked with "The Mahatma" about the possibility of owning multiple clubs at different levels as a way of capturing talent at a lower price than bidding for it on the open market. Rickey remembered, rethought the economics, and realized that the minor-league teams wouldn't necessarily have to be profitable. Spreading the conceptual net value of the big-league club's player-acquisition effort over the whole operation could justify a net loss in the minors.

There were side benefits. Scouting became cheaper and more thorough because all a team's top prospects were in a few locations. Flexibility went up because now it was easier to fill a roster or bank an extra player you didn't have room for on the big club, meaning you could, when useful, swap two players for three, or vice versa. Through the early 1920s, Rickey built the first farm system, teams on every level whose players were trapped in the Cardinals' domain.

As Leonard Koppett explained:

Hundreds of players could be examined in tryouts and assigned to minor league teams at various levels, with the minor league team committed by contract to give the Cardinals the first crack. . . . *You didn't have to guess which of the hundreds of hopefuls would turn out to be major leaguers; they would identify themselves in the process of progressing through the system. The ones you wanted, you'd keep; the other good ones, you'd sell off at a profit . . . and whenever you had a replacement ready for a respected veteran, you could trade or sell the veteran for more profit.*[62]

The Cardinals that Rickey started building with his first farm club in 1921 went to and won the 1926 World Series with almost all homegrown talent. That quick payback indicates how powerful the Hedges-Rickey idea was.

When I worked at Microsoft, it was small and innovative enough to have a farm system, although it wasn't a conscious initiative. The company had a ton of talented, not-well-paid people in technical support, workers who had deep people skills and solid technical knowledge. Occasionally, the company would realize how valuable one of these contributors was and promote him to a development role. Some of the most talented people I worked with were tech-support "farmhands."

Ultimately, Rickey's part in bringing up Jackie Robinson in 1947 and integrating baseball was probably more an extension of his search for innovative methods to capture lots of baseball talent inexpensively than it was a political statement. But his results again made a franchise dominant, and almost as quickly as you could say Jack Robinson.

The lesson is powerful for any contemporary organization. If you're willing to examine, analyze, and then cherry-pick a pool of people others won't, you get a comparative advantage in obtaining undervalued talent—be it African Americans, women engineers, or shorter-than-average people. The more averse other organizations are—10 teams stayed segregated for five more years, and the Tigers and Red Sox for another decade—the faster one can accelerate away from them, as Jackie Robinson, Don Newcombe, and Branch Rickey proved. The more seasons the diversity-averse stick to their guns, the fewer competitors you have to share your boon with. The harder it is for competitors to follow you in your innovation, whether it's operationally complex like the farm system, or emotionally complex like having to overcome personal biases, the more persistent the innovation's advantages are.

When Innovation Doesn't Spread: Bucky Harris, Firpo Marberry, and Charlie O. Finley

In the Stephen Jay Gould paleontology model I discussed in chapter 12, most of the designs that come into existence through mutation aren't effective survivors in that moment. They just fail. And that's fine as long as you haven't committed all your resources to that one test succeeding.

Sometimes the inventor takes a chance with a complex system even though the outcome can't reasonably be judged until it's deployed. So there's a prerequisite for a manager who intends to innovate: fearlessness. Sparky Anderson managed World Series winners in both major leagues. He believed that the single overriding requirement for managing in a dynamic system is being fearless—fearless of what people might say if your call doesn't work, fearless of being fired, fearless of acting on your conclusions.[63] By necessity, innovation will fail to turn out well far more often than it will meet your expectations.

Very few ideas actually come to fruition. Some end up as abject failures. Some are hijacked by another manager who takes the core of an idea and twists it beyond recognition. Some work but no better than the idea they were meant to replace. Self-control in the face of "failure" separates successful innovators from those who never get to home plate safely. That's the reason you can't master change until you've mastered third base, self-awareness.

The most tragic kind of failed innovations are the ones that are good ideas that no one accepts. I call these "Day-Glo" ideas after a whiz-bang one Charlie O. Finley had. Finley owned the Kansas City and then Oakland Athletics, and was one of the great innovators in business and baseball, but in this case, "great" means prolific. His difficulty in getting his ideas implemented was based largely on the fact that almost everybody, owners and players alike, couldn't stomach this difficult self-made man.

Finley exemplified the innovator with a high rate of idea production. His "Eureka!" moments were sometimes triggered by actual problems and sometimes by the need to change things to see what would happen. While he occasionally slugged one out of the park, a lot of his ideas were what I call "Yreka" moments—windy whiffs. Dick Williams, his manager for the A's, remembered the 1972 exhibition game where Finley changed the rules to speed up the game and keep people entertained. Every batter started with the count at 1-1, functionally making two strikes a strikeout and three balls a walk. According to Williams, the A's pitchers couldn't master the rhythm of what amounted to some suddenly introduced 1887 rule and walked about 20 batters.[64]

Innumerable great, functional innovations die before getting a fair trial, and then are resurrected years later. When Bucky Harris, the rookie manager of the 1924 Washington Senators, invented the modern relief pitcher, the practice didn't take hold.[65] The '24 Senators were an anomaly for Washington teams—they won the World Series. And one of the reasons Harris got them there was his new way of using Fred "Firpo" Marberry.

Marberry was a young starter with only one tough pitch he could throw for strikes. On the '24 Senators, he was a reliever/starter, which means he was a spot starter the manager didn't have much faith in, so most often he came in to mop up in lost causes. As the season progressed, though, Harris decided he liked Firpo's stuff, so he started using him the way modern relief aces are applied: entering a close game to preserve a victory.

This hadn't happened before, and it worked. Firpo notched 35 relief appearances and would have had 15 saves, enough to lead the league, if such a stat had existed. The next year, he appeared as a reliever 55 times and none as a starter. Bill James pegs Marberry as the first true reliever in baseball history and believes the reason the sorry Senators had a run of success was Harris's fresh Firpo finesse.

You know what usually happens with an innovation made by an outfit that wins: everybody jumps on the bandwagon, even if the innovation wasn't the cause. In this case, *no one* jumped on Harris's bandwagon. Competitors stuck with their old reliever patterns: broken-down old guys, failing starters, and then at the end of a really important game, their best starter (the way the M's, Diamondbacks, and Yanks have used Randy Johnson in a handful of late-season contests).

James believes that the lag occurred because the power of success couldn't overcome conventional assumptions. Managers' assumption that relief pitchers are "not good" meant that anyone who pitched in relief as a main task was, by the definition of the time, "not good." A "great relief pitcher" was an oxymoron, as inconceivable as "Best Buy customer service." So, James notes, competitors reinterpreted Firpo's accomplishments as a failure to be good enough to be a starter.

RULE 14.01a. Don't irrevocably dismiss changes that don't catch on. You can sift through viable ideas, yours and others', that didn't work or worked but didn't stick in previous contexts. In a new environment, they might well have a better outcome.

Harris came back to his innovation in 1947. At the helm of the 100-win Yankees, he made Joe Page a tough, close-game reliever, and when Casey Stengel took over the team as manager, he followed Bucky's blueprint, applying Page as a key ingredient in the first of many teams he would take to the World Series. Now it was all different. These were the Yankees. The practice took root everywhere and stuck. It wasn't *what* that diffused the innovation, it was *who* had done it.

In driving change, context is powerful, especially when your innovation is not based on an immediate necessity, as Rickey's development of the farm system was.

Left-Handed One-Batter Relief Specialists—Flamingos Meet Tony Phillips

In chapter 12, I told you about Mel Ott, the perfect Polo Grounds hitter who was merely pretty good elsewhere. I called him a "flamingo," a term I use for a person or tool that's perfectly engineered for a single environment in a way that makes him or it of little use in others. Flamingos are perfect adaptations to an immediate situation but barely functional elsewhere. They can't move just anywhere and expect to succeed, or make it through a multiyear drought.

In baseball, most teams have a flamingo on the roster, a left-handed relief pitcher stored in the bullpen to get a sequence of left-handed batters out in a tight situation late in a game. Opposing managers, knowing this, either flip-flop their lineups to avoid consecutive left-handed batters, or pinch-hit for one of them with a right-handed batter when the lefty specialist takes the mound. Therefore the lefty specialist usually becomes a one-batter walk-on. Understandably, teams don't want to invest a ton in a one-batter reliever, so they tend to end up with a player who is effective against lefties only, meaning that's the only way they can use him. A flamingo. A few flamingos are really good at what they do and also have the ability to learn to do whatever else you throw at them. Those are royal blue flamingos—rare and expensive.

In contrast, you have Tony Phillips, the switch-hitting infielder-outfielder, speedster–power hitter, versatility incarnate (chapter 5), a flexible, intelligent, driven human being with no single Hall of Fame skill. Whatever you need, you can plug him in and he can help you. What he doesn't know how to do now, he will learn. Organizations that need to adapt need talent that thrives at adaptation.

If you want to be an organization capable of change, you need a few well-positioned flamingos (experts) and more Tony Phillipses. Your specialized experts give you deep skill in a specific area, and that's great, but in a situation that needs to cope with change, the environment that is so superkind to them can turn ugly pretty quickly. Tony Phillipses adapt; few flamingos can.

Phillipses have another ingredient not always appreciated by hiring managers. *They have fun at work.* To be innovating is to be playful, to fiddle with the sequences or objects that make up work. Effective innovation and having fun use almost identical recipes. Mike Veeck, partner in many minor-league teams, believes that "fun is good" at work, and has made a model of moving staffers around, forcing them to be utility players, so they can grow and he can promote them. Veeck has made a lot of money running clubs and has made a lot of customers happy with original promotions that have included Richard Nixon Night; Silent Night (fans with sealed lips held up signs with "Boo," "Yay," and "Hey Beer Man" on them); and George Costanza Night, where everything ran backward, ninth inning to first. He has dozens of tools in his kit, laid out in his book *Fun Is Good*.[66]

Staffing functions tend to strap on their blinders and seek out all flamingos all the time. In 1988, before the first year of Baldridge Awards had been awarded, an acquaintance pointed out to me a recruiting ad for a billion-dollar food processor seeking a coordinator for their award-entry team. One of the requirements was having been a project manager on at least one food processor's successful entry for a Baldridge—at a time when, since no such award had been granted, zero qualified candidates could possibly exist.

Filling up positions with ten-years-of-increasingly-responsible-work-in-becoming-a-flamingo develops organizations that become brittle in the face of change. Hire experts by all means. If you can hire experts with a track record of shifting expertise, as Rex Barney would say, "give that flamingo a contract." But your chance to succeed in times of change hinges on your recruiting utility players who can fit in anywhere and whose diversity of experiences allows them to import innovations from other disciplines they've known before.

Process and equipment can be flamingos, too. Alternatively, you can create well-designed processes that are easy to change when you need to, as they do at Toyota. That requires commitment to designing processes that are flexible enough not to force you to throw them away and start from scratch every time you need to tweak or revolutionize a system. Equipment is a trickier issue, but Toyota has proven you can succeed with that, too, if you're determined.

RULE 14.99. Fun drives effective change. An organization that wants to drive change has a better chance if it promotes playful attitudes and ideas. Nonfun shops can drive change, but it's hitting, unnecessarily, into the wind.

Change Incarnate:
Ed Barrow, the Man Who Invented Babe Ruth

As I explained in chapter 1, Ed Barrow triggered the end of the Deadball Era by inventing Babe Ruth. As big as that change he triggered was, he innovated much more. I call Barrow "The Anti-Flamingo," and when I tell you his background, you'll see why. He started working full-time at age 16. His first management job was as the circulation supervisor for a daily newspaper, where he developed first-base skills: marketing, route planning, and other logistics and the benefit/cost ratios of efforts to increase results. There, he organized his first baseball league, a newsboys' circuit that increased part-time temporary employees' involvement with the organization (second base). He left to pursue marketing and sales, trying to commercialize his brother's soap invention (home plate) but failed (third-base lesson), and ended up being the assistant manager for a Pittsburgh hotel, a job where you learn advance scheduling, provisioning, facilities management and maintenance (first base) as well as staffing and dealing with customers (second base).

His hotel experience hooked him up with Harry Stevens, the first ballpark concessionaire (his company still serves ballparks), and together they started a minor league (home plate) where their mutual provisioning experience integrated the profitable business of food service with facilities and the game on the field (home plate again). They diversified into owning the Wheeling, West Virginia, franchise, so Barrow learned how to operate a single club, and when their league folded, he became the team's sole owner and field manager and moved it to a different league (home plate).

Barrow learned to scout, signing Honus Wagner, and to promote—he tried a night game under lights, hired boxing champs like Jim Corbett as umpires, and hired a woman to pitch (first base and home plate). He learned to manage from the dugout well enough that when he lost 14 of his players from his 1900 team, he managed to rebuild beautifully enough to win the league in 1901 anyway (all four bases). He field managed for other teams; quit baseball and went back into the hotel business, apparently to court his future wife (third base); then became a league president; then went to work in the majors as a field manager in Detroit. He and the Tigers' owner didn't get along, so he left (third base) for Boston after starting a rebuilding initiative that contributed to Detroit's winning three league championships starting three years later. As manager of the Boston Red Sox he made pitching star Babe Ruth an everyday outfielder (all four bases), applying his past experience in field managing and in route planning to invent the switch.

Barrow was baseball's first GM as we know it. Before Barrow took the Yankee general manager job in 1920 and paired with legendary field manager Miller Huggins, a team's field manager ran scouting and trades, while the GM was purely a business manager. Barrow took on the handling of personnel because he was The Anti-Flamingo. As a former field manager, he could speak Huggins's language. As a scout, he'd recruited a couple of future Hall of Famers. He could integrate the talent and the business the way none had before because he knew a hundred ways a ball club could make or lose money, and a million ways to reorganize efforts to squeeze value out of resources. But more than anything else, he knew that the talent was the product. Where most baseball operations tried to limit the star system to save money, Barrow saw boosting it as a conduit to team profits.

That's one of the reasons he invented putting numbers on players' uniforms. From his hospitality experience he innovated letting fans keep foul balls instead of "watching the ushers wrestling with the customers and building up a thousand dollars of bad will over a two-dollar ball." [67] And he was an astute enough recruiter of managers to hire Joe McCarthy, now considered by many experts the greatest field manager of all time. The McCarthy-Barrow combine led the Yankees to eight pennants in 16 years.

Barrow's life points out an upside in the shift from the one-company-for-life model of yesteryear to today's many-companies-in-your-career lifestyle. What you learn in one job can have a huge impact when you take those skills to a new setting—and put *you* in the position of the outsider who can see the needed innovations that lifers can't.

To drive change, you need to listen to those steeped in the work, observe other lines of work to see if there are pieces of their lineup you can borrow to advantage, test in controlled experiments—and do it all fearlessly. Staff for change, with versatile contributors and a few specific experts to anchor you in the now. Change *will* happen . . . and if you don't knock it out of the park, it'll knock *you* out. But for Cobb's sake, have some fun—change is almost never successful in shops that aren't having fun.

There's nothing quite so satisfying as rounding all the bases and touching home plate, knowing you've achieved your goal as a four-base manager. But as in baseball, the quest for home plate is not a final goal. It's only the beginning of your efforts to run up the score.

Epilogue
But, but, but . . .

It's only the Big Inning, it's only just the start.
—*Chicago Transit Authority*

You've circled the bases with me, and that's a fine start to a summer day. Sip a lemonade, reminisce about knuckleballs tossed, line drives hammered, pickles successfully executed, lessons learned. But let's play two, as Ernie Banks would say. I encourage you to join the community at the *Management by Baseball* Web site (www.ManagementByBaseball.Com). I keep additional resources there. I'm hoping it will be valuable to all of us as a mutual learning community, a place we can pool our knowledge and ideas and become better, more capable managers.

With book in hand, you can register for some special privileges and access to some extra materials and Web pages where the interested can carry on conversations about advancing our craft.

But what about when you really have crossed home plate and become one of the 5 percent who achieve adequacy at all four skill clusters. Then what?

It's a given in business writing that things don't start and end; things *cycle*. We're all familiar with the overhead slide that shows the three or four points with arrows that connect them into an endless cycle of infinite purification, the final point connecting to the first so the process can start all over. In American business, it's an article of religious faith that this treadmill represents reality.

In some cases, it does. But I've sat in too many slide-deck design and refinement sessions where someone shoehorned the information on a slide into a three- or four-step cycle because: (1) the cycle is an unquestioned assumption, (2) the software that most people use to produce slide decks includes the cycle format as a canned feature, and (3) you almost never see a slide deck without a cycle slide unless the author was technically primitive, so if you don't include it yourself, people will think you don't know how to use the feature. Moreover, in the consulting world anyway, the treadmill model generates more, nay, an eternity more, work.

So what about our baseball diamond. Do you just stop? Yes, and no. It's true that every significant change you adapt to or drive ripples through the other areas. You will alter your operational setup, but if you're good, you do that anyway, even without significant change, constantly using feedback as a guide to improve what you do. You will tweak the way you manage individuals, learning more about the individuals who work with you, starting from scratch with new people from new cultures. And as new subgenerations come into the workforce, mastery requires keeping up with their assumptions, preferences, fears, and cultural icons (you don't manage the average person born in 1952 the same way you do the average person born in 1964 or 1975). And if you're adequate at change adaptation, the self you examine in self-awareness won't have changed much. (If you're not self-aware, you're unlikely to master change, because invisible assumptions frequently block one's ability to succeed at change.) Yes, change, even change you've created and driven intentionally, is likely to change your environment enough to put some ripples in your inner force, but the necessary adjustments usually require existing, not new, observations.

So at the risk of being forced into a tiger cage at Guantánamo by the Consultingland Uniformity Enforcement Authority, I suggest that you don't merely repeat this process.

There are three main "places" to go when you've achieved at least adequacy at all four corners of the diamond.

One, work on improving the weakest of your skill sets. If you go to the *Management by Baseball* Web site, you'll see I've organized the recommended readings by skill set, so if reading is a way you learn well, pick out a few of those volumes and keep advancing your abilities.

Two, apply the change skills you've mastered to *yourself*, growing in your ability to adapt as a human being to the real world outside work. Yes, a bit ambitious for a 162-game season, or a 16,200-game season for that matter—it's a lifetime achievement, requiring more Erik Erikson than Scott Erickson, more Carol Gilligan than Junior Gilliam.

Three, choose other people to mentor. While you can score only one run yourself circumnavigating the diamond, you can run up the score by helping others in your organization score, too. I know this advice is likely to run counter to the social norms and expectations of your organization, but few organizations outside of government persist. People do. Long after you've left the employ of your current workplace, the people you mentored will be replicating your cognitive DNA. After your current organization has melted down or been reorganized into a tax-free e-shell in the Grand Caymans, merged, LBO-ed, or has simply forgotten you, the people you mentored will utter your name, channel you.

Like the National Pastime, managing and mentoring offer the possibility of a permanent record in the memories of all who saw you play.

Notes

1. http://www.cio.com/archive/091503/reality.html.
2. Data from baseball researcher George Lindsey, based on two seasons' worth of games. danagonistes.blogspot.com
3. Leonard Koppett, *The Man in the Dugout* (New York: Crown Publishers, 1993), pp. 4–6.
4. Earl Weaver, *It's What You Learn After You Know It All That Counts* (New York: Fireside Books, 1983).
5. Bill James, *The Bill James Guide to Baseball Managers* (New York: Scribner's, 1997), p. 99.
6. John Monteleone, *Branch Rickey's Little Blue Book* (New York: Macmillan, 1995)
7. In some organizational settings, highly educated workers with long-term goals may feel micromanaged if you direct their slack time, even if the only reason they have any is because you've captured it for them. Employees need to, and want to, have a lot of autonomy over their schedules, and as long as you're getting extraordinary productivity out of your team and meeting the objectives you need to, you can suspend this effort. But stay vigilant; if productivity lags or starts to drift away from objectives, you'll need to resume it thirdwith.
8. Mike Scioscia, interview, September 13, 2005.
9. He's right. For example, when there's a runner on first and no outs, followed by a single, if the runner stops at second base, the probability of the team scoring is 61 percent, but if the lead runner makes it to third base, it goes up to 87 percent. With one out the probability moves from 43 percent to 63 percent. (Dan Fox, danagonistes.blogspot.com, November 5, 2003.)
10. Go to the *Management by Baseball* Web site to see an example under the link "Base-Out Probabilities."
11. *New York Post,* May 30, 2004.
12. Koppett, p. 254.
13. Baseball Prospectus's Expected Runs Matrix for 2005, www.baseballprospec tus.com.

14. Featured in Alan Schwarz, "When the Dream Becomes a Reality," *Baseball America,* January 8, 1992.

15. Bill Bavasi, interview, September 12, 2005.

16. James, pp. 48–57.

17. James, pp. 60–63.

18. Stepping in the bucket is when a batter strides on a swing and ends up with the front foot farther away from the plate, opening up so the front of the body faces the pitcher. This leaves the average person prone to pulling inside pitches foul and having no chance at all on pitches outside. As with every other standard rule of batting (and life), there are some people who do it the "wrong" way and have success anyway because it works for them.

19. James, p. 65.

20. A manager who wants to institute a system can be at a significant advantage if the organization previously had *no* method. In most organizations there are two groups who will automatically resist replacing an existing system: those innately fearful of change in any form, and those who are defensive and believe a shift is an admission that the status quo was a failure.

21. Frank Frisch as told to J. Roy Stockton, *Frank Frisch, the Fordham Flash* (Garden City, NY: Doubleday, 1962), p. 22.

22. Frisch, p. 27.

23. Earl Weaver with Terry Pluto, *Weaver on Strategy* (New York: Collier Books, 1989), p. 59.

24. Twice in one season with the O's, Kelly went back on a long fly ball near the wall, mistimed his jump, thrust his glove at the ball, and actually propelled it over the fence for a home run that would not otherwise have been a four-bagger. José Canseco was notorious for doing this a decade later, but he was not nearly as balletic in his spontaneous combustion as Kelly.

25. Thirteen percent may not seem like much, but would you be skeptical if a basketball player was reported to be 8 feet 1 inch tall (13 percent over the NBA-topping 7 feet 2 inches), or if you heard that someone ran a mile in 3:14 (13 percent better than the current record of 3:43)? When it comes to bending the known limits of physical constraints, 13 percent is a truckload.

26. Ray Miller, interview, July 16, 2005.

27. *Total Baseball,* 3rd ed., John Thorn and Peter Palmer, eds (New York: Harper-Collins, 1993), p. 2385. For "defense," I'm using that book's rating system, "fielding wins." The traditional measure of fielding ability is fielding average—

an almost useless number for most players, since it tracks an event that is very rare for most fielders: the error. For 90 percent of regular players, the difference between the highest fielding average at a position and the lowest is about an error every 40 games. There will be an occasional exception, a deviant of massive fielding incompetence but with offensive skills who is allowed to play the field to get his bat into the lineup, but this is rare. The norm in fielding averages between players at the same position is very narrow, under 2 percent of chances.

There *are* significant differences in fielding ability that are not measured by fielding average (FA), because FA measures only the rate of errors a fielder makes once he gets to a ball and tries to make a play on it. For a condensed amble through defensive measures, I have a summary of contemporary fielding metrics, what they tell us, and what they don't, on the *Management by Baseball* Web site.

28. Torre's lineup featured some everyday fixtures, including Derek Jeter at shortstop, Bernie Williams in the outfield, and some starting pitchers.

29. Joe Torre, *Joe Torre's Ground Rules for Winners* (New York: Hyperion Books, 1999), p. 22.

30. Koppett, p. 87.

31. Monteleone, p. 24.

32. Monteleone, p. 24.

33. Perhaps baseball really excels at firings because the Elysian Fields, the name of the Hoboken, New Jersey, ballpark where the first baseball game played by the Cartwright rules took place in 1846, was named after the western suburb of Greek mythology's Hades, where dead heroes went to spend eternity. If baseball's beginning location was named for a place where people go after the end, how can baseball *not* have internalized lessons about life, birth, and death?

34. Not manager firings, which can be highly political. I believe I know but have no hard proof for a theory as to why. The range of abilities between the best baseball players in the majors (say, Barry Bonds) and the worst (say, pitcher Tim Redding) is significantly broader than the variation between the best and worst skippers. Ergo, turning over the manager will seem less risky, since the shear-off in the case of a botched decision will be probabilistically lower.

35. Chris Snow, "Appeal is Upheld; Wells Is Irate," *Boston Globe,* August 30, 2005.

36. Baseball Prospectus, Expected Wins table. www.baseballprospectus.com.

37. Ray Miller, interview, July 16, 2005.

38. James, p. 197.

39. Dick Williams, *No More Mr. Nice Guy* (San Diego: Harcourt, 1990), p. 6.

40. Williams, p. 273.

41. There's a lot of work about family-of-origin issues in the workplace, and none of it sings to me. I think the most useful book for further background is Brian DesRoches, *Your Boss is Not Your Mother* (Morrow, 1995).

42. The irony of this nickname is lovely, redolent of 1930s nicknames, like Charles "Gabby" Hartnett, who as a young player allegedly was less likely to speak than Silent Cal Coolidge, or Ernest "Tiny" Bonham (6 feet 2 inches, 235 pounds). The only thing sweet about Piniella was his truly sweet swing.

43. Williams, p. 251.

44. Williams, p. 35.

45. Material drawn from Baseball-Reference.com and David Quentin Voigt, *American Baseball* (Norman: University of Oklahoma Press, 1966). Note, too, that the league ranged in number of teams during those years from eight to 12. There are more extreme stories about Freedman, but founded only on the press of the time, which seemed to be solidly unified in finding his ethnicity offensive. I'm agnostic enough about these ax-to-grind allegations that I won't repeat them.

46. Glenn Stout, "A Curse Born of Hate," *Boston Baseball*, September 2004. Stout researched the series of Red Sox–Yankee trades made over a couple of seasons, trades that made the Yankees a powerhouse. Stout documented how Red Sox owner Harry Frazee, suspected of being Jewish by AL commissioner Ban Johnson, was isolated by most other American League owners for that reason. With no "market" for transactions, the Sox were limited in the kinds of trades they could make. The article is fascinating reading. It is also presented in another form in Stout's book *Red Sox Century* (New York: Houghton Mifflin, New York: 2000).

47. Standings at the end of April 2004. "WEST" is record against division rivals.

WEST	W	L	PCT	GB	WEST
Texas	13	9	.591	–	11–8
Anaheim	13	10	.565	0.5	11–8
Oakland	11	12	.478	2.5	10–9
Seattle	8	15	.348	5.5	6–13

48. Most singles in a season is an odd superlative because the value of singles hitters is built on an illusion puffed up by a conventional belief in batting average as a measure of offensive value. The singles mark is interesting, but a player could break the single-season singles record and still be a third less useful to his team than a player with fewer hits and a lot of home runs or doubles. The absence of power actually helps Suzuki attain these marks by reducing the likelihood of extra-base hits.

49. A quick history note. Of the 11 seasons on the list, nine are between 1920 and 1930, an era that was a veritable Chemical Brothers Dance-a-Thon of hitting. Only Ty Cobb's 1911 season and Suzuki's 2001 rookie campaign are exceptions. That 2001 Suzuki season was another example, I think, of intentional goal setting. When Suzuki came to the majors from a very successful career in Japan, no other Japanese-league position player had succeeded in the majors. There was widespread skepticism about his chances for success. And he was representing his country as well as himself. He sets himself objectives and pursues them relentlessly, and that 2001 effort was a glowing artifact of Ichiro's relentless rate-busting.

50. This is the toughest play a catcher has to make. He has to watch both the runner and the ball and they're 80–110 degrees apart.

51. Ichiro Suzuki, and Narumi Komatsu, *Ichiro on Ichiro: Conversations with Narumi Komatsu* (Seattle: Sasquatch Books, 2004).

52. Suzuki and Komatsu, p. 17.

53. As one of the most polymathic of baseball fans, Gould wrote in many places about the disappearance of the .400 hitter. If you want to read a deeper and more precise explanation, his book *Full House: The Spread of Excellence* (New York: Harmony Books, 1996) includes a roughly 50-page explanation, very literate, occasionally wonky. A collection of virtually everything Gould ever wrote about baseball, *Triumph and Tragedy in Mudville* (New York: Norton, 2004) includes an essay on this subject.

54. Gould wrote widely about punctuated equilibrium. His volume that most accessibly elaborates on the topic is *Wonderful Life* (New York: Norton, 1989), a good read, and the illustrations of sci-fi-looking life forms are fun even for postliterate folk.

55. OPS is a most useful single stat for measuring offensive output. To compare the decline from 2004 to 2005, expected by the pundits to be massive because

of the new antisupplements policies, was from .762 to .749, a normal variation of 13 points, compared to the 39-point decline between '63 and '64.

56. One-run strategies like these when executed properly marginally increase the chance of scoring a single run in an inning while also greatly diminishing the probability of scoring more than one run. The benefit/cost ratio is entirely based on context, and in most baseball post-1919, the context favors big-inning offenses.

57. The ban was not instant. The 17 pitchers who already had the pitch as part of their arsenal got to keep using it until they retired.

58. Since the Polo Grounds had actually been a polo field, the oval shape made for a challenging fit for a baseball field. Tiny down the lines (a distance Major League Baseball would now not allow) and immense to the power alleys and center, it was a distinctive place both to hit and to play outfield.

59. Koppett, p. 64.

60. Rob Neyer, "Angels rise was surprise but downfall is not," ESPN.com, August 14, 2003.

61. How about using more American metrics, like customer retention or return on sales?

62. Koppett, p. 94.

63. Koppett, p. 335.

64. Williams, p. 135.

65. This discussion draws heavily on work done by Bill James, and written up in his *Guide to Baseball Managers,* pp. 330–31.

66. Mike Veeck, *Fun Is Good* (Emmans, PA: Rodale Press, 2004).

67. Ed Barrow, *My Fifty Years in Baseball* (New York: Coward-McCann, 1951), p. 9.

Index

H

I

J

ABOUT THE AUTHOR

Jeff Angus is a management consultant specializing in work for entrepreneurial organizations in the business, nonprofit, and government sectors, with clients in and outside of North America.

Angus was an aide for the U.S. Senate Small Business Committee and for a U.S. Senator. He's also worked and managed in the transportation, agricultural, manufacturing, services, and technology sectors. He's reported on baseball for both the Associated Press and United Press International, and was a sportswriter for the *Seattle Sun*. His weekly column on sabermetrics appears in the *Seattle Times* during the season. He is also a regular columnist on management for *CIO Insight*, and has written commentaries on political economy and business evolution for the op-ed pages of many papers, including the *New York Times*, the *Baltimore Sun*, and the *St. Louis Post-Dispatch*. He's broadcast for radio stations in California, Ohio, and Washington. He plays right field for Jet City Messengers, when they field a team.

He was Director of Marketing Operations for Farallon Computing, a $45-million computer company. He founded and was Director of the InfoWorld Test Center, and was Director of Strategic Consulting Services for Lighthouse Consulting Group.

When he's not out on the road consulting or speaking, he makes Seattle his home.

A NOTE FROM THE AUTHOR ABOUT SABR

I'm a member of the Society for American Baseball Research (SABR), and if you enjoyed some of the historical studies, biographical sketches, and baseball anecdotes you read here, I urge you to join and participate. A noteworthy chunk of what I know about the game and its history is a result of belonging to SABR, spending time with its members, and reading the publications. Most members aren't experts; it's a membership group for all kinds of interests and levels of knowledge.

SABR's mission is to foster the study of baseball, to assist in uncovering the history of the game, to promote the distribution of research, and to stimulate interest in baseball. SABR, which is pronounced "saber" and whose acronym is the root of the word sabermetrics (mathematical tools to analyze baseball), is about more than stats. Many members pursue narrative history, collect relics, publish biographical material, and other specialties.

To join online, go to www.sabr.org and click on the link called "Membership."

To join by mail or contact the Society: SABR, 812 Huron Rd E #719, Cleveland, OH 44115. 1-800-969-SABR (7227).

Tell them Jeff sent you.